Venezuelan Politics
in the Chávez Era

Venezuelan Politics in the Chávez Era

Class, Polarization, and Conflict

edited by
Steve Ellner and Daniel Hellinger

LYNNE
RIENNER
PUBLISHERS

BOULDER
LONDON

Published in the United States of America in 2003 by
Lynne Rienner Publishers, Inc.
1800 30th Street, Boulder, Colorado 80301
www.rienner.com

and in the United Kingdom by
Lynne Rienner Publishers, Inc.
3 Henrietta Street, Covent Garden, London WC2E 8LU

Library of Congress Cataloging-in-Publication Data
Venezuelan politics in the Chávez era : class, polarization, and conflict / edited by Steve
Ellner and Daniel Hellinger.
     p.   cm.
   Includes bibliographical references and index.
   ISBN 1-58826-108-5 (hc : alk. paper)
   1. Venezuela—Politics and government—1999–   2. Political culture—Venezuela.
3. Political parties—Venezuela.   4. Châvez Frââs, Hugo.   I. Ellner, Steve.   II. Hellinger,
Daniel.

   JL3881.V464   2003
   987.06'42—dc21

                                                              2002073985

British Cataloguing in Publication Data
A Cataloguing in Publication record for this book
is available from the British Library.

Printed and bound in the United States of America

The paper used in this publication meets the requirements
of the American National Standard for Permanence of
Paper for Printed Library Materials Z39.48-1984.

5   4   3   2   1

With love and gratitude for their patience and support,
to our wives, Carmen Hercilia and Joann Eng

Contents

Preface

The abortive coup of April 2002 marks an appropriate stopping point for this study. The incident may have ushered in fundamental changes in Venezuelan politics and even signaled a new stage in the process that began with President Hugo Chávez's election in December 1998. Thus, for instance, in the aftermath of the April coup, Chávez and his supporters abandoned at least temporarily their aggressive style, toning down rhetoric and making concrete concessions to adversaries. Furthermore, President Chávez began to practice consensus politics, which had been the hallmark of the nation's political system since democracy's outset in 1958, and which the *chavistas* had thoroughly criticized in the past. The April 2002 coup attempt put in evidence an important aspect of the Chávez phenomenon that this book stresses, namely its unique features. The scenario of a mass turnout of poor people clamoring for Chávez's return to power, a movement that the troops refused to suppress and that put an end to a de facto government lasting but two days, has no equivalent in Latin American history.

This book is designed to give special weight to social factors, which have shaped political developments as well as the nation's political landscape during the 1989–2002 time span that we cover. For this reason, the topic of social movements is treated as a separate chapter titled "Civil Society: Institutionalization, Fragmentation, Autonomy," and not combined with the chapter on organized labor. Two other chapters further explore social dimensions: "Social Polarization and the Populist Resurgence in Venezuela" and "The Hugo Chávez Phenomenon: What Do 'the People' Think?" The book's introduction, and to a lesser extent several other chapters, also analyze the phenomenon of social polarization.

The editors would like to recognize the importance of institutional support that facilitated work on this study, particularly grants from the Faculty Research Program at Webster University and the Consejo de Investigación

of the Universidad de Oriente. Finally, the critical comments of two anonymous readers selected by Lynne Rienner Publishers suggested modifications that substantially enhanced the quality of all the chapters of the manuscript.

—Steve Ellner
—Daniel Hellinger

Prologue:
Venezuela's Permanent Dilemma

John V. Lombardi

This book focuses on the transformations of the last half of the twentieth century and the colorful challenges of the early years of the twenty-first. Although the dramatic rise of Hugo Chávez Frías from minor military conspirator to a self-proclaimed revolutionary and popularly elected presidential caudillo reads like a romantic adventure novel, the visible drama—with its coups and countercoups, street demonstrations and hyperinflated rhetoric, and constitutional revisions and dramatic policy shifts—often distracts observers from the fundamental structural issues of economy, class, and polity. The exceptional studies of the Chávez phenomenon included here, which offer broad and penetrating insight into the structure and context of Venezuela's turbulent and difficult recent transformations, gain added significance when seen within the larger frame of Venezuela's historical experience.

Each cycle in Venezuela's independent history follows similar profiles, although the rhetorical styles, the ideological concepts, and the technical, political, and economic details differ substantially. The cyclical nature of this process reflects a set of limitations on the range of alternatives available to the country and its leaders. The rhetoric of change often implies the opportunity to permanently set things right, to construct the Venezuela often dreamed of, to finally bring the order and progress that defines prosperity. We can easily imagine that by just doing the right things, Venezuela will rise into the ranks of the world's prosperous nations. This chimera informs much of the impassioned debate and underlies the cyclical transformations of Venezuela's political landscape since independence. The place we call Venezuela, nonetheless, lives and has lived within a set of constraints that effectively, if not theoretically, limit its rate of change, its progress.

The first of these is the Hispanic extractive engine itself. Originally perfected in the eighteenth century to produce and export cacao, it expanded to encompass coffee throughout the nineteenth century. In the early decades of the twentieth, with the decline of Venezuela's competitiveness in coffee and the rise of petroleum, the extractive engine began to produce oil, which remains into the twenty-first century the country's primary export product. This extractive engine produces not only exports for the international market but also the government's revenue. As many observers have noticed, Venezuela taxes its exports to operate its government. Taxes of all other types are low by any standard, and this makes the country's political elite dependent on the success and effectiveness of the Hispanic extractive engine. When that engine falters with declines in world prices for Venezuela's tradable commodities (cacao, coffee, or oil), the government is immediately in trouble and whatever its party or ideology, it readjusts its expenditures or acquires revenue elsewhere to sustain itself. If it fails, the government falls, replaced by new actors who assume control of the export engine and attempt to revive its effectiveness using new techniques and new policies.

The dependence on this extractive engine severely limits the government's ability to reconfigure Venezuela's economic model. In an almost desperate cycle, the government shores up the export model to generate sufficient revenue to operate the bureaucracy and, with the revenue that remains, make progress on improving society and diversifying the export economy. The extractive engine ties the government almost completely to world market prices for Venezuelan commodities, and those fluctuate on short-term cycles. Consequently, the government has only a short time to do what it can before the price falls and a new cycle begins. It often borrows money to prolong or speed up progress, and in borrowing money becomes even more dependent on the extractive engine to generate the funds to pay the country's debts.

The economic realities of this process, by debilitating institutional development, pose a second constraint on the system. After the disappearance of Spain's infrastructure for law, order, stability, identity, and nationality between 1810 and 1830, Venezuela re-created as much of the Spanish system as it could within the context of a liberal representative republican model. However innovative and creative the writers of constitutions and laws might be, they could not reinvent the traditional stability and effectiveness of the Spanish imperial institutions.

The republican version of order failed the primary tests of stability and permanency. The litany of caudillos and regime changes throughout the period from José Antonio Páez until Juan Vicente Gómez serves as incontrovertible evidence of the fragility of Venezuelan order. That these movements contained within them remarkable efforts by people at all levels of society to find a better way to improve their status in life is a given. So too is it given that this continuous and irregular form of regime change taught Venezuelans an important lesson about prosperity and individual progress under republican rule.

The lesson was simple: get it now, for whatever is possible today may not be possible tomorrow. Optimal personal progress depended on capturing the moment and translating that moment into personal wealth, because tomorrow's moment would likely belong to someone else.

With each new regime came a redistribution of some old resources (land in particular) and the creation of new opportunities related to the management of the extractive engine and the expenditure of the taxes derived from the export of its products. Most of the resources in play during each regime change involved benefits distributed by the central government, and so control of the capital city and its bureaucratic apparatus became the goal of each successive movement for reform, revolution, or retrenchment. Each cycle produced its set of winners and losers among the various elite groups and their followers. More important, each cycle further reinforced the permanence of the extractive engine as the source of national prosperity and slowed the continued development of institutional effectiveness that had occurred during the previous cycle. Each cycle cost the national treasury the surplus collected during periods of high export prices, leaving each successive regime dependent on both exports and loan arrangements with the international providers of capital.

On the scale of cacao and coffee, these cycles made relatively little impact on the world stage, and Venezuela, while an interesting place, did not engage the attention of the international community except in terms of issues such as the blockade of Venezuelan ports in 1902–1903 by the country's creditors or the ongoing international boundary dispute over Guayana. Oil catapulted Venezuela into an internationally significant actor, as the chapters in this volume make so abundantly clear. Oil not only proved to be the extractive engine's most valuable product, but also served as a strategic material for the world's primary powers. Venezuela, by virtue of its large and early production of petroleum, became a very important place. Oil not only made Venezuela significant to its external markets, it offered the possibility of creating true and permanent wealth for the Venezuelan government. Recognizing this opportunity, Venezuelans began to imagine that they could escape the trap imposed on them by the Hispanic extractive engine and the fragility of their postindependence institutions. If money was the problem, oil could surely resolve it.

Oil also raised the stakes of the game, although it initially did not appear to change the rules. From Juan Vicente Gómez through Marcos Pérez Jiménez, Venezuelans cycled their leadership in ways remarkably reminiscent of the last years of the nineteenth century. With the advent of the electoral democratic regimes in the 1960s, Venezuela began a forty-year project designed to construct a series of institutions and establish practices to fundamentally change the Hispanic extractive engine and replace the weak institutional infrastructure inherited from the past. Nurtured by the revenue from oil, informed by the best thinking in economics and social development worldwide, the Venezuelan political and economic leadership moved rapidly toward the long-sought order and progress.

As the chapters in this collection explain, the dramatic progress rested on a variety of unsustainable assumptions. One was that the oil wealth alone could transform the Hispanic extractive engine into a modern diversified economy by recycling the petrodollars into other enterprises, selected by the state and sustained by state subsidies. Another was that the prosperity and economic dynamism accompanying the rapid expansion of state spending reflected real economic wealth rather than the expenditure of the rents exacted from the international petroleum market. These assumptions took their most impressive form in the 1970s when Venezuela, benefiting from a boom in oil prices, began a massive expenditure program. Investing in everything imaginable—from social and educational programs to housing and sanitation, from subsidized industries to roads and bridges, and from airports to health care—Venezuelans saw the context of their lives improve dramatically in a short period.

The enemy of this progress was time. These investments and expenditures came from the rent on high oil prices. When prices declined as all commodity prices do (even when buffered by cartel management), the government borrowed to sustain its expenditure and investment programs, increasing the need to rely on the extractive engine to pay its debts. By the end of the twentieth century, as the studies included here illustrate so clearly, the historical continuities of Venezuela's past imposed themselves on the oil-financed transformations, and the country passed through another regime change that promised to reconfigure, restructure, and reinvent Venezuela's institutions, law, order, policies, and economy.

Each successive regime change in Venezuela's republican history has begun with the anticipation of using political techniques to reconfigure the country's economic landscape, to change the cycle of export-driven growth or decline. While these changes often modified and on occasion dramatically improved the political and institutional culture of Venezuela, they failed to substantially change the economic base. Venezuela's comparative advantage in petroleum exports proved so great that no alternative economic activity emerged. The immediate demands of social and economic improvements for all Venezuelans and the requirements of an ever growing public payroll overwhelmed the decision process that might have changed the basic economic structure of the country. Rushing to improve life for its various constituencies, each regime ran out of time to address the structural issues of the economic system when the inevitable downturn of oil prices arrived, bringing economic hardships and yet another regime change. Throughout the twentieth century and especially after 1958, Venezuela dramatically modernized its society and its political and social institutions. It greatly enhanced its technical capability to manage its oil production and marketing systems, but it never succeeded in substantially modifying its historically derived, export-commodity, economic engine.

Within the large frame of Venezuela's modern history, the Chávez movement offers a variety of remarkable innovations. Coming as it does within the context of the democratic tradition established after 1958, this movement has the distinction of failing as a traditional military uprising and succeeding as a popular electoral movement. As the studies in this volume illustrate, the remarkable success of the *chavista* alliances after the failed uprisings testifies not only to the extreme dissatisfaction of Venezuelans with their traditional party system and its practical performance but also to the strong preference of Venezuelans to manage change through formally democratic means. The organized opposition that continued through failed coups and into a successful electoral campaign also signals a remarkably strong and coordinated coalition capable of sustaining defeat and continuing organization, shifting tactics, and achieving success over an extended period.

Although the Chávez coalition followed traditional Latin American forms in creating a new government and issuing a new constitution, the energy for this transition flows much less from constitutional formalism and much more from an apparently opportunistic combination of ideologies, policies, and theories drawn from a wide range of sources with a decidedly social reformist slant. Many observers struggle with the effort to identify a coherent political and ideological philosophy that joins the groups that support the Chávez transformation. Some, noting the significant involvement of the left-wing generation that failed to capture a leadership role in the post-1958 political arrangements and remained marginalized throughout the Punto Fijo period, identify the *chavistas* as leftist revolutionaries. While this has some plausibility, particularly given Hugo Chávez's personal enthusiasm for Fidel Castro and things Cuban, the actual behavior of the government in matters of economic and social policy has been substantially less radical or revolutionary than the embrace of Cuba might imply. Whether the regime will become significantly more radical in practice, or whether it will choose to continue and improve its current form of realistic and perhaps opportunistic pragmatism, remains to be seen, but the rhetorical radicalism of the *chavista* revolution greatly exceeds its practical implementation.

The effective exploitation of the media to develop constituency and maintain the currency of the leader's identification with the people has been another hallmark of the Chávez regime, although the reliance on a media-driven public presence has made the *chavistas* vulnerable to an opposition that itself employs considerable media expertise. Nonetheless, in spite of the relatively modest performance of the *chavistas* in delivering their agenda of major social and economic improvement for the people, Hugo Chávez himself remains remarkably popular even as his government's record draws much less enthusiastic reviews. This split between the leader's and the government's popularity reflects the continuing truth that Chávez's rhetoric, for all of its literary failings, speaks to an agenda of complaint and concern that a majority of Venezuelans recognize as legitimate expressions of their own plight. This reasonably successful separation of the leader from the popular judgment of the government's performance created a challenge for an opposition that had to struggle to attach responsibility for the technical and performance inadequacies of the regime to Chávez himself. Indeed, when export revenue from petroleum sharply declined in late 2001, Chávez became more closely identified with the results of his government.

Perhaps the most dramatic consequence of the Chávez phenomenon is its demonstration of the bankruptcy of the post-1958 political tradition. The rejection and dissolution of the Punto Fijo political consensus, while not total, are nonetheless remarkable. Few if any leaders from that tradition retain popularity. Indeed, perhaps the enduring nature of Chávez's popularity owes more to the absence of alternative legitimate political voices than it does to the effectiveness of the *chavistas*. As new political actors emerge, as the coalition that supports the Chávez regime divides and splinters in the face of economic difficulties and doctrinal disputes, alternative political groups will acquire a legitimate voice, separate from the past failures and in opposition to the aggressive rhetorical content and style of Hugo Chávez. The military coup and countercoup of April 2002 dramatically illustrate both the fragility of the Chávez movement and the political immaturity of the newly emerging opposition.

Whatever the outcome of these political transformations, however, Venezuela's aspirations and national goals will rest on the successful management of the country's principal international comparative advantage in petroleum products. Whether the new political structures and institutions currently forming to replace the collapsed Punto Fijo tradition will have technical competence sufficient for Venezuela to compete successfully in the global market and political skill adequate to translate the gains from that competition into a better, less corrupt, and more effective economic system for all Venezuelans remains to be seen. Venezuela can control what it does at home, it can choose where to invest its petroleum rents, it can manage its distribution of wealth, but it cannot easily change the dynamics and the structure of the international marketplaces that arbitrate wealth and prosperity and determine the comparative advantage of nations. The detailed analyses in this volume offer an early assessment of the fundamental nature of the changes brought by the Chávez phenomenon, and serve as an essential base for understanding the transformations to come.

I

Introduction:
The Search for Explanations

Steve Ellner

The year 1989 was a watershed for Venezuela. The mass disturbances of the week of February 27 signaled a sharpening of social tension, which would reflect itself in everyday life and specifically on the political front in future years. In addition, immediately after his inauguration, President Carlos Andrés Pérez (1989–1993) implemented neoliberal reforms in accordance with the "shock treatment" formula, which also represented a sharp break with the past. Previously, the government had followed a strategy of intervention in the economy and protection of national industry, an approach initiated by Pérez's own Acción Democrática (AD) party at the outset of the democratic period in 1958. The shock treatment, which sacrificed national debate, also marked an abrupt end to the "consensus politics" that had been the bedrock of the Venezuelan political system since 1958. Pérez was ultimately impeached on grounds of corruption, but in large part he was forced from office because of mass repudiation of his economic policies, even by leaders of his own AD party. Pérez's removal also marked a major change for Venezuela, which went from three decades of relative political tranquillity to a nation torn by discord and subject to military involvement in politics.

Prior to 1989, Venezuela was Latin America's "near perfect" democracy. At least it met the political conditions (regular elections, alternation of parties in power, respect for civic rights, etc.) that political scientists have generally considered basic to long-lasting, well-functioning democratic regimes. Certain features of the Venezuelan economy and society were also conducive to political stability.

Most important, Venezuela's oil-based economy molded the nation's democratic system and minimized class conflict. Since oil became the nation's number one export in 1925 until international petroleum prices plummeted in 1986 (a period during most of which Venezuela was the world's leading exporter), the nation was blessed by nearly steady economic growth. Charles Bergquist (1986: 14, 206) has argued that Venezuelan oil

7

workers, and the working class in general, historically had a prosystem mentality because the nation's main commodity was not subject to the sharp fluctuations in price and demand that had such damaging consequences for other third-world nations. These factors lent themselves to a widespread sense of optimism regarding the steady improvement in social benefits (a concept embodied in the nation's Labor Law)[1] as well as the perfection of the nation's democracy. Attitudinal studies demonstrate that Venezuelans believed in a veritable "American Dream" in which the quality of life for their children would be better than for themselves.[2]

Until 1989, political scientists writing on Venezuela viewed the nation's political party system as in many ways ideal. Indeed, some considered Venezuelan democracy largely unique for Latin America, and actually more comparable to the democratic systems of Western Europe. Over the years, these scholars underlined seven positive aspects that set Venezuela off from most of Latin America:

1. *A two-party system with minimum ideological differentiation.* The social democratic AD and the social Christian Comité de Organización Política Electoral Independiente (COPEI) alternated in power after 1958 while the programmatic differences between them were significantly reduced. After 1973, AD and COPEI nearly monopolized electoral contests, particularly at the presidential level, where their combined vote reached about 90 percent. This pattern is a good sign according to such renowned political scientists as Maurice Duverger (1954) and Giovanni Sartori (1976), who posited that the U.S. model of two dominant parties lacking in major ideological differences is the most likely to achieve political stability.

2. *Political leaders committed to democracy who avoided ultranationalistic rhetoric.* The democratic convictions of Venezuela's major political leaders were never seriously placed in doubt, as were those of such outstanding political figures elsewhere as Juan Domingo Perón, Getúlio Vargas, and Víctor Raúl Haya de la Torre. For some political analysts, Venezuela's friendly relations with the United States further confirmed the democratic orientation of AD and COPEI (Alexander, 1964: 136–141; 1982: 524). Indeed, AD's standard-bearer, Rómulo Betancourt, played a leading role in the hemispheric offensive against Cuba's Fidel Castro in the 1960s.

3. *A mature political leadership that, learning from past experiences, discarded sectarian attitudes and formed interparty agreements.* The political leaders of AD, COPEI, and several smaller parties established coalitions to defend the nation's fledgling democracy after 1958 and then reached a formal agreement for top positions in Congress and organized labor in

1970. Political scientists praised Venezuelan parties as well as those of Colombia for pioneering what they called "pacted democracy" and for "political learning," whereby the intense party rivalry that had previously paved the way for military coups was largely avoided (Levine, 1978: 93–98). Only in the 1980s did pacted democracy and political learning become important features of the democratic transitions in the rest of Latin America. Several writers have pointed out that the Venezuelan leaders who engineered these accords were more pluralistic and acted in a more genuinely democratic fashion than did their Colombian counterparts (Herman, 1988: 5–9; Hartlyn, 1998: 111–116).

4. *Major parties of multiclass composition with a predominately middle-class leadership.* Terry Karl (1987: 69–71) and Daniel Hellinger (1984) argued that Venezuela's oil-based economy weakened the oligarchy, the peasantry, and the working class, which were thus unable to build their own political organizations, such as the ones created in Colombia, Chile, and elsewhere. The immense revenue derived from oil generated an exceptionally large middle class, which predominated in the leadership of AD, COPEI, and other parties, even though they also had sizable worker contingents. Karl and others considered this model the most conducive to maintaining stable democracy and containing class conflict.

5. *An emphasis on party discipline within AD and COPEI.* As far back as the 1930s, Rómulo Betancourt realized that a powerful labor component within his party could generate disruptive internal conflict. As an antidote he created a highly centralized party structure and took strict measures against internal dissension (Ellner, 1999b: 122). Even though AD's Labor Bureau played an influential role within the organization, it obeyed party dictates, unlike its more autonomous counterpart in the Peronista party in Argentina (Martz, 1966: 214–222; Kornblith and Levine, 1995: 41–42).

6. *A political system sufficiently open to provide attractive opportunities for junior coalition partners and other small parties.* Daniel Levine (1973: 236–252) pointed to the advantages of shifting government coalitions, which characterized Venezuelan politics in the 1960s, in that there were no permanent losers. Similarly, beginning in the 1970s, the AD-controlled Confederación de Trabajadores de Venezuela (CTV; Confederation of Venezuelan Workers—the nation's major labor confederation) followed a "generous" policy of allowing small leftist parties with minimal worker influence to be represented in its National Executive Committee (Ellner, 1993: 54). Inclusionary practices, reinforced by the system of proportional representation for all elections, undermined the appeal of extremist leaders and contributed to stability.

7. *Parties that were highly institutionalized rather than vehicles for ambitious leaders.* AD, COPEI, and other parties established close links

with the labor, peasant, and neighborhood movements as well as universities (Levine, 1973: 214–223). Political scientists have long considered this relationship a sine qua non for healthy democracy in Latin America.

Due to the apparent solidity of the Venezuelan political system, the political turmoil and radical changes of the 1990s took political analysts and Venezuelans in general by surprise. Indeed, many Venezuelans initially reacted to the 1989 disturbances and the February 1992 coup attempt with statements like "it can't happen here." Subsequently, they began to question the applicability of the "Venezuelan exceptionalism thesis,"[3] which viewed the nation as radically different from its Latin American neighbors either because of the maturity of its politicians or because of its status as an oil producer. The widespread reaction to the harsh realities the nation faced resembled that of many Argentines to the Falkland Island fiasco of 1982, which served as a reminder that the country after all belonged to the South American continent, not Europe.

1990s: Traditional Parties Exit

History repeated itself when President Rafael Caldera (1994–1999) turned to neoliberal formulas halfway through his term, just as Carlos Andrés Pérez had done at the outset of his own term. In both cases, the Venezuelan presidents discarded their electoral promise to maintain a large state presence in the economy, in opposition to the platforms of their electoral rivals, who favored a laissez-faire approach. Pérez deregulated banking, lifted most price controls, privatized the national telephone company, the port system and a major airline, and opened the oil industry and other strategic sectors to private capital. Diverse social groups reacted strongly against Pérez and his *el paquete económico* (economic package), as his neoliberal program was pejoratively labeled. Slum dwellers participated in the nationwide disturbances of February 27, 1989, which were followed by two attempted military coups in 1992—the first led by Hugo Chávez in February and the second staged in November—and then street protests (known as *cacerolazos,* which also involved the middle class) calling for Pérez's resignation. Caldera's political fate was different, in part because he adroitly followed a policy of national consultation, for which purpose he created a tripartite commission of labor, business, and state representatives. Caldera continued Pérez's privatization program by selling the national steel company and revamping the social security system to allow for private participation in health insurance plans and pension funds.

During the 1990s, the expressions of widespread discontent went beyond spontaneous disturbances, mobilizations, and insurgency, and led to a radical overhaul of the nation's long-standing political party system. Both AD and COPEI were defeated in the 1993 presidential elections, thus breaking a pattern dating back to 1958. President Caldera, who had until recently been COPEI's undisputed leader, formed a broad coalition that for the first time allowed leftist parties to share power. In other novel developments, the three leading contenders in the 1998 presidential elections were not professional politicians, and one of them received eleventh-hour backing from AD and COPEI (which dropped their support for other candidates). The biggest rupture with the past, however, occurred shortly after Chávez took office, when COPEI faded from the political scene at the same time that the president's Movimiento Quinta República (MVR; Fifth Republic Movement) replaced AD as the nation's largest party.

During this period, several parties were rewarded at the polls for assuming an intransigent stand toward traditional parties and traditional politics. Thus the Causa Radical (Causa R) party, which suddenly emerged after 1989, embraced an antiparty discourse and spurned alliances with all parties, including those of the left. As a result of having captured the general mood, Causa R's standard-bearer, former steelworkers head Andrés Velásquez, nearly won the presidential election in 1993. As soon as Causa R abandoned its go-it-alone approach, however, and entered into an alliance with COPEI and the Movimiento al Socialismo (MAS) in Congress in 1996, its popularity precipitously declined. Similarly, Chávez's two major opponents in the 1998 elections saw their presidential aspirations dashed the moment they accepted the endorsement of AD and COPEI.

Venezuela's painful decade of political turnover, instability, and military involvement contrasted with its own past as well as with the rest of Latin America. Venezuela's three-decade history of stability after 1958, and the above-mentioned auspicious characteristics of its political institutions highlighted by political scientists, made the nation an unlikely case for the disruptions it faced after 1989. In contrast to Argentina, Peru, and Chile, where voters reelected incumbent presidents and ruling coalitions, the implementation of neoliberal policies in Venezuela did much to destabilize electoral politics. In another contrast, the active role played by military officers in Venezuelan politics in the 1990s differed from much of the rest of Latin America.

Institutional Explanations for the Crisis

Ironically, the very factors that political scientists identified as the root causes for the success of Venezuelan democracy from the 1960s through the 1980s were used to explain the political crisis and instability of the 1990s (Ellner, 1997: 202; Crisp and Levine, 1998: 28). According to these scholars, the practices, institutions, and established beliefs that were conducive to lasting democracy after 1958 had by the 1990s become so inflexible that they blocked the incorporation of new actors with a decisionmaking capacity into the political system. Scholars who stressed these now unpromising features of Venezuelan democracy reached the same basic conclusion: the antidote for the nation's overly centralized and rigid political system was state reforms that would transfer decisionmaking authority to the private sector and local arena. Some of these writers went so far as to demonize the central government and embrace neoliberal-style formulas.

Political scientists blamed the following developments, which had previously been regarded as having contributed to democratic stability in the course of three decades, for the political crisis of the 1990s:

1. *Party pacts.* Venezuelan specialists were influenced by scholars who, writing in the 1990s on other Latin American countries, questioned the view that pacts shaped the democratic transitions of the previous decade in a positive way. Some writers noted, for example, that in spite of agreements between parties and the outgoing military government in Brazil, the nation's democracy was no more stable than in Argentina, where no such accords had been reached. Indeed, both explicit and tacit agreements involved concessions that (particularly in the case of Chile) held back democratization at a future date (Hartlyn, 1998: 108–111; Hagopian, 1990: 164–166). Venezuelanists, for their part, noted that the elitist nature of party pacts reached from above contributed to the centralist and exclusionary political structure, which flawed the nation's political system from the outset (Crisp, Levine, and Rey, 1994: 150).

2. *Political party institutionalization.* Those who viewed strong parties as essential to a healthy political system now recognize the danger of their becoming "overinstitutionalized" and rigid (Diamond, Hartlyn, and Linz, 1999: 27; Mainwaring, 1999: 336; Levine and Crisp, 1999: 156; Crisp, 1997: 161). Venezuela's AD, for instance, dominated organized labor and other organizations to such an extent that civil society was deprived of independent decisionmaking capacity. Some political scientists called Venezuela a "partyarchy" to refer to the all-encompassing power wielded by the top leadership of AD, COPEI, and other parties that failed to create viable mechanisms to consult their respective rank and file (Coppedge, 1994).

3. *Political learning.* What political scientists writing on Venezuela formerly called "political learning" Jennifer McCoy (1999) and Francine Jácome (2000) now characterize as "overlearning." According to them, AD and COPEI leaders after 1958 overcame the interparty discord of previous years by closing ranks, but went overboard in that new actors were kept from decisionmaking spheres. Furthermore, the learnt need to develop a

strong central government became a dogma, which obstructed decentralization and state reform in general.

4. *Oil-exporting status.* Toward the end of her otherwise upbeat, seminal essay of 1987, Terry Karl (1987: 88–89) recognized that oil-mediated
economies such as that of Venezuela have a downside. In *The Paradox of
Plenty* (1997), Karl takes up where she left off ten years earlier by pointing
to the multiple ways that Venezuela's status as an oil exporter held back
political and economic development. Most important, oil-derived revenue
encouraged the state to create a large, highly unproductive bureaucracy at
the same time that it borrowed money from abroad to finance unrealistic, if
not quixotic, megaprojects.

5. *The system of proportional representation.* For a long time, political
scientists credited Venezuela's constitutionally established practice of proportional representation (PR) for bolstering legitimacy and discouraging
insurgency in that it helped the government draw members of the far-left to
electoral politics (Levine, 1973: 46; Kornblith and Levine, 1995: 59).
Indeed, the low entrance requirements of the PR system in Venezuela provided even minuscule parties with representation in the national congress.
By the 1990s, however, scholars argued that the system of slates, which
went hand in hand with PR, encouraged elected officials to place party loyalty ahead of the interests of their constituencies. As a consequence,
Congress took the form of a rubber-stamp body whenever the president's
party enjoyed majority representation. The resultant skepticism regarding
politicians in general led to high levels of electoral abstention (Crisp, 2000:
11, 195).

6. *Multiclass parties.* In the context of the intense social animosities of
the 1990s, traditional multiclass parties may have undermined democratic
credibility. Although designed to contain class conflict, multiclass parties
failed to prioritize the demands of the lower strata of the population, which
suffered the most from two decades of economic stagnation (Buxton, 2001:
222). Specifically, AD abandoned the redistributive policies that it had
embraced during its early years, in spite of the influence of its powerful
Labor Bureau. The inability of traditional parties to identify themselves
effectively with the lower classes undoubtedly contributed to the erosion of
the system's credibility.

The first five of the above factors point in the direction of extreme centralism in which the national political elite is largely free of pressure from the
rank and file as well as private sectors. While the first two points favor the
growth of a "partyarchy," the fourth and fifth points are conducive to
hyperpresidentialism. The third point is compatible with both.

Political scientists differ as to the extent to which this institutional
rigidity is entrenched in Venezuela. Daniel Levine and Brian Crisp have

argued that the acute conflict and tension that have characterized Venezuela are mere growing pains generated by the system's renewal, not signs of the "exhaustion of the model" (Crisp and Levine, 1998: 27). On this basis they oppose the pessimism common among scholars and commentators: "What the doomsayers failed to appreciate was the ongoing process of democratization within democracy itself" (Levine and Crisp, 1999: 156). They point to the impeachment of the highly controversial Carlos Andrés Pérez as an example of the system's "resilience" rather than its decay (Crisp and Levine, 1998: 32). More important, reformist legislation and the emergence of new actors who worked for change within the system attest to democracy's capacity to respond effectively in a situation of crisis. In stressing these inroads, Levine and Crisp attempt to refute those works by political scientists who belittle the effectiveness of state reform.[4] Not surprisingly, Levine and Crisp oppose theoretical approaches resting on deterministic assumptions (themselves inherently pessimistic), which attribute political developments to dependence on oil (Terry Karl) or to cultural factors (Anibal Romero). Similarly, they oppose the "top-down fashion" of framing the issues that centers on institutions without taking into account mobilization and other rank-and-file activity (Levine and Crisp, 1999: 159; Levine, 1994: 161).[5]

The editors of this book are in basic agreement with Levine and Crisp regarding the far-reaching significance of the reforms enacted since 1989 and the emergence of new actors. Indeed, the breadth of this legislation and the inroads made by those who have recently come on the political scenes are impressive. Some commentators unjustly belittle the importance of the changes by claiming that governments have failed to vigorously carry out the proposals formulated by the Presidential Commission on State Reform (COPRE) in the 1980s. They single out the Law of Decentralization (1989) as virtually a dead letter. But a brief glance at the sectors that the law slated for decentralization demonstrates the contrary. The central government has transferred total authority of the port system, the salt industry, and several airports, as well as administrative control of the health system (in various states); at the same time, state and municipalwide housing authorities and municipal police forces have been created throughout the nation. Expenditures at the state level have accordingly increased at the expense of budgetary outlays by the central government (De la Cruz and Barrios, 1998: 231–232). In addition, governors and (though to a lesser extent) mayors have emerged as major political actors who have bolstered the legitimacy of the democratic system at critical moments and even wield considerable power in their respective parties (Ellner, 1996b: 91). This diffusion of power may have compensated, at least in part, for the appointment of influential technocrats (particularly under Pérez) who spurned existing neocorporatist decisionmaking bodies (Crisp, 1998: 33).

The pessimism that Levine and Crisp criticize is most pronounced among political analysts who defend neoliberalism as a dogma. Thus, for instance, neoliberal writers were skeptical of the market reforms enacted under Presidents Pérez and Caldera (Romero, 1994: 66–70). They expressed fear that since both presidents were interventionists at heart who adopted neoliberal formulas out of necessity rather than conviction, they would discard economic reforms such as privatization once the economy began to recover. Nevertheless, both Pérez and Caldera steadfastly defended these policies up to their last days in office.

Not only were the neoliberals excessively pessimistic about Venezuela, but they also stressed centralism as a basic cause for the nation's ills, to the exclusion of other more compelling factors. Neoliberal writers such as Anibal Romero, Moisés Naím, and Roberto Smith Perera (1995) posit that centralism is deeply ingrained in Venezuela and thus not likely to be readily overcome. The paternalist mentality created by easy oil money induces Venezuelans to look to the central government, which administers the revenue, for quick solutions to their problems. Romero (1997: 32; 1986: 44–45) calls this combination of paternalism, centralism, and populism "degraded democracy," which he dates back to the initiation of the democratic period in 1958, and not just the oil boom years of the 1970s. Naím (1993: 19–29; Naím and Francés, 1995: 176–182) also stresses the influence of national actors that reinforce centralism, specifically the nation's main business and labor organizations and the traditional parties, all of which benefit greatly from their intricate ties to the state.

While the pessimism that Levine and Crisp criticize goes beyond neoliberal thinking and characterizes much recent scholarship on Venezuela, so does the emphasis on centralist and rigid institutions as a root cause for the nation's problems. Centralism, of course, has long been recognized as endemic in Latin American countries and associated with underdevelopment (Véliz, 1980: 279–306), but there is a tendency to overstate its responsibility for the acute crisis of recent years. Several schools of thinking do just that. In addition to the cultural focus of many pro-neoliberal writers (Wiarda and Kline, 1996: 534–536; Romero, 1994: 22–28), two major theoretical approaches to Venezuelan democracy lead to the same basic conclusion regarding centralism. In her staple theory of "petrostates," Terry Karl maintains that "oil exacerbated the already high degree of centralization of authority in the executive [and] aggravated the form of presidentialism that could be found elsewhere in Latin America" (1997: 90; 1995: 35). Those scholars who posit leadership as a key independent variable also view centralism as an adverse result of party pacts. They argue that interparty accords fashioned by national elites, and the consensus among their signers in favor of an interventionist government, laid the foundation for a lethargic state that has consistently blocked badly needed political and economic reforms (Jácome, 2000: 108–109).

If Levine and Crisp are correct in their assertion that the nation's institutions have actively responded to the challenges of recent years, then the stress on centralism as a cause for crisis is misplaced. Certainly the issue of institutional reform in favor of decentralization was of major concern only to a small segment of the population. The unpopular Pérez embraced such reforms; furthermore the discourse of Caldera and Chávez was more pro-centralist than their rivals in the 1993 and 1998 presidential elections—and they won anyway. Thus the allegedly slow pace of state reforms cannot be blamed for the disillusionment and rage that were behind "destabilizing" events: the February 27 disturbances (which in turn influenced the 1992 coup attempts), the protests against Pérez and his "economic package," and the electoral triumph of Chávez.

Factors other than resistance to state reforms provide better clues to the concerns of those who repudiated traditional politics and ended up backing Chávez. Most important, traditional politicians were held to blame for the perceived failure of Venezuela's long-standing strategy of "sowing the oil," which left the nation without a viable alternative path of development. Venezuelans were keenly aware of the nation's privileged status as an oil producer and its good fortune of being endowed with other valuable raw materials. This notion was reinforced by the memories of the prosperity of the 1970s, which Venezuelans constantly harked back to. As Patricia Márquez discusses in Chapter 11, the "trickle-down" effect of the 1970s, which benefited the poorer sectors of the population, contrasted with the social polarization of the 1990s.

The neoliberal wave after 1989 never created the popular enthusiasm that interventionist policies had in the past. While interventionism had culminated with the nationalization of the oil industry in 1976, which was applauded by the entire nation and stimulated national pride, the neoliberal period saw the wholesale transfer of entire industries to foreign ownership. The presidential elections of 1988, 1993, 1998, and 2000 represented popular mandates to avoid the neoliberal approach, which both Presidents Pérez and Caldera ignored.[6] Popular disillusionment toward Caldera due to his reversal in 1996, when he embraced the neoliberal "Venezuela Agenda," recalled general attitudes toward Carlos Andrés Pérez, as a result of his "Great Turnabout" on economic policy in 1989.[7] Chávez, while failing to devise a coherent alternative economic policy, inveighed against neoliberalism and its tendency to exacerbate inequalities.

Perhaps the neoliberal-inspired measure most rejected by nonprivileged sectors was the elimination of the "retroactive" provision of the system of severance payments in 1997 (Ellner, 1999a). According to this arrangement, the worker's last monthly salary and the period of time on the job determined his or her severance pay. Retroactivity dated back to the Labor Law of 1936 (ironically drafted by a twenty-year-old Rafael Caldera) and was widened in scope over the years. Venezuelans came to consider retroactive severance pay as virtually a sacred right; legal terms associated with it became household words. A tripartite commission, which included the AD-dominated CTV, drafted the Labor Law Reform, which gutted the system of its retroactivity. The reform's endorsement by AD, COPEI, and the CTV did much to discredit these organizations in the eyes of the workers and was constantly referred to by the *chavista* movement as a veritable betrayal.

In short, Venezuela's two-decade economic contraction created tension throughout society. Pressure from abroad, from popular sectors, and from the rank and file of different organizations, as well as the consciousness of elites regarding the need for change (Martz, 1999–2000: 658), brought about important reforms designed to transform political institutions. That these changes were not as forthcoming or profound as may have been hoped for does not mean that the resistance to them was the main cause of political crisis. Political scientists need to prioritize the importance of sources of the discontent in order to understand why system legitimacy was questioned, beginning with the 1992 coups. This volume represents a departure from past writing in that it gives considerable weight to socioeconomic factors in looking for answers to these issues.

The book underlines the failure of political parties to respond to the economic challenges posed by a protracted economic crisis. As a result, the political party system in the 1990s became increasingly inefficacious while the nation's emerging civil society failed to take its place by becoming an important interlocutor, particularly at the national level. Indeed, one sign of this institutional weakness was that none of the nation's presidents after 1989 enjoyed solid political party backing. President Pérez faced resistance to his reform program from his own party, Caldera ruled with a coalition consisting of small and minuscule parties, while Chávez's MVR failed to develop a cohesive internal structure or link up with civil society. Furthermore, the nation's two main traditional political parties—as well as the party-controlled labor movement—lost prestige and credibility; for the first time since 1958 neither of the two captured the presidency in the 1993 elections. The decline of Venezuela's largest and most well-organized party, AD, was largely due to the conspicuous contradiction between its professed support for the traditional banners of social democracy and state interventionism, on the one hand, and its defense of the neoliberal program of the Caldera administration, on the other. Indeed, AD's response to *chavismo* reflected this lack of programmatic definition. From the outset, AD opposed Chávez's slogans in favor of a constituent assembly and state control of the oil industry and other sectors, but failed to formulate alternatives or to clarify its position regarding the role of the state in the economy.

Social Polarization

Scholars who seek to explain Venezuela's political difficulties must look for sharp contrasts and go beyond the facile explanation that political institutions were simply worn out as a result of protracted democratic rule. According to this view, other Latin American nations were at an advantage in the 1990s due to the newness of their democracies and the popular enthusiasm for the system after years of military rule. Socioeconomic factors are more compelling as explanations for the disruptions of the 1990s. Most important, they suggest significant differences with the nation's past and (although to a lesser extent) with trends in the rest of the continent.

First, Venezuela's economic performance was more disappointing than that of the rest of Latin America. The Economic Commission on Latin America (ECLA) called the 1980s Latin America's "lost decade," largely because of economic stagnation and the lack of an economic strategy to overcome underdevelopment. According to ECLA, production increased a mere 1.2 percent and in Venezuela it actually declined by 0.7 percent. In the 1990s, Latin America's growth picked up, although its 1.5 percent increase per inhabitant was far behind the expectations generated by the radical market reforms that were introduced. The continent's bright spot, however, was the increases in cost of living, which by the end of the decade were the lowest in fifty years. In contrast, Venezuela's annual production level after taking into account population growth was a negative 0.1 percent, thus falling for the second decade in a row. Furthermore, for the first time in modern history Venezuela suffered from soaring inflation, reaching 100 percent in 1996. Ecuador was the only other South American nation with a consistently high inflation rate over the decade. Market reforms in Venezuela took a particularly heavy toll on employment, as the number of industrial jobs between 1988 (the year Carlos Andrés Pérez was elected president) and 1997 (the year before Chávez's election) decreased by 15 percent. Indeed, urban unemployment throughout the decade was 31 percent higher than in Latin America as a whole (CEPAL, 2001; 1999: 64–65, 75, 95, 319–323).

The most significant contrast, however, is between the disappointing behavior of the Venezuelan economy during the last two decades of the century and that of the 1970s. The oil price boom of the latter period generated sudden wealth, which filtered down to the lower classes in the form of populist benefits decreed during the first Pérez administration (1974–1979). Thus the 1970s demonstrated the nation's enormous potential. The prosperity of the decade would be a constant point of reference for Venezuelans in future years and form part of their collective consciousness, making it difficult to cope with the hard times that fell upon them.

The sharp fluctuations in international oil prices in the 1980s and 1990s contrasted with the product's historical pattern of stability. The downturn in the economy served as a painful reminder that Venezuela had not overcome its dependency on petroleum, despite fifty years of well-publicized efforts to "sow the oil" through diversification. Indeed, as Karl (1987: 65) points out, OPEC countries are even more dependent on their main export product than are other third-world "single-commodity" nations. As a result, Venezuelans began to question the viability of the thesis of "Venezuelan exceptionalism," which highlighted the nation's privileges and successes. At the same time, they blamed politicians for failing to harness the nation's oil revenue, a point that was driven home when the much touted state-run steel and aluminum complexes were placed on the auction block and assessed at only a small fraction of what had been invested in them.

Social polarization, which was set off largely by the explosive growth of the informal economy (representing 53 percent of the work force by the turn of the century—see Chapter 3), galvanized tensions. In the words of the president of an important community-based nongovernmental organization: "After the February 27 disturbances, the poor came to consider the affluent communities enemy grounds. Any businessman who is successful is assumed to be corrupt, but the distrust is mutual. The middle class fears that the poor are about to invade their communities" (personal interview with Santiago Martínez, Caracas, September 14, 1999). The intensification of social animosities represented a sharp break with the past, as until then Venezuela had been socially one of the most fluid societies in Latin America. Particularly alarming due to its political implications was that Venezuela, in the words of one scholar, "experienced one of the world's largest increases in inequality during the 1990s" (Naím, 2001a: 31).

Social friction reflected itself on the political front. Indeed, Venezuela became an exception to the generalization formulated by political scientists that class cleavages are of minor importance in understanding Latin American politics, particularly over the last two decades (Mainwaring, 1999: 46–60; Dix, 1989: 33–34).[8] The rise of Causa R and the MVR broke Venezuela's historical pattern of multiclass parties, which had long contained social conflict (Myers, 1998: 514–516). Not only did both parties draw support predominately from the lower classes, but they were also unpopular among privileged sectors, even intellectuals who traditionally identified with leftist movements and causes. The president of Causa R, Pablo Medina (1988: 64–65), recognized his party's failure to gain middle-class support at the same time that he criticized intellectuals, including pro-

gressive ones, for "assuming false commitments which are highly question-
able from the workers' point of view."

Perhaps the incident that first put in evidence the importance of the
social component of Venezuelan politics was Rafael Caldera's much
acclaimed congressional speech on the day of the February 4, 1992, coup
attempt (cited in Chapter 2). Caldera implicitly rejected the notion repeatedly expressed that day in Congress and elsewhere, even by some leftists,
that power-hungry officers determined to destroy the nation's democracy
had spearheaded the rebel movement. Instead he attributed the coup in
large part to the deterioration in the nation's standard and cost of living,
and the social devastation unleashed by neoliberal reforms. Thus one of the
main architects of the modern democratic system refused to close ranks
with AD, COPEI, and MAS, or to place institutional preservation ahead of
the plight of the poor. The speech was particularly significant because it
signaled the political comeback of the veteran Caldera and paved the road
for his election as president the following year.

Scholarly work should carefully examine the sources of popular frustration and privilege the lower classes, which played a central role in the
above-mentioned destabilizing events. The central issue that explained
their behavior was not the economy per se but the nature of the economic
crisis, which aggravated social polarization and singled out the very poor
for special treatment (Myers, 1996: 252). That the underprivileged sectors,
which supported Chávez from the outset of his political career, continuous-
ly voted for him in 1999 and 2000 in spite of the nation's ongoing economic slump demonstrates that their political responses were not mechanically
tied to economic performance (Canache, 2002b: 150). Following his original electoral triumph President Chávez relied increasingly on the support of
the marginalized sectors, as demonstrated by the antigovernment strike of
December 10, 2001, when only members of the informal economy showed
up to their workplaces in large numbers. Significantly, the large rallies and
marches of Chávez's supporters were organized in the poor, western sector
of Caracas, unlike those of the opposition, which took place in the affluent
eastern part of the city.

For the first time since 1958, politics was perceived as a zero-sum
game in which the poor and the privileged had conflicting interests. Thus,
for instance, much of the middle class believed that Chávez was bent on
eliminating private education. Furthermore, when Chávez justified squat-
ting, he was favoring the lower classes at the expense of others. At least
that is the way his remarks were perceived. Naturally, Chávez was not the
first Venezuelan president to appeal directly to the lower strata of the population, but he was the first one who came from the ranks of the nonprivileged and who constantly reinforced this association. When Chávez's main
rival in the 2000 presidential elections, Francisco Arias Cárdenas, used a

rooster to symbolize the president's alleged cowardice in a series of contro-versial television spots, he was well aware that the middle class would con-sider the ads crude and in bad taste. Arias ran them anyway in hopes of making inroads into the lower classes (personal interview with Eduardo Pozo, national leader of the Izquierda Democrática, Caracas, June 5, 2000). Venezuelan politics had never been like this, at least not since 1958.

In short, social polarization found expression on at least five fronts:

1. The growth of the informal economy and the aggravation of social inequality.
2. Mutual resentment between lower classes and relatively privileged sectors of the population.
3. The emergence of parties that appealed disproportionately to lower classes, thus breaking with the nation's tradition of multiclass par-ties.
4. Political leaders such as Chávez whose discourse and to a certain extent actions favored the poor at the expense of privileged groups. The style and rhetoric of these same leaders appealed to the lower classes, and at the same time alienated the middle class.
5. Strong preferences on the part of both lower- and middle-class vot-ers for certain presidential candidates (in contrast to previous elec-toral contests), and for certain policies (as demonstrated in Table 2.1 in this volume).

Social polarization increased the distances and the tension between the unorganized sectors of the population and organized and privileged ones. This trend, however, did not contribute to class consciousness on the part of the underprivileged, who lacked a well-defined political vision, organiza-tional skills, and a sense of organizational discipline. These shortcomings and deficiencies impeded the task of building a cohesive political party to represent the underprivileged, as well as the new structures for society envisioned in the constitution of 1999.[9]

From Social to Political Polarization

Social polarization, which became increasingly acute in the 1980s, fed into political polarization. Five major candidates participated in the 1998 presi-dential campaign, but toward the end, voter preference for Chávez's oppo-nents centered on Henrique Salas Römer, the one with the best chance of winning. Indeed, in the final week AD and COPEI withdrew support for their respective candidates and endorsed Salas Römer. This polarization has deepened even more following the 1998 elections. The middle class became more undivided in its opposition to Chávez and vehement in its opinions about him and his movement than in 1998. Navigating Internet pages, the preserve of relatively privileged sectors, revealed this class bias. When the daily *El Nacional* polled its online readership about various propositions in 2000, Chávez's positions were defeated by about four to one.

The polarization was aggravated by the positions assumed by both sides of the political divide and the rhetoric they employed. MVR leaders, including Chávez, displayed considerable aggressiveness toward adversaries (a style that may be geared to lower-class supporters). This attitude of intolerance is reflected in the MVR's stormy relations with its allies, specifically the Patria Para Todos (PPT) and MAS. The opposition maintained an intransigent stance of its own, and thus consistently opposed all of Chávez's positions, beginning with his proposal for a new constitution at the outset of his first term. A more neutral space, which could have consisted of center-left parties (such as Causa R and Izquierda Democrática) that avoided total opposition but which was independent of the governing coalition, was left largely unoccupied.

Political polarization in which opposition to Chávez became increasingly harsh was also evident in the coverage provided by the U.S. media, particularly after his first six months in office. Leading newspapers such as the *New York Times* and the *Washington Post* referred to Chávez as "Venezuela's rambunctious president" and a "firebrand," his policies as "Jacobin," and his movement as containing "anti-American elements." The articles in both newspapers vividly described the militarization of the government, the politicization of the armed forces, the reliance on populism, and the "purging" of all cultural institutions. Sometimes Chávez was systematically compared with Peru's Alberto Fujimori without reference to the basic differences between the two regimes. The *New York Times* (unlike the *Washington Post*) hailed the April 2002 coup that momentarily ousted Chávez from office (Werz, 2001: 151–152; *New York Times,* January 20, 2001, p. 19-A; August 30, 2000; April 13, 2001, p. A-4; April 24, 2001, p. 1; April 13, 2002; *Washington Post,* May 28, 2000, p. B-1; April 23, 2000, p. B-2; April 14, 2002).[10]

This book as a whole avoids extreme positions with regard to Chávez and his movement and instead puts forward a more nuanced analysis. Kenneth Roberts (Chapter 3) and Patricia Márquez (Chapter 11) accomplish this by placing the rise of *chavismo* in a socioeconomic context. Both authors demonstrate that social polarization preceded Chávez's advent to power and was thus not the product of his fiery rhetoric, as is sometimes alleged. Márquez uses an anthropological approach in order to illustrate changing attitudes, particularly among the poor, for the purpose of gaining insights into the surprising turn of events in recent years. She points out that in the 1970s a youngster from the barrio could end up going to Harvard, and concludes that what she calls the "trickle-down process" of oil windfall revenue worked for the poor during those years. Roberts presents a wide range of economic indicators to demonstrate that 1980 marked a sharp reversal of the trend of improved living standards of popular sectors over the previous two decades. The examination of these long-term socio-economic trends serves as a corrective to the focus of numerous studies that posit *chavismo* as basically the product of political deterioration over the previous two or three decades.

Several chapters put in evidence the institutional errors and shortcomings of the "revolution" that Chávez purported to have carried out. Angel Alvarez (Chapter 8) points to the failure of the Chávez government to build on state reforms such as decentralization, which were designed in the late 1980s and only partially carried out by Presidents Pérez and Caldera in the following decade. Deborah Norden (Chapter 5) shows that while the new constitution promoted institutional accountability in general, it granted the armed forces a dangerous degree of independence and autonomy, beginning with the system of promotions. Steve Ellner (Chapter 9) discusses how the temptation of *chavista* labor leaders to rely on the political backing of the government accounted for their vacillations regarding the strategy of working within the existing trade union structure. Party building was a particularly slow and awkward process. Margarita López Maya (Chapter 4) describes the rudimentary organizational state of Chávez's MVR, which, designed for electoral purposes, failed to deepen the participatory practices of its predecessor, the Movimiento Bolivariano Revolucionario 200. María Pilar García-Guadilla (Chapter 10) demonstrates that the MVR was unable to organize Chávez's followers into a viable social movement to serve as an underpinning for the "revolutionary" process. Nevertheless, under Chávez and in large part stimulated by the process of drafting a new constitution, organizations of civil society did assert themselves and assumed greater autonomy than in the past (a similar observation is made by Ellner with regard to organized labor).

The chapters by Daniel Hellinger, Bernard Mommer, and Julia Buxton address policies that could either enhance or undermine the democratic credibility of the Chávez government. Only by changing policies in fundamental ways could Chávez demonstrate that his "revolution" was more than just empty rhetoric in order to avoid the mass cynicism and apathy that prevailed until 1998 and that did much to discredit the democratic regime. Chávez's foreign policy and its new role in the Organization of Petroleum-Exporting Countries (OPEC), as analyzed by Hellinger (Chapter 2) and Mommer (Chapter 7) respectively, represented a fundamental break with the past. On the other hand, in her discussion of economic policy, Buxton (Chapter 6) shows that Chávez failed to clearly define and apply his "third

way" between socialism and capitalism, although he avoided the mass privatization carried out by the Pérez and Caldera administrations.

Political changes in Venezuela from 1989 to the present have far-reaching implications for the rest of Latin America. The Chávez government's
position on economic policy, for instance, may influence the rest of Latin
America, whose sacrifices resulting from neoliberal formulas have not
translated into desired results. Chávez, more than any other Latin American
president, lashed out at neoliberal economic policy, but stopped short of
embracing nationalization or the statist model in general. Buxton calls
Chávez's approach "mixed" in that it spurned traditional left-wing policy as
well as the formulas of the neoliberal right. Chávez's government moved in
the direction of designing an alternative to both strategies, and those
searching for a novel model elsewhere on the continent have undoubtedly
noted his policies.

Other developments in Venezuela since 1989 represent a rupture with
the past and are bound to have repercussions—or are a reflection of future
trends—in the rest of Latin America. Social cleavages, which so strongly
impacted political struggles during these years, were previously less important in explaining political life throughout the continent. Does the transformation of Venezuela's political landscape under Chávez foretell a new pattern of social struggle for the rest of Latin America? Similarly, the Chávez
government's effort to replace the AD-dominated labor movement with one
created and controlled by its own followers, which incorporates workers of
the informal economy, may be repeated elsewhere on the continent. The
prominent role the Venezuelan military played in political party politics,
which has few parallels in Latin American history, may not necessarily be
an isolated chapter in one nation's history.

The social focus of this book is made more compelling by the events
surrounding the attempted overthrow of Chávez in April 2002. The mass
march of the opposition on April 11, which set off the coup attempt, originated from wealthy sectors of Caracas and consisted mainly of members of
the middle class. In contrast, worker response to the antigovernment general strike called by the CTV and business groups was at best mixed.
Furthermore, slum dwellers constituted the bulk of the participants in the
concentrations that made possible Chávez's return to power.

Indeed, in the immediate aftermath of the abortive coup of April 2002,
the social focus became more relevant than ever before. Social polarization
in Venezuela is more pronounced than ever, reflecting recent trends
throughout the third world. Furthermore, the great expectations that *chavismo* generated among the popular classes have not been dampened in any
way. This is particularly troublesome because, despite their setbacks, the
traditional parties have not responded to recent events by reexamining their
strategies and ideological positions. Indeed, Chávez's special appeal to the

marginalized sectors of the population may form part of a new populist strategy throughout the continent in which political leaders prioritize this social bloc.[11] In short, events in Venezuela since 1989, and particularly during Chávez's rule from 1998 to 2002, beg for a fresh look at the recent past, as the editors and authors of this book have set out to do.

Notes

1. Article 3 of the Labor Law states that "under no circumstances is a norm or disposition that favors the worker revocable."

2. See reference to the study "Conflictos y consenso" undertaken in the early 1960s in Ellner, 1993: 100–102.

3. The term "Venezuelan exceptionalism" was first used by Steve Ellner (1989; 1993: 224–231) to question the validity of the tendency among scholars and Venezuelans in general to exaggerate the propitious aspects of the nation's democracy, and to ignore the nation's status of dependence, which it shared with the rest of Latin America.

4. Political scientists who defend this position (Naím, 2001a; Buxton, 2001: 226) also point out that political actors lacked the courage to forcefully defend market reforms that were closely associated with political reforms. In fact, presidential candidates Eduardo Fernández, Oswaldo Alvarez Paz, and Claudio Fermín campaigned on the basis of a platform of neoliberal reforms, but as a result were penalized at the polls.

5. Levine and Crisp (1999: 159; Levine, 1995) criticize Daniel Hellinger (1991) and Richard Hillman (1994) for adhering to this top-down approach, for failing to appreciate the importance of rank-and-file movements, and for being overly pessimistic. In fact, both Hellinger and Hillman discuss social movements and underline their potential for radical transformation (see, e.g., Hellinger, 1991: 168–184; 1996: 111, 127; Hillman, 1994: 162–170).

6. Scholars have differed among themselves regarding the role of substantive issues in Venezuelan politics over the years. Michael Coppedge (1994) minimizes the importance of ideological and even programmatic positions and stresses personal power struggles and institutional rules. Steve Ellner (1996b: 107, n. 1) argues that while personal ambition is a constant in politics, positions on specific issues also mattered.

7. According to David Myers (personal interview, State College, Pennsylvania, March 17, 2001), survey data actually show that Venezuelans felt more deceived by Caldera's sharp reversal on economic policies than by Pérez as a result of his "Great Turnabout." Venezuelans were particularly resentful of Teodoro Petkoff, who was one of the main architects of the "Venezuela Agenda." Petkoff had been a guerrilla leader in the 1960s and went on to become one of Latin America's most prominent leftist theoreticians. For the attitudes of the popular classes toward the neoliberal reforms of the 1990s, see Table 3.1 in this volume.

8. Previously, political scientists had pointed to the Venezuelan case as a prime example of the validity of the elitist focus that discarded the impact of social cleavages on politics (Neuhouser, 1992: 117).

9. These characteristics contrast with other sectors of the population. Middle sectors, for instance, over the previous three decades had organized autonomous neighborhood associations, which embraced decentralization and state reform. The

organized working class, for its part, belonged to a nationally structured union movement, which generally defended state-sponsored intervention in the economy and at one point put forward proposals of worker participation in company decisionmaking, referred to as *cogestión*.

10. The basic differences between the Chávez government and the "delegative" democracy represented by Fujimori are discussed by Ellner (2001).

11. Kenneth Roberts (1995) and Kurt Weyland (1996) have developed the concept of "neopopulism" to refer to governments with strong backing from marginalized sectors of the population.

2

Political Overview: The Breakdown of *Puntofijismo* and the Rise of *Chavismo*

Daniel Hellinger

Venezuelan democracy as founded by the Pact of Punto Fijo (1958) and consolidated in the constitution of 1961 rested upon a material basis: the distribution of international oil rents through a system of clientelism. Political scientist Juan Carlos Rey (1972) captured this idea famously in his phrase "populist system of reconciliation." This system was crafted by a generation of political leaders who since 1936 had championed electoral democracy as the key to asserting sovereign control over oil (the subsoil) and creating a sustainable nonoil economy. This was its ideological basis, its basis of legitimacy. The oil boom of 1973–1983 and nationalization of the foreign oil companies in 1976 were the culmination of this project associating democracy, oil nationalism, and development.

On February 28, 1983, a day known as "Black Friday" in Venezuela, the government of President Luis Herrera Campíns devalued the bolivar, signaling the beginning of not only a material but also an ideological crisis from which the country never recovered. The explosive "Caracazo" of February 1989, which engulfed nearly every city in the country (not just Caracas), punctuated the collapse of the populist system of reconciliation. Less clear was what would take its place.

In retrospect, the period after 1989 can be seen as a chaotic, fluid political interlude, not yet concluded, in which various sectors put forth incomplete projects to restore faith in the developmental potential of democracy. Three distinct social forces (with some fluidity across the boundaries separating them) sought to fill the vacuum left by the collapse of *puntofijismo* (to be discussed in detail below): an *obrerista* movement that gave rise to Causa Radical (Causa R), the first political party to contest the electoral hegemony of the Punto Fijo parties; a managerial sector consisting of executives associated with the Petróleos de Venezuela, Sociedad Anónima (PDVSA), and various lesser groups associated with the middle and profes-

27

sional classes; and the military, especially the Movimiento Bolivariano Revolucionario (MBR) of Hugo Chávez Frías. Each force propelled forward organic electoral movements and candidates, each articulating an outlook consonant with its corporate or class interest but each one also seeking, in terms articulated by Antonio Gramsci, "to get beyond that moment of their historical development and become agents of more general activities of a national and international character" (1971: 15).

Chávez and his Bolivarian movement, with origins in the military, seized the initiative in the 1990s, but the attempted coup of April 11, 2002, clearly indicated that the competition to advance projects to replace the exhausted Punto Fijo system was not over. Political initiatives launched from the sinews of the social and labor movements and from ranks of the business and middle classes left their mark on Venezuelan politics, shaping both *chavismo* and the opposition. Oil policy, struggles over the distribution of rents, and the character of democracy remained intertwined both materially (in conflicts over spending) and ideologically (in debates over neoliberal policy alternatives).

Oil Nationalism, Development, and *Puntofijismo*

Between 1945 and 1948 the Acción Democrática (AD) political party, led by Rómulo Betancourt, attempted to implement a program of rapid modernization of Venezuela. Certain political fault lines in contemporary Venezuelan politics have their origins in the civilian-military coup that inaugurated this *trienio*. The *trienio* government was legitimated by landslide victories in three elections, but President Chávez frequently alluded to the fact that AD initially came to power as the result of a military coup against the liberal, nationalist regime of General Isaías Medina Angarita. Betancourt's influential writings portrayed this coup of 1945 as necessary to pave the way for democracy. The founder of AD portrayed Medina's oil reform of 1943 as a sellout of national interests, while he depicted his own policies of "no more concessions" and "fifty/fifty" (equal shares of oil profits between the state and the companies) as the beginnings of oil nationalism (Betancourt, 1978: 61–106). It could be no other way. To suggest that a military ruler (Medina) had defended Venezuelan sovereignty would violate the underlying assumption that *only* a democratic state could exercise effective control over the subsoil and use oil rents to modernize the country in a manner that would benefit everyone.

An undercurrent of political resentment with origins in the period 1941 to 1948 ran just below the surface of Venezuelan politics during the Punto Fijo era, only to resurface with the crisis of legitimacy after 1989. Luis Miquilena, right-hand adviser to Chávez after 1994 and first secretary-general of the Movimiento Quinta República (MVR; Fifth Republic Movement), began his political career in the Communist Party (leaving sometime in the 1950s), which supported Medina and until the *trienio* competed with AD for hegemony in the labor movement. Another supporter of Medina was Salvador de la Plaza, whose defense of the 1943 oil reform and critique of Betancourt's *trienio* oil policies inspired the views of Alí Rodríguez Araque, Chávez's first minister for energy and mines, later secretary-general of the Organization of Petroleum-Exporting Countries (OPEC), and then, after the abortive coup of April 2002, president of the state oil company. Rodríguez was the chief architect of Chávez's nationalist oil policy (see Chapter 7).

The Pact of Punto Fijo was an attempt by elites to prevent a repetition of the coup of 1948, which ended the *trienio* and paved the way for the dictatorship of General Marcos Pérez Jiménez. The pact was not only inclusionary but also exclusionary. Specifically, it excluded the Communist Party, then a considerable force in Venezuelan politics. The pact and the resulting political system survived military coup attempts against the Betancourt presidency (1959–1964) and a decade-long insurgency inspired by the Cuban Revolution of 1959. The Comité de Organización Política Electoral Independiente (COPEI), founded by Rafael Caldera in 1946 as a Christian democratic opposition to the secular, positivist ideology of AD, shed its character as a confessional party. As president from 1969 to 1974, Caldera made it a policy to pacify the country, and much of the left began to abandon insurgency. After 1973, former guerrillas began to appear as members of Congress or even cabinet ministers, some of them as members of AD. From then on, Venezuelans could say, ruefully or not, "We're all *adecos* now."

The hegemonic status of the *adeco* project during the Punto Fijo era benefited from the consolidation of liberal internationalist hegemony in the United States after World War II. In exile during the dictatorship of Pérez Jiménez, Betancourt assiduously courted the approval of liberal foreign policy elites, notably Nelson Rockefeller, with whom he had developed a friendship during the *trienio*. After 1958, under his "Betancourt Doctrine," the Venezuelan president "urged non-recognition of *de facto* regimes and their expulsion from the Organization of American States" (Ameringer, 1977: 336–337), a policy aimed at both Cuba and rightist regimes, but often limited to symbolic gesture. Venezuela served Washington's interests as a foil for the Cuban regime and as a model for the kind of "transitions to democracy" preferred by U.S. policymakers (e.g., Merkel, 1981). That is, the minimalist democracy established by the Pact of Punto Fijo was a polyarchy, a form of weak democracy preferred by U.S. elites to more radical, participatory, egalitarian regimes (see Robinson, 1996).

An optimistic prognosis for democracy and development prevailed

after the December 1973 election brought President Pérez to office for the
first time. Within two years the Venezuelan oil industry had been nationalized, and Pérez and his planners imagined the imminent transformation of
Venezuela into a great industrial power (Coronil, 1997; Karl, 1997:
71–188). Unlike the cases of Peru, Chile, and other countries where nationalization of natural resource industries was part of a nationalist agenda,
anti-imperialism in Venezuela did not have state ownership of foreign companies as a goal. Never in his prolific writings over a half century did
Betancourt envision a Venezuela without foreign capital, nor was nationalization of this sort urged by other political forces. The main debate
revolved around how to best take advantage of the expiration of vast oil
leases, which was slated for 1983. A national oil company was created to
participate in but not monopolize the oil industry. Suddenly, because OPEC
had wrested control over pricing and levels of production from the companies, the path was cleared to full nationalization (Mommer, 1988:
157–198). To a nation flush with petrodollars, poised to make a great leap
forward into developed status, the need to regulate the relationship between
capital and the natural resource seemed obsolete. As Bernard Mommer
shows in Chapter 7, the failure to understand the new situation had disastrous consequences.

The influx of petrodollars during the OPEC boom (1973–1983) far
exceeded the capacity of the country to absorb capital. The institutions of
democracy, especially the judiciary, seemed incapable of coping with the
competition for rents. Certainly the wealthy profited the most, but the corruption was prolific, embracing toll takers on the highway, military con-
tractors, social service providers, presidents, and their mistresses. Thus the
corruption was "democratic" in a sense. *Puntofijismo* ensured that some
rents percolated down to all social strata, and there was optimism that the
country was advancing. It was measurable in daily life and in opportunities
for the children of urban migrants and workers (see Chapter 11). After the
devaluation of 1983, however, the distributive capability of the system
waned, and with it confidence that *this* democracy would spur development
and opportunity.

Several studies (Coppedge, 1994; Crisp, 2000) have demonstrated how
the political parties increasingly lost much of their ideological coherence
and became vehicles for contesting control over patronage. As the first generation of party leaders gave way to the next, party factionalism increased.
The divisions within AD were made more acute by the resentment that the
party's old guard felt toward Pérez's patronage of a group of economic
elites (the so-called twelve apostles and especially the banker Pedro
Tinoco) whose fortunes were largely made and expanded during the Pérez
Jiménez regime or later. Significant policy and group interests were often at
stake (Ellner, 1996a), but personal factionalism seemed paramount in inner-

party struggles. The parties became the antithesis of Gramsci's notion of organizations in which individual and corporate interests are put aside in favor of a broader political perspective (Hellinger, 1984).

As the parties became more clientelist, a structural weakness became more salient. Venezuelan parties had never fully institutionalized their internal procedures for choosing presidential candidates and filling party lists *(planchas)* with nominations for national, state, and local offices. The focus of competition was always the presidential nomination, but the rules of the game were rarely clear from the outset. Central party organs, a national party conference, or a primary vote might determine the nomination. Bitter fights over procedures could be costly to the eventual candidate, as in 1968 when Caldera triumphed over an AD candidate weakened by the defection of much of its labor to a sizable splinter party. More often, however, divisions within party ranks were assuaged by common interest in gaining the largest share of power in the rent-seeking and rent-distributing state. As oil rents contracted, what would hold the parties together? What future could they hold out to voters?

End of the Illusion

On February 2, 1989, outgoing president Jaime Lusinchi handed the presidential sash to his fellow *adeco,* Pérez, who began his second term with a lavish inauguration lending credence to the popular notion that the flamboyant Pérez, popularly known as "CAP," would restore the good times of a bygone, populist era. Only after the ceremonies were complete did Pérez announce that he had already negotiated a structural adjustment agreement, the so-called *paquete* (package), with the International Monetary Fund. On February 27 came the Caracazo, a popular uprising set off by anger at *por puesto* drivers who, facing a 30 percent fuel hike, attempted illegally to double fares and to refuse student discounts. The rioting spread to nineteen other cities and lasted until March 5. The army was called to quell the revolt; when it was over, medical personnel estimated 1,000 to 1,500 deaths, well above the official count of 287. The mass opposition against dictatorship in 1958 had united people across class lines. In contrast, the Caracazo of 1989 was the first mass action with strong class overtones since 1935, when the death of Juan Vicente Gómez sparked rural and urban unrest.

On February 4, 1992, a second blow to *puntofijismo* was delivered by the coup attempt of Lieutenant Colonel Hugo Chávez. The *golpistas* achieved their military objectives almost everywhere, but they failed to capture Pérez in Caracas or to spark a civil uprising, as some leftists insisted was necessary (see Chapter 4). However, defeat was turned into political victory for the MBR in the electrifying moments when Chávez appealed on national television for the revolting troops to surrender. He accepted sole responsibility for the defeat, something that impressed Venezuelans accustomed to politicians dodging accountability. His statement that the objectives had not been met "for now" stirred popular hope that the struggle had only begun. On the streets, civilian supporters, especially younger parts of the population, began appearing in red berets similar to those worn by the paratroop commander and his troops.

Margarita López Maya has shown that the ensuing period was marked by a variety of protests demonstrating that "the political parties and unions had been losing their dynamism and capacity for popular representation and mediation, exhausted by the way they exercised power in the context of abundant money and resources of the Petro-State of the 1970s" (1999: 212). For the next ten years, until the decisive triumph of Chávez in the 1998 presidential election, the major political actors attempted in vain to find new footing. They agreed to implement some institutional reforms delayed since the 1980s, but the relegitimation of the governing elite would have been difficult under any circumstances. Having been told for fifty years that the country was rich, and now fully sovereign over oil, how could Venezuelans not conclude that their impoverishment was the fault of the politicians and the elite linked closely to them?

The congressional session following the February 4 military uprising brought forth a good deal of fiery rhetoric about the duty to defend democracy, including a cry of "death to the *golpistas*" from David Morales Bello, a prominent *adeco* senator. Then former president (and senator-for-life) Rafael Caldera dared to call the emperor naked, noting that the people had not poured into the streets in defense of democracy, a notable contrast to recent events in Eastern Europe, the Southern Cone of South America, the Philippines, and Tiananmen Square:

> It is difficult to ask the people to burn for freedom and democracy while they think freedom and democracy are not able to feed them and impede the exorbitant increase in the cost of subsistence; when it has not been able to deal effectively with the blight of corruption. The golpe is censurable and condemnable, but it would be disingenuous for us, without giving attention to their aims, to think that we are dealing with merely a few ambitious officers precipitously launching an adventure on their own account. (translated from *El Universal,* February 4, 2001)

The constitution of 1961 and the *puntofijista* party system were left gravely wounded. Congress removed Pérez from office after the Supreme Court had ruled there was sufficient evidence to try him for illegal diversion of funds into the campaign of Nicaraguan presidential candidate Violeta Chamorro. He was later convicted, but the relatively inconsequential weight of this scandal compared to other incidents of corruption that went unpunished (including previous accusations against Pérez) makes it clear that the action was really a desperate attempt to remove from office the highly unpopular president—highly unpopular due to his neoliberal economic policies—before *puntofijismo* collapsed altogether. The distinguished historian Senator Ramón Velásquez finished out the last few months of Pérez's term.

During the Lusinchi administration, the Presidential Commission on State Reform (COPRE) had made various proposals to decentralize state administration and democratize the internal workings of the parties. President Pérez accelerated some of these reforms after the Caracazo, implementing in 1989 the first direct elections of governors and mayors. The resulting decentralization of political and administrative power opened the way for new actors to emerge and enhanced the influence of personal factors in voting (Naím, 2001b).

The constitutional thread was barely intact. So much cannot be said for the party system. COPEI was the first of the two major parties to implode. In 1993, Caldera refused to run against his former protégé turned rival, Eduardo Fernández, in a primary contest he thought would be controlled by the party machine. He then split from the party he had founded to run as the candidate of the left-leaning Movimiento al Socialismo (MAS) and a coalition of sixteen other small parties, nicknamed *"chiripera"* after small insects that together make a noisy racket when they chirp together. COPEI ultimately nominated the governor of Zulia, Oswaldo Alvarez Paz, who offered, according to some, "neoliberalism light" and defeated Fernández in the primary contest. AD nominated Claudio Fermín, former mayor of a Caracas municipality, over the opposition of its powerful secretary-general, Alfaro Ucero. The Causa R candidate was Andrés Velásquez, leader of an insurgent labor movement and governor of the important industrial state of Bolívar.

As Chapters 1 and 8 show, these résumés put the lie to the idea that no significant reform had taken place in Venezuela. Direct election of governors and mayors, initiated in 1989, had advanced the careers of all the candidates and strengthened their ability to compete against preferred candidates of national party leaders. This procedure wrested the nomination process from politicians who controlled party machines. From 1974 until 1993, AD and COPEI together controlled no less than 81 percent of the seats in the lower house and 88 percent of the seats in the Senate. The percentages would have been even higher had not the system of allocating seats been proportional and allowed for a quota according to national totals (Crisp, 2000: 44–46). In 1993, the totals had shrunk to 53 and 60 percent, respectively, with three other parties sharing most of the rest of legislative power.

Caldera assumed office with a mandate from only 30.5 percent of the voters. Official returns showed Velásquez finishing fourth, only 8 percentage points behind the winner. Causa R maintained that its candidate had actually won the election. Bitter and sometimes violent conflict over charges of fraud broke out in several state elections. AD and COPEI had been undermining the independence and technical capacity of the Supreme Electoral Council for some time. Wherever smaller parties were unable to monitor voting procedures, the hegemonic parties could steal votes by altering the results (the *actas*) reported at the polling places. The phrase *"Acta mata voto"* had become a cliché. Julia Buxton's study of the 1992 local elections found that leaders of AD had issued explicit instructions to members on how to "easily convert a defeat in the urns into a victory in the *actas*" (2001: 81). Tactics included using bribes and liquor to ply military officials in charge of polling places, lining up party voters early to create a long wait for other voters, distracting witnesses, and trying to alter ballots cast for organizations with no witness. Entire *actas* could be nullified due to irregularities, which happened often in areas of Causa R strength. Ballot boxes containing results favoring Causa R were found in garbage dumps. Buxton concluded, "This disenfranchisement is not due to any failings on the part of the electorate, it is due to the politicization of table members which prevents the basic task of counting votes from being carried out in a fair and neutral manner" (2001: 89).

Caldera used his stature, political sagacity, and the political capital obtained from his 1992 speech to reduce political tensions somewhat. He moved boldly to replace the high command of the military with loyalists. Then he freed Chávez and his coconspirators and declared amnesty for exiled officers involved in a second (November) coup attempt in the tumultuous year of 1992. However, the patriarch had no answer to the long-term economic decline that fed popular discontent. A major banking crisis in his first months of office exhausted what little room he had for economic maneuver and placed him at the mercy of international financial forces. After two years of improvisation, Caldera embraced the idea of opening the oil sector to foreign capital (the *apertura*) and announced a program of structural adjustment, "Agenda Venezuela," little different from the hated *paquete* of CAP. Various subsidies and wage increases to the public sector were intended to lessen the blow, but they failed to halt the further deterioration in the quality of life.

Caldera's stature gave *puntofijismo* only a temporary reprieve; the economic crisis and social polarization continued apace. Although visible tension had eased, the proportion of Venezuelans seeking "radical changes" as opposed to "partial reforms" in the system continued to increase between 1995 and 1998 (see Table 2.1). As the 1998 election approached, it became

Table 2.1 Percentage of Population Favoring Radical Changes, Partial Reforms, or No More Changes, 1995–1998

	1995 3rd qtr.	1996 1st qtr.	1997 2nd qtr.	1998 1st qtr.	1998 3rd qtr.
Radical changes	51%	55%	55%	60%	63%
Partial reforms	26	27	25	20	27
No more changes	17	13	13	13	7

Source: Consultores 21, 1998.

clear that the major parties were in difficult straits. What might replace them was less clear.

Three Contenders to Succeed *Puntofijismo*

A proliferation of new political personalities and political forces appeared in the decade of agony for *puntofijismo*. In retrospect, however, the roots of these insurgent candidacies can be found in three sectors that sought to step into the vacuum: labor, professional and managerial sectors, and the military.

The Rise and Fall of Causa R

The 1993 campaign of Velásquez and Causa R (Radical Cause, with the *R* reversed in the party logo) posed the first serious challenge from a party seeking to break from the Punto Fijo system. Unlike other contenders, Velásquez had a fairly developed program rooted in a decade of patient organizing, especially in the labor movement. The grand strategy of Causa R was rooted in the thought of its late founder, Alfredo Maneiro, a former guerrilla leader. Maneiro was almost unique among Venezuelan leftists in emphasizing the importance of building social and worker movements from which leadership would emerge organically. This was a departure from the prevailing notion on the left, which emphasized, even within the ranks of the ideologically innovative MAS, capturing control of the state and existing social groups, especially the Confederación de Trabajadores de Venezuela (CTV; Confederation of Venezuelan Workers).

Causa R had its greatest success in the area around the new industrial zone of Ciudad Guayana, where the hegemony of the *adeco* union leadership was less established (see Hellinger, 1996). By the late 1980s, Causa R's union movement, Matanceros, had won control of several key metallurgical worker organizations, including the steelworkers, which was the largest union in the country. A close, consultative relationship with workers was key to the party's resistance to the tactics of co-optation, legal intervention, and repression, which usually permitted the traditional parties to beat back challenges to their hegemony. The most prominent union leader, Velásquez, used this struggle as a springboard for a stunning victory in the state of Bolívar in the first direct gubernatorial elections of 1989. The party achieved a presence in Congress as well as control of the mayoralty of Caracas. These victories raised the prospect that an *obrerista* organization, part party and part social movement, not unlike the Workers Party (PT) in Brazil, might play a prominent role in a post–Punto Fijo regime.

Causa R offered what might be described as "leftist pragmatism." During his term of office in Bolívar, Velásquez and his associates governed in a consultative style resembling the movement-oriented politics of the PT, the Revolutionary Democratic Party (PRD) of Mexico, and the Sandinistas in the early years of the Nicaraguan Revolution (Hellinger, 1996). Where it controlled unions (e.g., in the metallurgical sector and the state-owned telecommunications company, CANTV), it resisted privatization but compromised and negotiated transitional benefits for workers. In Congress, Causa R consistently supported the call for a constituent assembly— although it resisted the popular demand to replace proportional representation with a single-member district system *(uninominalismo)*. This earned the party criticism from social movements, especially middle-class neighborhood organizations that saw in *uninominalismo* a way to break the grip of the *cogollos* (political coteries) on local politics. Causa R enhanced its mass appeal as a fresh alternative by eschewing alliances with traditional parties, but this also earned it a reputation for sectarianism from other leftist parties.

Why, then, did Causa R falter after 1993, culminating in its division in 1997? Organizationally it failed to reconcile the need for internal discipline with the democratic, open relationship it sought with workers and other social forces. On the one hand, its ranks were open to whomever was willing to declare commitment to its democratic principles; on the other hand, power was retained by a small group of veteran leaders who operated by an informal but highly centralized decisionmaking process. As its star rose, especially in states where it had barely existed, opportunists joined party ranks. At the same time, it failed to extend debate about tactics and strategy beyond the ranks of its veteran leadership, whose personality differences deepened.

The decision to leap ahead with a challenge for national power seems to have overtaken the longer-run, grassroots organizing that had made Causa R a promising alternative in the early 1990s. Velásquez might very well have been denied victory by fraud in 1993, but his very run for office was contradictory to the more strategic vision that had been laid out by

Maneiro, which was predicated on building strong, grassroots organizations, not immediately seeking state power. In fact, some important leaders in the party were also pursuing military routes to power, claiming that the political establishment and military would never let them come to power through elections (Buxton, 2001: 162–163). Pablo Medina, secretary-general of Causa R until 1997, acknowledged that they sought to organize civilian support to give the 1992 golpe a "civic-military" character. Eventually, the Velásquez faction forced out Medina and his followers, who then founded the Patria Para Todos (PPT) in 1997. This division obscured a more fundamental shift on the part of both factions from organizing a broad, democratic mass movement to seeking state power (Hellinger, 1996; Buxton, 2001: 176–179).

In the Chávez era, Causa R maintained some influence primarily through the Nuevo Sindicalismo (New Unionism) labor movement, which remained aligned with Velásquez. Somewhat contradictorily, the party initially backed a technocratic independent, Irene Sáez, in the 1998 election before switching to its own candidate. In the 2000 election it supported the main opponent of Chávez. For its part, the PPT backed Chávez in the December 1998 elections but left the Polo Patriótico (PP; Patriotic Pole), the alliance of parties supporting the president, just before the megaelections of 2000, only to return again in 2001. The PPT retained control of the Ministry of Energy and Mines because of the success of the oil policies and prestige of Rodríguez, even after Medina openly broke with Chávez in early 2002.

With the division of Causa R, the prospect that a political party rooted in social movements and democratic reform of labor might emerge as a viable contender for executive power and an influence in the national legislature receded. As Steve Ellner shows in Chapter 9, Chávez and the MVR were more successful in forcing the CTV to accept democratic reforms than in organizing unionized workers to support their own vaguely defined Bolivarian project. As a consequence, the polarization of Venezuelan society and politics occurred more along an axis defined by conditions of life and poverty than around relations of production. As Chávez moved into his third year as president in 2002, most of the labor movement allied itself with the opposition. Chávez found himself confronted by labor conflicts that tested his credentials as a revolutionary and left him strategically vulnerable.

Business and the Middle Sectors

The search for a caudillo was not limited to Venezuela's poor; the middle class also sought its man (woman?) on horseback. In mid-1997, the Consultores 21 polling firm asked a cross section of the population what model of president they preferred (see Table 2.2). Although Fidel Castro was most popular among the most marginalized sectors of the population, his 25 percent paled compared to the enthusiasm of the middle and upper classes for a leader in the mold of Peru's Alberto Fujimori.

The collapse of the rentist model had a severe impact on domestic capitalists and the middle class. Financial crises, unemployment, administrative corruption, rising crime rates, limited opportunities in professional fields, and declining salaries all contributed to the contraction of the middle class (see Figure 2.1). The replacement of foreign oil by the state subtracted from the business world the strongest private sector of capital. Groups of professionals and survivors from the shrinking middle class launched political projects, but most were little more than romantic forays into cyberspace. The campaign of Irene Sáez is emblematic of the mercurial nature of movements and parties launched within this sector.

Sáez had parlayed her fame as Miss Universe and as a spokesperson for a major bank (Consolidado) into a successful run for mayor of Chacao,

Table 2.2   Preferred Model of President by Social Class, June 1997

	Total	Popular Lower	Popular	Popular Middle	Middle	Middle Upper
Alberto Fujimori	43%	10%	32%	53%	49%	50%
None	18	27	23	14	15	27
Fidel Castro	16	25	17	13	16	4
Others	18	19	19	16	18	15

Source: Percepción 21, vol. 2, no. 2 (Caracas: Consultores 21, June 1997): 6.

Figure 2.1   Shrinkage of Middle Class, Growth of Marginal and Low Sectors, 1989–1999

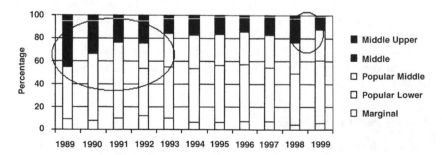

Source: Consultores 21, 2000.
Note: Percentages are based on first-quarter data.

a wealthy municipality in the Caracas metropolitan area. Her administration was respected for transparency and efficiency. To seek the presidency she launched "IRENE," yet another personalist electoral movement intended to demonstrate a candidate's independence from *puntofijismo.* Throughout most of 1997 she was far ahead of any other candidate in the polls and seemed a good bet to become Venezuela's next president, which prompted COPEI, facing dismal electoral prospects, to place her name at the head of its ballot. Her candidacy offered the prospect of an antiparty candidacy consistent with the middle class's desire to participate in a globalized capitalist economy.

That the Venezuelan parties had been notoriously resistant to increasing the representation of women in political life (Friedman, 2000) certainly did not help Irene Sáez's prospects. Pageants may be popular in Venezuela, but to the masses she was a former beauty queen from a wealthy enclave in the capital. Sáez was more a technocrat than either a mother figure or caudillo, and she refused to offer a program, neoliberal or otherwise. Early in the campaign this ambiguity was an advantage, but it became a liability once voters began to listen for clues to what a Sáez presidency might mean. Her acceptance of the nomination of COPEI deprived her of the luster of an outsider. By contrast, the charismatic Chávez drew on his humble origins to feed his "man-of-the-people image." Chávez rose as Sáez fell in the polls. Many in the business and professional community cast about for an alternative.

Even while Sáez was still riding high in the polls, speculation in the media centered on a candidate from the only sector of Venezuelan business that seemed to be prospering—the state oil company. Although he always denied interest in the nomination, Luis Giusti, president of PDVSA and chief architect of the *apertura,* was being discussed in late 1997 as *presidenciable* by some leaders of Causa R, COPEI, MAS, and AD (*El Nacional,* May 16, 1997; May 21, 1997; January 15, 1998; *El Universal,* May 18, 1997). Giusti had campaigned to convince the *adeco* caudillo, Alfaro Ucero, to reverse the traditional hostility of AD toward foreign investment in oil. Ucero not only endorsed the *apertura* but also reportedly came to see Giusti as a possible candidate for his party (*El Nacional,* July 27, 1997). A Giusti candidacy also attracted interest from financial groups and international investors (*El Nacional,* April 15, 1998; April 20, 1998).

Well before nationalization, the oil companies that would become PDVSA had "Venezuelanized" their management. Perhaps it is more accurate to say the companies had "Westernized" the outlook of the native managerial strata. The "Generation of Shell" was how one journalist characterized the managers that embarked on the oil *apertura* and pressed for Venezuela's departure from OPEC, perhaps preparing ultimately for privatization of PDVSA (Arrioja, 1998). The gap between these executives and the majority of Venezuelans was not only economic but also cultural. Andrés Sosa Pietri, former president of PDVSA under Pérez, described membership in OPEC as nothing less than the rejection of Western modernity: "Our country was never a colony, not of Spain nor of any other power," he argued on the eve of Chávez's 1998 victory. For Sosa, Venezuela was "discovered," not "conquered," because the country's territory was, he claims, "thinly populated by tribes living close to a state of nature. The wars of liberation in Africa and Asia were to preserve cultures often thousands of years old, whereas the Independence War of Venezuela was more a civil conflict among a population with European ethical and religious values." Had it not been for OPEC, argued Sosa Pietri, "we could have aspired, because of our origins, cultural roots, and territorial wealth, to convert ourselves quickly into full associates of the so-called 'first world'" (Sosa Pietri, 1998).

The collapse of oil prices in 1998 dealt a severe blow to the prestige of Giusti and the company. The previously untouchable reputation of PDVSA management now came into question. The removal of Giusti became a popular campaign promise for Chávez *(El Universal Digital,* September 14, 1998). The professional and managerial sectors turned to Henrique Salas Römer, a former businessman, once a member of COPEI, and the popular, independent governor of the state of Carabobo. Like Sáez, Römer offered "neoliberalism light," comparable to the option offered by President Fernando Henrique Cardoso of Brazil. He supported the *apertura* but unlike Giusti did not dogmatically defend the model. Like Sáez, Römer was respected for competence as an elected official, but he was more adept politically.

The business sector in Venezuela was ill prepared to confront a resurgence of populism in Venezuela. AD's hegemony had already been shaken so profoundly by the events of 1989 to 1992 that the opportunity of co-opting a populist party to implementation of neoliberalism, as Carlos Menem did with Peronism in Argentina, was blocked. Pérez had already tried that route with disastrous consequences. At the same time, the military's status as a contender for state power had been enhanced, not discredited, by recent historical experience.

The Military

The February 4, 1992, rebellion and a second failed coup on November 27 revealed a deep chasm between the civilian politicians and the military, one of the key sectors incorporated into the Punto Fijo agreement. Considering the role the military had played in suppressing the Caracazo, this was entirely unanticipated. Shortly after the Caracazo, Arturo Sosa Abascal, editor of the Jesuit *Revista SIC* and a keen observer of the Venezuelan scene, wrote: "In a moment in which the faithfulness of the military was vital to its survival, the Armed Forces reacted as a fundamental (and founding) ally of the political system installed in Venezuela after 1958" (1989: 104).

Indeed, the military itself had seemed quite adept at rent-seeking. While the economy had been failing in the 1980s, the military budget had actually tripled, reaching 3.6 percent of the gross national product in 1987. With 50,000 men under arms in ten brigades and five divisions, Venezuela had 103 active brigadier generals and 30 generals of division, in contrast with Brazil, whose army was five times larger and had only 116 generals altogether. Congress decided annual promotions. Although this reinforced civilian supremacy, it also enhanced the importance of the partisan affiliation of officers. Promotions, like everything else, fell under the influence of the *cogollos* and were tainted by corruption. Several embarrassing scandals indicated that officers were intricately enmeshed in the system of patronage and corruption that had discredited the politicians (Hellinger, 1991: 163–168).

The military rebellions of 1992 demonstrated that some officers, particularly those who formed the MBR, had not assimilated North American geopolitical doctrines nor been fully integrated into the structures of *puntofijismo*. Chávez and his collaborators were the first cohort of officers to have attended civilian universities and not to have undergone training at U.S. counterinsurgency schools. In the 1980s Chávez made contact with several guerrilla commanders, including one, Douglas Bravo, who had never renounced armed struggle (Garrido, 1999; Blanco Muñoz, 1998; Gott, 2000; López Maya, Chapter 4 in this volume). Chávez himself acknowledges that they influenced the MBR ideologically (Blanco Muñoz, 1998: 272–276).

The nationalism incubating in the MBR drew upon a deep tradition of populist caudillism in Venezuelan history. The least known but possibly most emblematic of the trinity of heroes in MBR rhetoric (which includes Simón Bolívar, the great leader of Latin America's emancipation from Spain, and his philosopher/teacher, Simón Rodríguez) is Ezequiel Zamora, a Liberal caudillo assassinated in 1860, allegedly from within his own ranks during the Federal War (see Banko, 1996: 169–183). During the 1960s, leftists such as the folk singer Alí Primera built a mythic reputation around Zamora, even if most Venezuelans otherwise knew little of his history. Chávez, from the llanero region of Barinas, where Zamora achieved his greatest following, exalted the Federalist martyr and appropriated his antioligarchic rhetoric, which resonates in his mass rallies, televised speeches, and weekly radio broadcasts. This egalitarian discourse is often vague on specifics, laced with racial overtones, evocative of the resentment of the masses, and threatening to elites. *"Horror al oligarquía"* was a popular Federalist cry to rally the underclass of peons and former slaves, most of African ancestry. Chávez resurrected the slogan to appeal to the poorest Venezuelans, who despite relatively relaxed social barriers are disproportionately blacks and pardos. Humberto Celli, a prominent leader of AD, captured the significance of race in commenting on the scene that greeted Chávez as he delivered his victory speech from the presidential palacc to a throng gathered in the plaza below: "When I saw Chávez triumphant on the 'People's Balcony,' greeting the multitude, and the TV cameras focused on those delirious faces," said Celli. "I said to myself, 'My God, those are the *negritos* of *Acción Democrática*'" (Colomina, 2001: sec. 2, p. 8).

The MBR had espoused abstention from elections, but this stance began to give way after 1994 as the movement began to more openly interact with civilian sectors. Francisco Arias Cárdenas, a popular hero in the February 4 golpe because of his successful seizure of the governor's palace in the Maracaibo, Zulia, showed the electoral potential of the MBR by winning the governorship of that state in 1995, with the backing of Causa R. Chávez initially disdained electoral politics, but in prison he found a political tutor in Luis Miquilena, and he first made the acquaintance of María Isabel Rodríguez, a society columnist, whom he would later marry and who would emerge as a significant political figure in her own right. After his release from jail in 1994, Chávez lived for a year in the apartment of Miquilena, then a relatively minor figure in Venezuelan politics, but a veteran practitioner with connections in the banking and insurance industries, some of whom helped finance the candidate's 1998 campaign (Santodomingo, 2000). When Chávez decided in 1997 to seek the presidency, he converted the MBR into the Movimiento Quinta República, attracting legions of new members, including refugees from the sinking *puntofijista* ship. The PPT, MAS, and some smaller parties joined with the dominant MVR to form the Polo Patriótico.

The penultimate lineup of candidates in 1998 included Sáez, backed by her own electoral movement (IRENE) and COPEI; Ucero, who used his control of the AD party machine to secure its nomination; Salas Römer, who called his electoral movement Proyecto Venezuela; and Chávez, backed by the PP. In an effort to test the electoral waters and save candidacies from being overwhelmed by the appeal of Chávez, the major parties advanced local and state elections by a month. When the MVR ran well, traditional parties panicked. Governors, no longer cowed by central party authorities, took the lead in moving the parties to abandon their candidates and back Salas Römer. Barely a week before the election, too late to modify the ballot, COPEI withdrew its support from Sáez. AD, in the face of bitter resistance from the old caudillo, withdrew the candidacy of Ucero and likewise endorsed Salas Römer. The ugly denouement probably did little to help the Carabobo governor. Chávez defeated him by a margin of 56.0 to 39.9 percent.

Where the business sector, social movements, and organized labor had failed, the military succeeded in striking the final blow against the Punto Fijo regime. This does not mean, however, that the military was united behind the project of Chávez, or that the other sectors ceased seeking to advance their own agendas for the future. In fact, the military itself became increasingly politicized and internally divided, a tendency encouraged not only by the character of the Chávez government but also by the opposition, which sought to widen and exploit internal divisions within its ranks.

New President, New Constitution, New Politics?

After the elections of November and December 1998, the traditional parties held sufficient seats in Congress to shape, if not block, attempts to convene a constituent assembly to write a new constitution. Chávez moved quickly to call and win a popular referendum calling for an elected assembly to write the new document. With the exception of three seats designated for indigenous peoples, the assembly was elected by a first-past-the-post system, a radical departure from the proportional list system of the Fourth Republic. The PP controlled 121 of 131 assembly seats. After winning resounding approval for the new "Bolivarian" constitution, Chávez called for "megaelections" in July 2001, so named because all elected officials at the national and state levels were required to stand for reelection. The PP swept to victory, achieving large majorities in the new, unicameral legislature. Chávez himself defeated his closest challenger, Arias, now promoting himself as a moderate alternative, by a margin of 21 percentage points (59 to 38 percent).

In the 1998 campaign, Chávez separated himself from Salas Römer by assuming an unequivocal position in favor of a constituent assembly to draft a new constitution. The traditional parties had always opposed such an assembly, and by criticizing it Salas Römer lost some of his appeal as an antisystem candidate. This was an institutional issue, but it was one that resonated more strongly with the young, with men, and with the lower classes. Although Chávez appealed to all strata, these sectors supported him most strongly (e.g., see Datanalisis poll, *El Universal,* April 6, 2000). The presidential race between Chávez and Arias was even more polarized, with the Datanalisis poll showing that Chávez was preferred by a wide margin among the poorest social sectors. Arias, on the other hand, enjoyed the support of two-thirds of those in the wealthy and middle-class sectors (*El Universal,* April 6, 2000).

When the smoke had cleared after the megaelection in July 2000, the opposition was in total disarray. The closest competitor to the PP was AD, which held only twenty seats in the assembly. Subsequently its delegation split into two factions divided on whether to assume a hard-line or pragmatic approach in opposition. COPEI had virtually been extinguished as a national force. Neither Salas Römer nor Arias emerged as poles of opposition. On the other hand, Chávez had devastated the old party system, but his own political movement had yet to prove it had an institutional vitality apart from the charisma of the president.

The deployment of troops in "Plan Bolívar 2000" was a bold attempt to fuse military capabilities with those of other public institutions to attack social problems with programs of sanitation, health, indigent care, public transport, housing, and the like. The programs delivered immediate, short-term relief to many and demonstrated how the military could aid and not simply repress the population. In this way, Chávez hoped to consolidate the character of government as "civic-military." However, Plan Bolívar also undermined decentralized control of social programs by the states, still controlled in many cases by representatives of the "old" regime (Melcher, 2000: 266–269). Furthermore, repeated use of the military in such projects was controversial within the ranks of the armed forces and problematic in terms of civilian control of the military. Thus although the military ultimately emerged as the actual sector to topple *puntofijismo* with the victory of Chávez, it was far from unified, as Deborah Norden discusses in Chapter 5.

Supporters of Chávez could point to his landslide victories between 1998 and July 2000 as proof of the democratic nature of his putative revolution. No one doubts that the elections were won overwhelmingly by the PP and the MVR, but it became the turn of the traditional parties to charge that the electoral process was manipulated and corrupt. In addition, the abstention rate, something that had early signaled the deterioration of *puntofijismo,* remained high. In the hotly contested election between Chávez and Salas Römer, it fell, but the two referendums and election of delegates to a national assembly all had abstention rates significantly above 50 percent (see Table 2.3). In the megaelection the abstention rate was 43.5 percent. Some of this can be attributed to electoral fatigue, but polls in the run-up to the 1998 and 2000 presidential elections found that the poorest parts of the population, despite the populist appeal of Chávez, were least likely to vote. In December 2001, in an election that was a combined referendum on Chávez's labor reform and municipal election, abstention soared to over three-quarters of the electorate, a significant setback for the president.

In the 1998 election and in sweeping away the 1961 constitution, Chávez seemed to have triumphed like an avenging angel over the institu-

Table 2.3　Rates of Abstention in Elections, 1988–2000

	Type of election	Abstention rate (%)
1988	Presidential	18.1
1989	Regional, municipal	54.5
1992	Regional, municipal	50.7
1993	Presidential	39.8
1995	Regional, municipal	53.9
Nov. 1998	Regional, municipal	45.6
Dec. 1998	Presidential	36.5
Apr. 1999	Referendum	62.2
July 2000	Megaelection	43.5
Dec. 2000	Labor referendum, regional, municipal	75.0[a]

Source: National Electoral Council, except as indicated.
Note: a. Estimate based on news reports of preliminary counts by the National Electoral Council.

tions and leaders of the old regime. In reality, the victory was far from complete. Many of his opponents never accepted the legitimacy of the process by which the constitution had changed. A large number of his old collaborators in the MBR split from his government, complaining that he was practicing the old politics of *puntofijismo*. Although *chavismo* dominated the state apparatus, his opponents were well organized in civil society, especially in the media. Rapidly improving the standard of living of his followers would require a major overhaul of the economic system and a revolutionary break with Washington, something Chávez had promised to avoid. What sustained the president's popularity was his ability to tap into the deep reserve of popular resentment toward the old political class and his ability to pursue an independent foreign policy that reinforced his revolutionary credentials.

Tercermundismo at Home and Abroad

Various ideological influences shaped the worldview of *chavismo*. Chávez and his fellow conspirators came in contact with leftist professors at the major Venezuelan universities. Chávez read widely and deeply across a spectrum that runs from Fidel Castro to Norberto Ceresole, a self-exiled Argentine international relations expert who offered a neofascist critique of the post–Cold War dominance of the United States. Ceresole posits caudillism as a kind of democratic tradition uniting the military and people in defense of national values. However, Chávez's admiration for Fidel Castro, his refusal to disavow liberal democratic norms and civilian control over the military, and his pragmatic attitude toward the United States alienated

Ceresole. The Argentine broke entirely with the Venezuelan president after José Vicente Rangel, a muckraking journalist and former leftist presidential candidate, was named minister of defense in February 2001 (Garrido, 2001).

The Venezuelan president challenged Washington by refusing to cooperate with the U.S. drug war in Colombia and maintaining friendly relations with Colombian guerrillas. After devastating floods destroyed the transportation infrastructure along the littoral, Chávez would not allow U.S. military engineer units to deploy and help in the rescue and rebuilding efforts. At the Summit of the Americas in Quebec City in 2001, Chávez refused to endorse the resolution that would have tied participation in a hemispheric free-trade zone upon electoral democracy. Alone among Latin American presidents, Chávez criticized the United States for causing civilian casualties in its bombing campaign in Afghanistan.

What Chávez's actions have in common is resistance to unipolar domination of the world by the United States. Relations with countries like Iraq and Libya can be explained on a pragmatic basis—the need to coordinate oil policy. However, the *chavista* strategy on oil also corresponded to a broader geopolitical agenda. Chávez, much as Simón Bolívar and José Martí before him and Fidel Castro today, perceives the United States as a threat to a unified, free Latin America. Like Ceresole, he opposes Washington's desire to refashion the Latin American military into an instrument of hemispheric defense of U.S. hegemony under the guise of defending democracy. This resistance faced a major challenge after the attacks upon the World Trade Center in New York and the Pentagon on September 11, 2001. Washington made clear its expectation that allies were expected to cooperate militarily against groups and countries the United States considers "terrorists" or "rogue states," respectively, and this threatened to raise the stakes for Chávez's determination to maintain an independent foreign policy.

This most visible success of Chávez's foreign policy was the Second Summit of Heads of States and Governments of the Member Countries of OPEC, which took place in Caracas in September 2000. Points 12, 13, and 14 of the resultant "Declaration of Caracas" reaffirmed OPEC's commitment to leadership of the entire underdeveloped world, sought substantial reduction of the developing countries' debt, and called for the "just and equitable treatment of oil in the world energy market" in negotiations over environmental, fiscal, and energy problems. This independent foreign policy has, like everything else, deeply divided the country. The contrasting visions of the "modern" middle class and the masses who support Chávez are reflected in the rhetoric surrounding OPEC. By contrast, the "modernized" oil executives pose the most articulate and powerful resistance within Venezuelan civil society to the third-world outlook championed by Chávez.

The struggle between the Ministry of Energy and Mines and Petroleos de Venezuela over a proposed organic law ended with a victory for the ministry when the president decreed new oil legislation in November 2001, despite the overwhelming opposition of the middle class and professionals. For reasons that Bernard Mommer makes clear in Chapter 7, there are economic and international pressures that may still turn momentum back toward some form of privatization.

If the foreign policy of President Chávez significantly broke from the pro-Washington outlook of *puntofijismo,* it was less evident that his exercise of power at home was as clear a break as his rhetoric suggested. For all of his revolutionary rhetoric, candidate Chávez attracted support from sectors of the business community who provided indispensable financial help for the 1998 campaign. The degree and nature of the quid pro quo was unclear, but by some reports he owed much to insurance interests, public relations firms, developers, and even fugitive bankers eager to return to Venezuela once Caldera departed (Ojeda, 2001; Santodomingo, 2000).

Chavismo in power was altered by subtraction. Decisions to investigate charges of human rights abuses and corruption, although praised by human rights organizations demanding action from the president, were factors inducing three of his closest collaborators from the MBR-200 period to launch the candidacy of Arias Cárdenas against Chávez in the 2000 megaelections. Discontent with the way the loosely organized but tightly controlled MVR designated candidates for legislative and local elections in the megaelection produced further defections, particularly among professionals who had hoped for a clearer break with traditional practices (Ojeda, 2001). Alliance politics meant that slates of candidates had to be configured through negotiations within the PP. The MVR failed to submit its nominations to voters in primaries, as it had promised. Often central party authorities overruled local MVR organs. Those pushed aside often charged that Chávez and Luis Miquilena disregarded their longevity or past efforts on behalf of the MVR in favor of candidates from alliance partners and financial backers.

Some critics accused Miquilena of corruption and of reinstituting the worst practices of the Punto Fijo era. His defenders said he was honorable and committed to leftist ideals, however much his style was aggressive and caustic. All agreed that the octogenarian carried much of the burden of day-to-day politics. Miquilena shepherded the new constitution through the Constituent Assembly, coordinated nominations and electoral strategy over seven campaigns in three years, negotiated alliances with other parties inside and outside the PP, and determined the timing and adjustments made to legislation during the transitional period and in the new, unicameral National Assembly. His adroit leadership reminded many of the politics associated with *puntofijismo*. After the July 2000 elections, Miquilena offered the Proyecto Venezuela of Salas Römer a vice presidency in the new assembly in exchange for legislative support. In early 2001 the MVR reached out to a majority faction of AD headed by Deputy Henry Ramos Allup for support on some legislation, while it threatened MAS with expulsion from the PP if it continued to withhold support from some initiatives (e.g., in education) opposed by the middle class. MAS subsequently split into factions supporting and opposing Chávez.

Miquilena seemed indispensable in holding the MVR together, but the power of the patriarch clearly emanated from Chávez. In July 2001 the president called for the reactivation of the MBR-200 and for people to join his grassroots-level Bolivarian Circles, leading some to believe that Chávez himself feared that the MVR practiced excessively the type of politics associated with *puntofijismo*. Such suspicions deepened after Miquilena resigned as minister of the interior in early 2002. Critics who once saw him as an ideologue now claimed his departure deprived Chávez of a moderating influence. In more practical terms, the MVR delegation in the National Assembly began to fracture, and even before the attempted golpe of April 2002 it became clear that Chávez could no longer count on automatic majorities in the legislature.

Although politically such deals evoked *puntofijismo,* they also belied the notion that Chávez, like Fujimori, intended to close Congress and spearhead an autogolpe. The president did take advantage of the new constitution's liberal provisions under which the National Assembly granted him broad powers of legislation. Certainly the use of his authority to issue decrees was not the most democratic way to implement reforms, but similar powers were often granted presidents during the Punto Fijo era. Still, critics accused the president of violating his own constitution and contemplating a grab for dictatorial power.

Almost to the end of 2001 the political opposition remained deeply divided and weakly represented in the National Assembly. The bitterest debates seemed to take place not in the legislature but in the major news media. Venezuela, in line with the universal trend in the late twentieth century, had seen the decline of parties capable of mobilizing voters through face-to-face contact by cadres and the concomitant rise of well-financed mass media campaigns. Chávez, with his intellectual acumen and understanding of popular culture, is a masterful social communicator. For this reason opponents sought to limit the president's authority to use state-owned television and command access to the entire national broadcast system. Several other contentious debates over legal regulation of the media raised international concern about press freedom in Venezuela, but underlying them was a basic struggle between the president to preserve his main channel of communication to his social base of support, and the opposition's desire to limit that capability.

Chávez combined his remarkable charisma and skill in the mass media with a highly personal distribution of rents. Many of the callers to his weekly radio program—*¡Aló, Presidente!*—sought to resolve problems in finding employment or obtaining a benefit from a particular social service agency. On the occasion of a presidential caravan to commemorate the ninth anniversary of the February 4 revolt, televised interviews with bystanders featured people pleading for redress of specific problems. Those interviewed often attributed their plight to the neglect or callousness of individuals associated with the old regime. The presidential office created a special bureau to attend to thousands of similar petitions arriving daily in the mail, by way of telephone calls to the president during his weekly radio program, and from people waiting in line outside Miraflores Palace, or La Casona, the president's official residence (*El Nacional,* January 26, 2001).

Celli's rueful comment on *"negritos"* evokes the manner in which class and racial identity are intertwined in Venezuelan political culture, something that Chávez has effectively appropriated to advantage. The racial, class, and cultural differences were much in evidence as the political situation polarized in early 2002. Opposition rallies and marches were organized in the more affluent eastern sections of the capital, with the middle class most visible. Supporters of Chávez responded with their own mass actions in the west, and the ranks of the demonstrators were largely drawn from the poor barrios. When organized labor participated in antigovernment civic strikes, many workers in the informal economy carried on business as usual (see Chapter 1).

Despite falling approval ratings in the polls, it was the poor Venezuelans, mostly pardos, who rallied to the president's defense and played a crucial role in thwarting the attempted coup of April 25, 2002. "Approval ratings" indicate dissatisfaction with a president; they fail to capture deeper sentiments that Chávez elicited. Venezuelans saw in the faces of the junta that claimed power on April 12 the image of the very oligarchy that they blamed for squandering Venezuelan's considerable oil wealth.

Gender politics likewise plays a role in the contemporary Venezuelan drama, and here the *chavista* record is mixed. Chávez chose a fair number of women as cabinet members (particularly by 2001), and for the first time a woman held the vice presidency. The president's spouse, Marísabel, was a prominent adviser and public relations asset to the MVR. On the other hand, public opinion surveys show that across all social classes men were more likely than women to support Chávez, which may become a significant political factor if the gap between the opposition and the president narrows. Women headed many of the social movements frustrated by the administration's failure to fully implement consultation with civil society. As with earlier efforts to incorporate women into party organization (see

Friedman, 2000), the MVR seemed intent on subordinating Bolivarian women's groups to other goals.

Much of Chávez's rhetoric is paternalistic, if not macho. However, the opposition also did not hesitate to appeal to baser prejudices in the culture, as it did when it sent women's panties to military officers, clearly implying that failure to rise up against the president brought into question their masculinity. The detention of a civilian who endorsed the panty protest in a letter to the editor evoked considerable protest from the opposition. Few seemed concerned that the action obviously was intended to provoke a coup against Chávez.

Although the poor rescued his administration in April 2002, the populist appeal of Chávez continued to exceed his ability to improve the material conditions of most Venezuelans. The underlying decline in living conditions had not been arrested. One opposition think tank, the Workers Center for Documentation and Analysis (CENDA), claimed that 90 percent of Venezuelan households had insufficient income to meet basic necessities, with 55 percent of the population in extreme poverty (*El Universal,* January 30, 2001, sec. 2, p. 1). Shortly after taking office, a Datanalisis poll showed Chávez enjoying an astounding approval rating of 90.3 percent (*El Universal,* March 20, 1999). Two years later the same poll showed that confidence in the ability of the president to deal with the country's problems had fallen from 66 percent, when he took office in 1999, to 42 percent in early 2001 (*El Universal,* January 27, 2001, sec. 1, p. 6).

By focusing his rhetoric on the oligarchy, Chávez attempted to avoid alienating the middle class, but bridging the gap between this group and *el soberano* is difficult. For example, *buhoneros,* the ambulant vendors who make up the largest single part of the informal sectors, want the government to make good on promises to create space for their activities in increasingly tense confrontations with municipal authorities and neighborhood associations opposed to their presence. Oil workers had successfully struck for higher pay, and other labor stoppages suggested worker militancy was rising. The survival of the president depended upon the conviction among the poor majority that Chávez remained the only political force in Venezuelan politics resisting accommodation to globalization at their expense. The middle class and wealthy viewed him as the main political force blocking their integration into a globalized world (see Chapter 12).

The failed coup of April 11, 2002, exhibited just how polarized Venezuelan society had become. The immediate catalyst for action was an attempt by Chávez to discharge the executive directors of PDVSA, a move interpreted widely as cronyism, but one that must be understood in the context of the struggle between the oil company and the government for control over oil policy. Sensing weakness, the main business confederation (Fedecámaras), the CTV leadership, and other opponents called for another general strike in support of striking employees at the oil company. The strike was at best a partial success and was faltering when the opposition called for a mass demonstration in front of PDVSA headquarters, located closer to more affluent neighborhoods in the eastern part of the city. The private Venezuelan media joined the protest by advertising calls for the demonstration at regular, ten-minute intervals.

A crowd numbering hundreds of thousands suddenly marched from the company toward the presidential palace in the city center after leaders called on them to sack Chávez. The crowd was met by Chávez supporters. Gunfire was exchanged and demonstrators died on both sides. Some military commanders said they shot under orders and attempted to stage a coup. They detained Chávez and announced prematurely that he had resigned. Despite a media blackout, word of the coup and initial resistance to it spread to the poorer barrios, especially in the western part of the city. Demonstrators flooded into the area around the presidential palace to demand the return of the president. Despite U.S. support for the coup, Latin American diplomats refused to recognize the new government. Some of the opposition withdrew active support after the interim junta announced it was suspending the constitution. Less than forty-eight hours after it had begun, Chávez returned again as president.

The attempt to remove Chávez evoked comparisons to the fall of President Salvador Allende of Chile in 1973, in which the United States played an important role. The United States denied involvement in the coup attempt, but suspicions abounded. Stratfor, a respected think tank on military and intelligence affairs, claimed that Washington had two parallel operations in support of the coup (*La Jornada,* April 16, 2002). The Venezuelan military itself was divided three ways: a hardened anti-Chávez faction, a pro-Chávez faction, and an institutionalist faction committed to defending the new constitution but not committed to the president himself. Although the Chilean military had an institutionalist sector, there was no significant pro-Allende sector within the Chilean armed forces. However, the coup also revealed that like Chile in the early 1970s, Venezuela was a highly polarized country, divided about the kind of democracy it would be, the way it might parlay oil wealth into a viable economic development strategy, and whether its natural allies in the world lay in the core or the periphery of the world system.

In August the Supreme Court refused to indict military leaders for their role in the attempted overthrow. In response, the president charged political interference, while his supporters went into the streets in indignation. As Angel Alvarez and María Pilar García-Guadilla show in Chapters 8 and 10, Chávez had elected to appoint the court through political bargaining in the National Assembly rather than fully involving human rights groups and other civic organizations, as the Bolivarian constitution provided. This decision proved costly as politicians shifted ground. In the months prior to the April events, the president's control over the National Assembly had weakened as the parties in the PP, including the MVR itself, began to divide internally. Within the legislature the opposition began to maneuver to replace the attorney general with someone willing to indict the president for responsibility for civilian deaths during the turbulent events of April, opening the door to his removal from office through an "institutional coup." At the same time, further military revolts were threatened. Drawing lessons from the violence of April, some middle-class groups and some Bolivarian Circles began arming themselves in anticipation of civil violence. These developments portended a period of political instability and continued polarization, regardless of whether or not President Chávez was to complete his term of office.

Conclusion

Puntofijismo was built on a vision of development made possible by democracy and oil rents. Bolivarianism was a response to disillusionment with the efficacy of that project, and it succeeded in sweeping away much of the old regime. Hugo Chávez capitalized on the profound mistrust and anger directed toward those associated with the old regime and the sense of Venezuela's poor majority that he is one of their own. This special appeal to the concerns of a sector of the population represented a break with pre-1989 politics, which was predominately multiclass and reflected the relative class fluidity characteristic of Venezuela over an extended period of time. The solidification of class attitudes and positions after 1989, although certainly far from absolute, provided the social backdrop to the rise of *chavismo*.

Thirty months after his initial election, President Chávez had yet to lose an election or legislative vote on a key priority. He had carried out grand institutional reforms and altered the direction of oil policy, but he had yet to develop programmatic alternatives to meet deteriorating living standards. *Chavismo* had not evolved into a party or movement that could transcend the charismatic authority of the president himself. After barely surviving the attempted coup of April 2002, Chávez was under pressure to tone down the rhetoric of *tercermundismo* at home and abroad, but this ran the risk of undermining his popular image and requiring an abrupt about-face from the nationalist trajectory that guided his ascent from junior military officer to the presidency.

Few leaders have so effectively dismantled a well-entrenched political class, challenged the hegemony of a superpower, and animated the desire for social justice of a people. Like the generation of political leaders who founded the Punto Fijo regime, Hugo Chávez Frías attempted to link oil nationalism and economic development to a conception of democracy. Whether he would succeed or instead find himself, as Bolívar put it, "plowing the seas" depended less upon his personal charisma than on his ability to harness other social forces that asserted themselves during the agony of *puntofijismo*.

3

Social Polarization and the Populist Resurgence in Venezuela

Kenneth Roberts

The stunning rise of Hugo Chávez to power at the end of the 1990s marked the definitive collapse of the party system that had dominated Venezuelan political life under the post-1958 democratic regime. What is less well understood is that *chavismo* also signified a repoliticization of social inequality in Venezuela. Class-based political distinctions had been highly salient at the dawning of Venezuela's democratic experiment, but they gradually dissipated over the course of the Punto Fijo system (Myers, 1998; see also Chapter 6 in this volume). Starting in the late 1980s, however, recurrent political and economic crises gradually polarized the political arena along an elite-mass cleavage for the first time in a generation. Like most populist experiences in Latin America, this new cleavage did not follow strict class lines; Chávez clashed with a labor movement that was still led by traditional parties, and Venezuelans of all social strata abandoned traditional parties in the 1990s to support a range of independent and "outsider" candidates. Nevertheless, Chávez's appeal was especially pronounced among the unorganized subaltern sectors of the population. The poor embraced his vitriolic attacks on the political establishment, while many from the middle and upper classes recoiled before the uncertain scope and depth of impending changes.

This revival of social inequality as an axis of political differentiation is doubly interesting, as it breaks not only with Venezuela's recent political history but also with the dominant trends in contemporary Latin American politics. Although social inequalities have deepened across most of Latin America over the past twenty years of economic crisis and free-market reforms, class cleavages have generally eroded in the political arena, a victim of fragmented labor markets, diminishing class-based collective action, and partisan strategies that de-emphasize class identities (see Roberts, 2002). Social polarization, in short, has found little expression in the political arena, and party systems have become increasingly detached from underlying structural inequalities. In Venezuela, however, the political salience of social inequalities increased as the party system decomposed and emerging populist figures competed to realign political loyalties. Although Chávez, unlike some traditional populist figures, did not organize his followers as a class, he nevertheless exploited and deepened a stratified social schism in political identities and policy preferences. This schism had become evident in the popular backlash against neoliberal reforms imposed by the second government of Carlos Andrés Pérez starting in 1989, and it congealed when the unorganized poor embraced Chávez as the embodiment of a rupture not merely with the dominant parties, but also with the entire post-1958 political order.

What is striking about the Venezuelan case, then, is that political cleavages—which had previously cut across class distinctions—moved over the course of the 1990s into greater alignment with social cleavages that progressively deepened as a result of an unresolved economic crisis and erratic market-oriented reforms. This process of cleavage realignment is traced below through an analysis of the transformation of class structures in contemporary Venezuela and their evolving patterns of politicization (and depoliticization). The interaction between social and political polarization, I argue, eventually led to the partial reconstruction of a class cleavage. The political loyalties of elite and popular sectors became more clearly differentiated, but they were very poorly organized in both civil society and the partisan arena, as Chávez made little effort to institutionalize his Movimiento Quinta República (MVR) and faced virulent opposition from labor unions that remained under the control of traditional parties.

The Politics of Social Class in Venezuela

As Robert Dix (1989) noted, party systems in Latin America have historically been weakly grounded in class and other social cleavages. Most parties have drawn support from heterogeneous multiclass constituencies, meaning that political cleavages were segmented rather than stratified— that is, they cut vertically across class distinctions rather than horizontally between them. Venezuela was unusual in that it did not develop a national party system during the oligarchic stage of development, given the prevalence of armed conflict and regionalized political fragmentation (Kornblith and Levine, 1995: 39), and when one finally congealed in the middle of the twentieth century during the onset of mass politics it quickly polarized along class lines. Acción Democrática (AD), like most populist parties, mobilized a heterogeneous social constituency, but its commitments to land reform, labor rights, and grassroots organization generated staunch support among workers and peasants and unrelieved hostility from traditional elites. Elite groups were frightened by the social reforms and hegemonic pretensions of the AD-led government during the *trienio* of 1945–1948, and they countered by organizing the conservative party Comité de Organización Política Electoral Independiente (COPEI) and supporting the military overthrow of the fledgling democratic regime. When democracy was restored a decade later, electoral competition was marked by class distinctions: lower-class communities voted disproportionately for AD, while better-off communities were more inclined to support COPEI (Myers, 1998: 502–503). This structural divide was buttressed by organizational patterns, as AD dominated the national labor and peasant confederations.

This stratified class cleavage gradually eroded over the course of Venezuela's post-1958 democratic regime, however. To facilitate elite acceptance of the democratic transition, AD moderated its stance and negotiated a series of social, economic, and political pacts with COPEI and other actors. These pacts excluded the Communist Party, a strategic ally in the struggle against Pérez Jiménez, and required that AD accept power-sharing arrangements, self-contain its capacity for social mobilization, and limit the scope of redistributive reforms (Karl, 1987; Peeler, 1992). Oil rents made it possible to induce business, labor, church, and military cooperation with the democratic regime, and they ultimately encouraged a programmatic convergence between the two dominant parties. AD and COPEI settled on a statist development model that protected the property rights of business and eschewed radical redistributive reforms, while bestowing patronage payoffs on the major organized interest groups in Venezuelan society. The surge in state-captured oil rents in the 1970s helped transform Venezuela's elite political pact into a deeper class compromise (Neuhouser, 1992): the accumulation demands of capital were accommodated by maintaining extremely low domestic tax rates and extraordinary public credits for private business, while the consumption demands of the working and lower classes were addressed by paying the highest wages in Latin America and establishing extensive price controls and subsidies on food, transportation, education, health care, and other basic goods. Labor militancy was kept in check by a combination of material concessions and partisan political controls, at the same time that the AD-COPEI duopoly relegated their contenders to the margins of the political system.

In this context of partisan political collusion and oil-fueled class compromise, elections were progressively drained of ideological and programmatic content, and the class cleavage that originally structured the axis of partisan competition gradually eroded (Alvarez, 1996a). Ideological moderation and control over state patronage resources enabled AD to broaden its appeal among the middle and upper classes, while COPEI established a significant minority position within the national labor and peasant confederations. Not surprisingly, public opinion surveys in the 1970s found that the membership profiles of AD and COPEI were not sharply divided along class lines (Baloyra and Martz, 1979: 184), and by the 1980s both parties were archetypal multiclass, catchall electoral organizations (Myers, 1998: 506–511). Venezuela's axis of political competition thus cut vertically across class distinctions, pitting alternative patronage machines with relatively undifferentiated social constituencies against one another.

Although this sociopolitical alignment seemed to be grounded in highly institutionalized party organizations and political identities (see Mainwaring and Scully, 1995: 16–17), it ultimately proved to rest on unstable material foundations. Indeed, the material bases of consent that undergirded both the elite political pacts and the class compromise began to erode in the early 1980s when the Latin American debt crisis reached Venezuela's shores and global market forces caused oil rents to plummet. Prolonged economic hardship frayed party-society linkages and undermined the programmatic convergence on the statist development model. The imposition of a strict neoliberal structural adjustment package in 1989 by AD president Carlos Andrés Pérez ruptured both the programmatic consensus and the social pacts that had bound diverse constituencies to the established parties. As explained below, this dramatic policy shift also redrew the fault lines of social and political conflict in Venezuela, eventually paving the way for a partial reconfiguration of a class cleavage as traditional institutions decomposed and political outsiders jockeyed to fill the vacuum.

Economic Crisis, Neoliberal Reform, and Social Polarization in Venezuela

The elite-mass cleavage that erupted on the Venezuelan political scene with the rise of Hugo Chávez at the end of the 1990s was preceded by an extensive process of social marginalization and disarticulation. These, in turn, were the inevitable byproduct of nearly two decades of economic decline and a traumatic decade of erratic, market-oriented economic restructuring. The social landscape of the Chávez era was thus markedly different from the landscape that underlay the multiclass partisan bases of AD and COPEI during their heyday. Four principal patterns of social change stand out: (1) a process of economic immiseration, reflected in declining living standards and rising poverty levels; (2) a related but analytically distinct increase in economic inequality; (3) a restructuring of the labor market and work force, marked in particular by the growth of informality; and (4) the fragmentation and diversification of civil society, seen especially in the declining capacity of organized labor to serve as the fulcrum of popular political representation and the resulting proliferation of politically unincorporated grassroots organizations and civic protest movements, as discussed in several other chapters in this book. These processes of change produced a growing detachment from traditional representative institutions, which was deepened by the growing disillusionment with corruption and the political stranglehold exercised by AD and COPEI. Taken together, these socioeconomic and political trends created a social milieu that was amenable to Chávez's mobilization of a populist backlash against the political establishment.

Economic immiseration began when the regionwide debt crisis hit in the 1980s and the oil boom turned into a bust, but it accelerated rapidly in the wake of structural adjustment policies at the end of the decade. The democratic regime had been able to sustain relatively steady wage increases between 1965 and 1980, and social spending had escalated sharply during the oil windfall of the 1970s (Neuhouser, 1992: 126, 128). These indicators began a downward slide in the 1980s, however, and continued their plunge in the 1990s. Per capita gross domestic product (GDP) actually peaked in the late 1970s, and by the mid-1990s it had declined by 20 percent (Crisp, 2000: 175), returning to levels last seen in the 1960s. Wages and social spending, which are especially relevant for sustaining popular living standards, fell even more rapidly than the national income. Both real industrial wages and the real minimum wage stood at less than 40 percent of their 1980 levels by the late 1990s (ILO, 1998: 43). The purchasing power of the minimum wage declined by more than two-thirds between 1978 and 1994, leaving it at a level below that of the early 1950s (Evans, 1998: 12). Likewise, per capita social spending by the state was 40 percent below the 1980 level in 1993, including real cuts of greater than 40 percent in education programs, 70 percent in housing and urban development, 37 percent in health care, and 56 percent in social development and participation (República de Venezuela, 1995: 40). Cuts in spending were especially pronounced during the period of economic adjustment in the late 1980s and early 1990s; whereas social spending accounted for 8 percent of GDP in 1987, it was only equal to 4.3 percent of GDP in 1994 (Evans, 1998: 12).

Sharp cuts in wages and social spending led ineluctably to an increase in poverty. Between 1984 and 1995 the portion of the population living below the poverty line increased from 36 to 66 percent, while the portion living in extreme poverty more than tripled, increasing from 11 to 36 percent (República de Venezuela, 1995: 23; Organización Panamericana de Salud, 1998: 5). Again, the biggest change coincided with the process of economic adjustment in 1989. In that year the poverty rate increased from 46 to 62 percent of the population, while those living in extreme poverty more than doubled, from 14 to 30 percent of the population (República de Venezuela, 1995: 23). Clearly, chronic poverty had remained a blight on Venezuela's development model even during the oil boom of the 1970s, but the economic crisis of the 1980s and 1990s transformed the scope and character of the problem. Whereas previously poverty affected a minority of the populace who had yet to share in the oil bonanza, by the 1990s it afflicted an absolute majority, who were systematically excluded from meaningful participation in the development model.

The political effects of economic decline were compounded by the fact that hardships were not evenly distributed. To the contrary, as the economic pie progressively shrank, it came to be distributed more unequally. The income share of the poorest 40 percent of the population fell from 19.1 percent in 1981 to 14.7 percent in 1997, while that of the wealthiest decile increased from 21.8 to 32.8 percent (CEPAL, 1999: 63). Indeed, all but the wealthiest quintile lost relative income shares over the course of the 1980s and 1990s. In short, during a period of generalized macroeconomic decline, income became more highly concentrated, and society became more sharply divided between elite and popular sectors.

Economic immiseration and social polarization were accompanied by important changes in the class structure of Venezuelan society. Two basic trends predominated: a shift of labor from agriculture and industry toward the services, and a shift from formal to informal modes of employment. Between 1980 and 1997 the portion of the work force engaged in agricultural activities declined from 16.1 to 10.0 percent, while the industrial labor force declined from 28.4 to 24.3 percent. In contrast, the highly diversified service sector increased from 55.5 to 65.5 percent of the total work force (CEPAL, 2000: 26; *Europa World Yearbook,* 2000: 4008). The flight from agriculture was especially dramatic during the first three years of neoliberal reform, between 1989 and 1992, when an estimated 600,000 persons abandoned the countryside (Bolívar and Pérez Campos, 1996: 52). Given the limited absorptive capacity of Venezuela's industries and fiscally strapped public sector, much of the surplus labor force flowed into the informal sector, where wages on average were 30 percent below those in the formal sector. The percentage of the labor force engaged in informal employment practices thus swelled from 34.5 percent in 1980 (Sunkel, 1994: 155) to 53 percent in 1999 (*Economist Intelligence Unit Country Report: Venezuela,* 2000: 16). Likewise, during this same time period open unemployment increased from 6.6 to 15.4 percent of the urban work force (CEPAL, 2000: 744). Taken together, these trends mean that fewer Venezuelan workers are employed in stable industrial or agricultural activities, while a growing number face a precarious existence marked by under- and unemployment.

These changes in the class structure and labor markets had important consequences for social and political organization in Venezuela, leading in particular to a growing fragmentation and diversification of civil society. During the heyday of the Punto Fijo system, AD could dominate popular political expression through its control of the national labor and campesino confederations, which were linked to the state through semicorporatist channels of interest intermediation. The political centrality and representativeness of these organizations gradually diminished, however, as the social landscape was reconfigured by economic crisis and market reforms. As labor flowed out of industrial and agrarian sectors that were historically organized and bound to AD, it flowed into informal arenas that are notoriously difficult to organize, given the diffuse and heterogeneous character of their economic activities and the ambiguity of their class positions. Unions belonging to the AD-dominated Confederación de Trabajadores de Venezuela (CTV; Confederation of Venezuelan Workers) were not effective at articulating the political identities or representing the interests of these informal workers. Consequently, a sharp decline in trade unionization occurred; according to the International Labour Organization (ILO) (1997: 235), the portion of the work force belonging to trade unions was cut nearly in half during the period of economic adjustment, declining from 26.4 percent in 1988 to 13.5 percent in 1995. Organized labor came to depend on the membership of relatively privileged workers in the public sector who had little in common with an increasingly privatized and informalized work force.

Even among workers who did belong to trade unions, the CTV became less representative, as a powerful opposition union movement emerged in the southern industrial state of Bolívar with political ties to a rising leftist party, Causa Radical (Causa R) (López Maya, 1997). This militant "new unionism"—which gained control of Venezuela's largest union, that of the steelworkers, in 1987—was sharply critical of neoliberal reforms and the political quiescence of the CTV. Indeed, the CTV's alliance with AD had prevented organized labor from taking a strong stand against the structural adjustment policies of *adeco* President Carlos Andrés Pérez in 1989. When Pérez's shock program triggered massive riots in Caracas and other cities that were repressed militarily at the cost of hundreds of lives, the CTV responded by declaring a national strike, but it quickly retreated to a less confrontational stance in order to maintain its ties to the governing party (Ellner, 1995: 148–152; Burgess, 1999). Some 5,000 protests occurred in the three years that followed the adoption of neoliberal reforms, but this social mobilization was not led by or channeled through organized labor (Ellner, 1995: 149). Instead, the protests were more often territorially based, emerging primarily in poor communities that had little or no organization beyond the local level (Salamanca, 1995: 386). AD had never penetrated these urban popular districts as thoroughly as it did the functional organizations of workers and peasants (Ray, 1969: 110–127), and when economic adjustment slashed state subsidies and public services that helped to sustain popular living standards, the barrios erupted with fury.

Clearly, by the 1990s the semicorporatist consultative and bargaining relationships that linked the state (and the dominant parties) to peak associ-

ations of labor and capital were no longer capable of articulating the interests of large groups of Venezuelan citizens who were either unorganized or
affiliated with a myriad of decentralized, community-based organizations.
The labor movement, in particular, was too organizationally narrow and
politically compromised to serve as the primary agent of popular representation in this more diversified, autonomous, and fragmented civil society.
The combination of social polarization and political detachment proved to
be highly combustible after 1989, as Venezuelans turned on the political
establishment and threw their support to a series of independent leaders and
protest parties. By the end of the 1990s, widespread disillusionment produced a ground swell of support for the consummate political outsider: a
former paratrooper commander who captured the popular imagination by
leading a failed coup attempt against a discredited democratic regime, then
ran for the presidency on a campaign pledge to dismantle the Punto Fijo
system and reconfigure the nation's political institutions. The process of
institutional decay and populist mobilization redrew the lines of social and
political cleavage in Venezuela, repoliticizing social inequalities for the
first time in a generation and thoroughly transforming traditional patterns
of political competition and representation.

The Repoliticization of Social Inequality in Venezuela

The Latin American experience provides abundant evidence that class
inequalities are not translated directly or automatically into political cleavages. Multiclass forms of political organization and competition have often
prevailed in the region (Dix, 1989; Mainwaring, 1999), both historically
and in more recent times, despite the existence of the most acute class
inequalities in the world. Although the Venezuelan experience of economic
immiseration and social polarization over the past several decades may
have been extreme, it is certainly not unique, as parallel trends have been
under way in other countries of the region as well (Inter-American
Development Bank, 1997). In most of these other nations, however, the
combination of economic crisis and neoliberal reform has dampened the
political expression of class cleavages by fragmenting and diversifying the
working class, weakening labor movements, and transforming labor-backed
parties into moderate, catchall electoral vehicles (see Roberts, 2002).
Parties with strong working-class traditions such as the Chilean Socialists
and the Argentine Peronists have de-emphasized their trade union ties and
sought to broaden their appeal among the middle class and independent
voters. What is distinctive about Venezuela, then, is the renewed political
salience of social inequalities even in a context of declining class organization. Class distinctions were repoliticized in the 1990s, bringing the axis of

political competition into closer alignment with underlying structural cleavages.

The first clear sign that Venezuela's long-dormant class cleavage was primed for reactivation came in February 1989, when the "shock program" of economic austerity measures imposed at the beginning of Carlos Andrés Pérez's second term in office produced an immediate social explosion. After running a campaign that evoked the populist symbols of his first presidential term during the halcyon days of the 1970s oil boom, Pérez abruptly changed course upon taking office. Advised by a team of neoliberal technocrats, he withdrew subsidies and price controls on a broad range of public services and consumer goods, liberalized foreign exchange and interest rates, slashed tariffs and other forms of trade restrictions, relaxed controls on foreign investment, and launched an ambitious privatization program. The initial price increases triggered by this *gran viraje,* or "great turn-around," sparked a five-day paroxysm of urban rioting known as the Caracazo, which punctured the myth of democratic tranquillity and class compromise. The riots stoked middle- and upper-class fears of plebeian hordes descending from the hillside slums to pillage and plunder, and they dealt a political blow from which Pérez and the new economic model would never recover.

The Caracazo became an enduring symbol of Venezuelans' resistance to neoliberal reforms, a phenomenon much noted (and often lamented) by scholars and political leaders (Romero, 1997; Naím, 1993). What is less widely recognized is the extent to which responses to the new economic model were differentiated by social strata. Although Pérez's reforms faced opposition from business leaders who depended on sheltered domestic markets and state-administered petroleum rents, their reception among the middle and upper classes in general was much more favorable than among the poor. Shortly after the reforms began, public opinion surveys discovered that nearly twice as many upper-class respondents supported the new model as opposed it, while lower-class respondents were more than six times as likely to reject the reforms as to support them. This gap narrowed slightly but remained highly salient throughout the peak period of reform between 1989 and 1991. In quarterly surveys conducted during this period an average of 51.5 percent of upper-class respondents favored the neoliberal model, while 30.7 percent preferred a return to the old model. In contrast, among lower-class respondents an average of only 23.8 percent supported the new model, while 55.1 percent had a preference for the previous one. Strong opposition to the neoliberal model was also manifested by lower-middle-class respondents, while the middle class tended to split more evenly (see Table 3.1). These divergent responses were not merely a function of political dynamics under the Pérez administration or the singular process of initial structural adjustment; instead, they appeared to be grounded in

Table 3.1   Support for Neoliberal Reforms Under Carlos Andrés Pérez by Social Class, Average 1989–1991

	Lower Class	Lower Middle Class	Middle Class	Upper Class
Support neoliberal reforms	23.8%	30.1%	40.7%	51.5%
Return to previous economic model	55.1	54.0	43.3	30.7

Source: Calculated from Consultores 21, "Estudio de opinión pública sobre temas económicos," eleven surveys between April 1989 and December 1991. Data from the September 1990 survey were not available.

durable and deep-seated class-based distinctions in policy preferences. A 1996 survey of political culture in Venezuela thus found once again that the poor were much less disposed to support economic liberalism. Among the poor, 30 percent said the state should "always" intervene in the economic activities of the people, 43 percent said the state should intervene "sometimes," and only 19 percent said the state should "never" intervene. Among the wealthy, on the other hand, 22 percent said the state should always intervene, 37 percent said it should sometimes intervene, and 40 percent said it should never intervene (Zapata, 1996: 156).

The new economic model was, in fact, highly divisive. Not only did it break the programmatic consensus that had been forged after 1958 around a state-led model of import substitution industrialization, but its reliance on insulated technocratic decisionmaking violated the consultative norms that had previously given a variety of interest groups institutionalized access to the policymaking process (see Crisp, 2000). Neoliberal reforms thus exacerbated the congenital factionalism of AD, since many party members (and officials) opposed the economic revolution imposed by a president from within their own ranks (Corrales, 2000), and it deepened the fissures both within the labor movement and between unions and other popular organizations. As AD and the CTV waffled on economic reforms, they became increasingly detached from the popular protest movement, opening new political space for Causa R and its affiliated, more militant labor unions, as well as independent and loosely organized neighborhood groups. Reflecting the broader process of social polarization, even the neighborhood movement split into separate organizations oriented toward middle- and lower-class constituencies (Ellner, 1999d: 79–81).

The depth of social polarization was manifested again in February 1992, when a military rebellion led by then–lieutenant colonel Hugo Chávez narrowly missed toppling the Pérez government. The political establishment was stunned by the degree of sympathy expressed for the coup attempt by Venezuela's popular sectors, who were clearly attracted by the anticorruption, anti-neoliberal thrust of the rebellion. The fallout from the coup attempt, however, temporarily dampened the political expression of Venezuela's social inequalities. Former president Rafael Caldera, a founder and historic leader of the conservative party COPEI, spoke out against the neoliberal model and rationalized popular frustrations with the democratic regime, then used his critique of the status quo to launch an independent bid for a second term as president in 1993. In a tight four-way race, Caldera used his establishment background and dissident message to draw support from across the social and political spectrum, narrowly defeating the candidates of Causa R, AD, and COPEI. Caldera made opposition to neoliberalism a centerpiece of his program, but after two years of heterodox policies and deepening economic crisis his government yielded to pressures for market reforms in 1996.

Following the 1989 riots, two 1992 coup attempts, and the 1993 impeachment of President Pérez on corruption charges, the electoral defeat of AD and COPEI in 1993 left little doubt that the economic and political crises were taking their toll on the party system. Caldera's victory, however, was a tentative, preliminary stage in the process of party-system decomposition. The electorate opted for an independent who had broken with the dominant parties, but Caldera hardly qualified as a political outsider. As an architect of the Punto Fijo system and a pillar of the political establishment, Caldera was a well-known and trusted politician with a populist message but long-standing ties to the business community. Indeed, he governed in tacit alliance with AD, without whose legislative support the minority government would have been paralyzed. Caldera failed to turn around the economy, however, and his personalistic government neither resuscitated the traditional parties nor constructed a viable new one to fill the political void left by their demise. As the Caldera government limped to its close in 1998, Venezuelans would be given a new opportunity to turn the clock back to the reign of the traditional parties or make a more decisive break with the past. They opted, overwhelmingly, for the latter.

Chavismo and Social Polarization in the Late 1990s

By the 1990s, Venezuelans of all social strata were abandoning the traditional parties. Parties consistently ranked at the bottom in surveys of confidence in national institutions, party identification declined, and voter abstention increased sharply (see Alvarez, 1996a). One survey discovered that 70 percent of the poor and 84 percent of the wealthy believed political parties created more problems than solutions, while 63 percent of the poor and 58 percent of the wealthy said they served no purpose at all (Zapata,

1996: 177). In the process of identifying new political alternatives, however, the rich and poor veered off in different directions. The 1998 presidential race was ultimately transformed into a contest between independents, but it was won by the candidate with the most impeccable outsider credentials and the most assertive populist message—Hugo Chávez. In the end, Chávez's mobilization of lower-class support overwhelmed the capacity of elite sectors and the political establishment to craft a less threatening alternative.

After being released from prison by President Caldera, Chávez began traveling across the country, using his contacts within leftist and former military circles to organize a new political movement that was committed to the nationalistic, "Bolivarian" ideals proclaimed during the 1992 military rebellion. Chávez attacked the corruption of the political establishment, the viselike grip of the dominant parties over the democratic regime, and the deleterious social consequences of the neoliberal model. His Bolivarian movement was slow to catch on, however. A year and a half before the 1998 election, Chávez had secured a base of support among the lower classes—12 percent of whom declared an intention to vote for him—but he could only claim 7 percent of the vote intention nationwide and a mere 2 percent among upper-class respondents. The early front-runner in the polls was former Miss Universe Irene Sáez, the popular independent mayor of a wealthy district in Caracas, who had the support of 24 percent of the poor, 42 percent of the middle class, and 33 percent of the upper-class individuals surveyed. Another independent, Henrique Salas Römer—a former governor from the state of Carabobo who had abandoned COPEI—had a profile that was the opposite of Chávez's, with support from 20 percent of upper-class respondents but only 8 percent of the poor (Consultores 21, 1997).

By mid-1998, however, the race had changed considerably. Chávez's support grew rapidly, while Sáez dropped in the polls, especially after accepting the endorsement of COPEI, and Salas Römer emerged as the most viable mainstream alternative to the former coup leader. The centerpiece of Chávez's campaign was a pledge to elect a constituent assembly that would draw the Punto Fijo era to a close and redesign Venezuela's political system. This proposal to break with the constitutional order, combined with Chávez's personal history of military rebellion, allowed his campaign to appeal to popular sentiments for radical change without specifying the form of the new political institutions or the content of his economic program. Shortly before the election, surveys showed Chávez with 45 percent of the vote intention among the poor, 38 percent among the lower middle class, and 32 percent among the middle and upper classes. In contrast, Salas Römer and Sáez combined for 32 percent of the vote intention among the poor, 43 percent among the lower middle class, and 43.5 percent among the middle and upper classes (Target Global Research, 1998). Statistical analyses of survey data have confirmed that Chávez drew support disproportionately among the poor and those who were less supportive of democracy, both at the beginning and at the end of his presidential campaign (Canache, 2002a).

At the end of the campaign, AD and COPEI abandoned their declared candidates and urged their supporters to vote for Salas Römer in a desperate gambit to derail Chávez, but the ploy only seemed to taint Salas Römer as the candidate of the establishment and buttress Chávez's outsider credentials. Chávez won a landslide victory, drawing heavy support from sprawling lower-class districts that more than offset Römer's sizable advantage in wealthy districts (see López Maya and Lander, 2000c: 23). Upon taking office, Chávez set out immediately to uphold his pledge to sweep away the institutional edifice of the old order.

In many respects, the ascendance of Chávez (like that of Caldera before him) fit a broader pattern of personalistic political leadership in Latin America's neoliberal era. In countries like Peru, Brazil, Ecuador, and Argentina, where traditional parties were either very fragile or weakened by economic crises, personalistic leaders with a populist style emerged, typically bypassing or subordinating political parties in order to cultivate a direct relationship with the masses (Roberts, 1995; Weyland, 1996; Torre, 2000). Like Alberto Fujimori, Fernando Collor, Abdala Bucarám, and Carlos Menem before him, Chávez played off public discontent with the status quo, portraying himself as a man of the people who had risen up to challenge the political establishment. In contrast to these other leaders, however, who mixed a populist style with austere neoliberal programs and mobilized very diverse multiclass constituencies, Chávez rejected neoliberalism and gave new political expression to the class antagonisms that had been present since the end of the 1980s.

Indeed, Chávez was more of a throwback to Latin America's earlier populist tradition, which was characterized by strident nationalism and opposition to U.S. hegemony, an ideologically ill-defined faith in state interventionism and redistributive economic measures, and a commitment to the social and political mobilization of subaltern sectors (Ellner, 2001). The main difference was that this earlier version of populism coincided with the onset of mass politics and the dawning of the era of import substitution industrialization (ISI), conditions that were conducive to the organization of mass parties or labor unions and the creation of developmentalist states. Chávez, on the other hand, emerged at a time when the ISI model had collapsed, developmentalist states had been bankrupted, global market and political pressures for economic liberalism were far stronger, and strategic political spaces had already been occupied by the mass parties and labor unions forged during an earlier generation of popular mobilization. Although unions were clearly in decline by the 1990s, they still retained sufficient presence to obstruct new organizational efforts sponsored by the Chávez government. As established parties and labor unions lost legitimacy, they seemed to taint the very idea of organized mass political representation, dampening popular enthusiasm for participation in alternative grassroots institutions.

Therefore, in contrast to classical populist figures like Juan Domingo Perón, Getúlio Vargas, Francisco Arias Cárdenas, and Victor Raúl Haya de la Torre, Chávez has not been able to use the labor movement as the organizational pillar of his popular constituency. To the contrary, during his first two years in office he repeatedly clashed with the AD-dominated hierarchy of the CTV, which resisted pressures from the government and pro-Chávez labor groups for internal democratic reforms. The CTV even turned to the International Labour Organization to shield itself from governmental interference. In December 2000 the Chávez government finally held a referendum that approved the temporary removal of existing labor leaders and paved the way for the reorganization of the labor movement. Nevertheless, Chávez failed to bring the labor movement under his control, as CTV leaders declared the organization to be on a "war footing" and supported a series of strikes against the new regime. In April 2002 the CTV joined Fedecámaras in the opposition protests that triggered the short-lived military overthrow of Chávez. The countermobilization of Chávez's military and lower-class supporters quickly brought down the business-dominated interim government, however, restoring Chávez to the presidency and providing graphic evidence of the political schism between organized labor and pro-Chávez popular sectors (see Chapter 9).

Given the organizational deficiencies of *chavismo* in both the labor movement and the partisan sphere, its mass base of support remains poorly institutionalized and highly contingent on fluctuations in public opinion and governmental performance. The aversion to institutionalization is certainly not as extreme as in Peru under Fujimori or Brazil under Collor, but Chávez has yet to demonstrate the capacity for institution building that Latin America's first generation of populist figures possessed. This also means that Venezuela's social polarization lacks the organizational dimension of a fully formed class cleavage (see Bartolini and Mair, 1990: 212–249). Although Chávez has given electoral expression to class-based political distinctions, these distinctions are not well organized on the basis of class in either political or civil society. They exist primarily as differentiated sentiments or preferences, rather than institutionalized sociopolitical alternatives.

Nevertheless, these divergent sentiments have heightened the salience of social class in Venezuelan politics. Social polarization was temporarily dampened during Chávez's early honeymoon in office, when his approval ratings hovered near 80 percent and his popularity clearly crossed class lines. Within his first year, however, his base began to narrow to his core constituency among the lower and lower middle classes, who comprised his earliest and most stalwart supporters. In the December 1999 plebiscite called to ratify the new constitution drafted by Chávez's constituent assembly, support for the founding charter was disproportionately low in wealthy districts (López Maya and Lander, 2000a: 23). When Francisco Arias and other former military leaders from the original Bolivarian movement broke with Chávez in early 2000, Arias was embraced by the middle- and upper-class opposition, which had no credible party to represent it and no effective political leaders. Arias then ran against Chávez in the presidential election called to "relegitimize" Chávez's authority. Surveys indicated that the poor supported the positions of Chávez over those of Arias by 47 percent to 23 percent; in contrast, the rich favored the positions of Arias by 40 percent to 29 percent (Alfredo Keller and Associates, 2000).

These sociopolitical distinctions were sustained by the actions of Chávez as well as his rhetoric and political style. His swift dismantling of established institutions and rebuilding of new ones that concentrated power in the hands of the executive and enhanced the political role of the armed forces proved unsettling to middle- and upper-class groups that were wary of radical change. Although Chávez devoted his first year in office to political and institutional reforms, following a pragmatic economic course that was devoid of major policy initiatives, the business sector clearly mistrusted the general thrust of the new president. Indeed, a survey of business executives found that 97 percent of them wanted the government to modify its policies (*Economist Intelligence Unit Country Report: Venezuela,* 2000: 9). The peak business association, Fedecámaras, was critical of the new constitution, which shortened the workweek for nighttime jobs, redefined the system of severance pay, restricted the privatization of social security and the oil industry, and generally prescribed a vigorous role for the state in economic development. Political distrust and uncertainty showed up clearly in the behavior of the business sector, as private investment declined 26 percent in Chávez's first year in office, foreign direct investment dropped by $1.7 billion, and capital flight totaled $4.6 billion (*Latin American Weekly Report,* February 1, 2000, p. 57). Two years later, business opposition began to take a more organized form, as industry leaders declared a capital strike against the government, encouraged opposition protests, and ultimately helped to orchestrate the April 2002 civil-military coup. The leader of Fedecámaras, Pedro Carmona, was named interim president during the coup, heading up a government of business elites that sought to dismantle the institutional edifice of the Fifth Republic before resigning in the face of a furious pro-Chávez backlash.

With respect to the core popular constituencies of Chávez, the focus on political reform and the severe recession that plagued the Venezuelan economy at the beginning of his term made it difficult to reward political loyalty with material benefits. Nevertheless, he initiated a major public works project known as Plan Bolívar, which was overseen by local military commanders and designed to generate employment and social services. Chávez also reasserted Venezuelan leadership in the Organization of Petroleum-Exporting Countries (OPEC), orchestrating a sharp increase in international oil prices that provided a huge financial windfall. These oil rents allowed the government to reactivate the economy and sharply increase public spending in 2000. The popular thrust of the government was also buttressed by constitutional provisions that encouraged grassroots forms of democratic participation, as well as legislative initiatives on behalf of land reform.

Chávez's leadership style and political rhetoric also drove a wedge between elite and popular sectors in Venezuela. Although most of his fire was concentrated on the parties and political establishment of the old order, his frequent public addresses and weekly radio and television appearances also directed criticism at the media, the conservative hierarchy of the Catholic Church, and the "rancid oligarchy" that benefited from an economic model producing egregious social inequalities. Chávez claimed to be leading a peaceful revolution on behalf of "the people," and he portrayed this revolutionary struggle in Manichaean terms. While campaigning for his new constitution, Chávez said: "We're in Apocalyptic times, there's no middle ground. Either you are with God or you are with the Devil and we are with God" ("Venezuela's Chávez Won't Tone Down Campaign for New Constitution," 1999). Traditional elites recoiled at this fiery imagery, but it clearly resonated among popular sectors who sought vengeance for past wrongs and were anxious for a new beginning. Chávez reveled in opportunities for direct contact with the masses, and given his modest upbringing, mixed racial features, blunt discourse, and penchant for playing baseball, he clearly struck a chord with popular sentiments.

A new popular political identity was thus constructed around the person of the president, giving political expression to social inequalities that had long lain dormant in Venezuela's public sphere. The elite-populist cleavage was readily visible during the dramatic events of April 2002, when the business-backed coup against Chávez triggered instant protests and looting in the slums of Caracas and a popular mobilization that restored Chávez's presidency. These events clearly demonstrated that opposition sectors—not to mention the U.S. government—had underestimated the depth of support for Chávez, the degree of social polarization, and the virulent popular backlash that would be produced by any effort to topple Chávez and install an elite-based, civil-military government.

Conclusion

Two decades of chronic economic decline, increasing inequalities, and social disarticulation created a context that ultimately facilitated the repoliticization of social inequalities in Venezuelan democracy. In contrast to other Latin American nations, where similar conditions spawned the emergence of new populist leaders who challenged the political establishment but diffused class identities, Hugo Chávez stoked class resentments and harnessed them to a frontal assault on the ancien régime. In so doing, he posed a vigorous challenge to the regional trend toward neoliberal reform, countering Latin America's embrace of the political and economic models sanctioned by U.S. hegemony. Although *chavismo* has not, to date, institutionalized the grassroots organizational dimensions of a class cleavage, it has clearly redrawn the axis of sociopolitical contestation in Venezuela by bringing it into closer correspondence with underlying structural inequalities. A generation of partisan-based, multiclass political competition has thus given way to a more stratified cleavage that is grounded in the polarizing figure of a president who has dismantled the inherited governing institutions and reconstructed new ones according to his design.

The elite civil-military coup against Chávez in April 2002 and the popular mobilization that quickly returned him to the presidency provide graphic evidence of the contentious volatility that accompanies this new sociopolitical alignment. Chávez's response to these events is likely to be decisive in determining whether the elite-popular cleavage will be assuaged or intensified and given a more institutionalized expression. The president can moderate his discourse and make concessions to his opponents in an effort to stabilize his regime, although this will undoubtedly place constraints on his ability to offer social reforms and political mobilization to his core lower-class constituencies. Alternatively, he can opt to deepen reforms and intensify organization from below while striking against the economic and institutional bases of opposition power, a strategy that will inevitably elicit hostility from the middle and upper classes in Venezuela. Although the international political and economic environment is decidedly unfavorable to the latter approach, the domestic dynamics of conflict and compromise will heavily condition the course charted by the Chávez presidency.

Whichever course this might be, the Venezuelan case provides a striking example of the enduring vitality of populist formulas in Latin America's deeply stratified societies and crisis-ridden political systems, even in a regional context of streamlined states and globalized markets. Although populism may recede periodically, it is capable of explosive reemergence in unforeseen forms and places. Whether or not Chávez's version of populism succeeds in founding a durable new political order, there is little doubt that it has dealt a deathblow to the old one.

4

Hugo Chávez Frías:
His Movement and His Presidency

Margarita López Maya

On the night of December 5, 1998, Venezuelans witnessed one of the most surprising electoral results in their democratic history. Hugo Chávez Frías, creator of the electoral organization Movimiento Quinta República (MVR; Fifth Republic Movement), who spearheaded a failed coup d'état against President Carlos Andrés Pérez in 1992, triumphed over his opponents with a whopping 56.2 percent of the vote. This percentage was only comparable to that obtained by President Jaime Lusinchi in 1983, in circumstances not without similarities. At that time, Lusinchi won as an opposition candidate to the social Christian government of Luis Herrera Campíns after the "Black Friday" of February 1983 cast the image of a failed government and a society confronting pressing difficulties. In 1998, fifteen years later, once again the image of a failed government and a society on the edge of an abyss favored strong electoral support for the option of change. In 1983, this alternative was Acción Democrática (AD); in 1998, it was a candidate and a movement entirely outside of the political establishment. In both instances, popular support was resounding with only a few percentage points of difference between them.

The change in political attitudes over fifteen years, which passed from massive support for an institutional system founded in 1958 to a radical rejection of that system, has been the object of much academic analysis. A combination of international and national factors has been emphasized in explaining the emergence of these political phenomena in Venezuela at the end of the twentieth century.[1] This chapter looks at another question that also warrants a discussion: Why did Chávez and his Fifth Republic capture the collective imagination and the confidence of the majority of Venezuelans, rather than other emerging parties such as Convergencia Nacional, Causa Radical (Causa R), or Proyecto Venezuela? Furthermore, in the elections of July 2000, following a year and a half of Chávez's government, the results were even more favorable as the president increased his share of the vote to 59.8 percent. Chávez's coalition moved from eight

73

governorships in 1998 to fifteen (plus two more governors who were sympathetic to the president's project). In addition, the MVR achieved a considerable victory when its candidate won the mayoralty of the newly created Metropolitan District of Caracas. This consolidation of popular confidence also merits an explanation.

Origins of the Bolivarian Movement

In Venezuela, the 1980s was the beginning of the end of the political system constructed since 1958. The import substitution model, fueled by petroleum income, showed the first symptoms of an irreversible decline, while the debt crisis that has plagued third-world countries since 1982 exposed Venezuela to changes within the world capitalist system (Roberts, 2001). For Venezuelans, the 1980s were years of failed reform efforts, economic contraction, social degeneration, and growing popular mobilization. The exuberant economic growth that occurred in Venezuela in the previous decade, stimulated by the boom in international petroleum prices, had promoted the diversification and increasing complexity of the social structure. The appearance of the first symptoms of recession at the end of the decade and the imposition of currency devaluation and exchange controls in 1983 provoked a growing change in the collective conscience. Venezuela began leaving behind the golden years, and entered what was then believed to be the "postpetroleum" era.

The severe weaknesses and perversions in the democratic system that became evident during the government of Lusinchi (1984–1989), along with the prolonged economic contraction, brought into question the viability of the modernization project based on policies of import substitution (Gómez Calcaño and López Maya, 1990: 39–55). Critiques of the role played by the state in different areas of social life, growing accusations of corruption in all public spheres, and demands for greater political participation by civil society were the major themes debated. At the outset of his presidency, Lusinchi decreed the creation of the Presidential Commission on State Reform (COPRE). Despite this initiative, the decade finished with few positive results toward reform, and with one of the most dramatic events expressing the frustration of Venezuelans: the Caracazo of 1989, which deepened critiques and revealed the ire and desperation felt by broad sectors of the population.

Venezuela's military sectors did not stay on the margins of the process of examination and debate. Various groups within the armed forces met on a regular basis to discuss politics and criticize the existing order (Gott, 2000: 61). These included the young Hugo Chávez and some of his friends, including Jesús Urdaneta Hernández and Felipe Acosta Carles, who in 1982 founded a clandestine organization called the Movimiento Bolivariano Revolucionario 200 (MBR-200). They later recalled swearing an oath beneath the historically famous tree known as the "Samán of Güere" in Maracay on December 17 of that year (commemorating the death of Simón Bolívar) that they would rescue the values of the fatherland, dignify the military career, and fight against corruption (Zago, 1992: 21).[2] How specifically they would comply with the pledge was not very clear in the beginning. They met to study military and national history and to discuss current political problems, but without a doubt they also intended to influence political processes (Zago, 1992: 21–36; Gott, 2000: 40–43). The MBR-200 was composed of very young officers. Most, like Chávez, were no more than twenty-eight years of age in 1982, but they had already begun developing political concerns. They discussed, for instance, the military coup against Salvador Allende and the Panamanian military experiment led by Omar Torrijos, and drew conclusions reflecting a leftist perspective (personal interview with Hugo Chávez, Caracas, March 25, 1996). Along the same lines, they sympathized with the experience of General Velasco Alvarado in Peru.

During the 1980s, the MBR-200 was fundamentally a clandestine cell of military officers, although on subsequent occasions Chávez claimed that it was never meant to remain so. Civilian ties during these early years were relatively scarce, but they significantly influenced the political orientations of the movement. Through relatives and close friends, the officers came into contact with activists and leaders of the leftist parties that were defeated during the guerrilla struggle of the 1960s. The most important contact, by virtue of its influence over the organization's subsequent thought, was the Partido de la Revolución Venezolana (PRV; Party of the Venezuelan Revolution), led by Douglas Bravo, who was the principal guerrilla commander of the western region of the country. Chávez's brother, Adán Chávez, belonged to the PRV and appears to have facilitated the first meeting between the two leaders at the beginning of the decade (Gott, 2000: 60). Early on, the Bolivarianos also contacted Alfredo Maneiro and Pablo Medina of Causa R, and groups like Bandera Roja (Red Flag) and the Liga Socialista (Socialist League) (personal conversation with Pablo Medina, New York, March 15, 1999). The meetings with these leaders appear to have occurred less frequently, even though Causa R's influence over the future movement manifested itself in various aspects of the MBR-200's organization and discourse in the 1990s.[3]

These leftist groups shared with the Bolivarianos the goal of organizing a civil-military alliance in order to stimulate revolutionary change, reformulating an idea embodied in Venezuelan guerrilla discourse in the 1960s (Bravo and Melet, 1991: 125–143). Besides former guerrillas, the MBR-200 contacted other prominent leftist intellectuals and activists, although this appears to have occurred somewhat later, at the turn of the

1980s. These included members of the Frente Patriótico (Patriotic Front) such as Luis Miquilena, Manuel Quijada, Lino Martínez, José Vicente Rangel, and Omar Mezza, and university figures such as Luis Fuenmayor, Héctor Navarro, Jorge Giordani, Trino Alcides Díaz, and Adina Bastidas. All would come to occupy positions in Chávez's government after 1998.

One point always emphasized by the military members of the Bolivarian movement is the type of university education they received. They point out that the "Andrés Bello Plan," which was introduced in 1971, provided future officers with a broader and more complex university education than that received in the past (Chávez, 1993). In addition, many would then undertake more advanced coursework or university degrees in social science fields at public Venezuelan universities (Gott, 2000: 41–42). These endowed the participants with an uncommon outlook in comparison to the military formation of their Latin American colleagues. Furthermore, many Venezuelan military officers came from low social strata. Indeed, the military career is one of the paths toward social mobility for poor, but ambitious, young men. During the 1980s, military salaries shrank as a result of inflation, but the military career continued to be a secure route toward social mobility, due to the education, social benefits, and opportunities for business contacts that the military offered its members. Thus, while other channels such as public education became closed due to budget cuts and the general deterioration of social institutions, the military career path remained open, training Venezuelans from the poorer sectors who were highly sensitive to the problems of those of similar social origins.[4]

From Sacudón to Prison

An important milestone for the MBR-200 as well as other emerging social and political groups were the disturbances of February 27, 1989, known as the Caracazo or Sacudón (Upheaval). This popular revolt, which covered practically the entire urban map of the country and involved paralysis and widespread looting, revealed the weakness of political institutions, at the same time that it contributed to their further weakening (López Maya, 2000). As a result of the chaotic institutional performance of February 27, it became clear that the government had survived almost exclusively due to the support of the armed forces, which at the time demonstrated unconditional backing for civil order.

The Sacudón became a turning point in the Venezuelan sociopolitical process. The weakness and lack of representation evidenced by the official and mediating institutions made it urgent to begin reforms, corrections, and adjustments in political relations. This did not happen to the extent that the situation required, and consequently the government, political parties, and organized labor lost credibility. The vacuum was partly filled by alternative organizations, which sought to reconstruct the bases of interaction. In particular, new leaders and institutions emerged from two sources. One of these was the process of decentralization. The other, unsuspected at the time, was in the barracks.

The end of the Lusinchi administration (which largely held back state reform) and the events of February 27, 1989, gave a stimulus to the decentralization process. In 1989, Venezuelans voted for the first time for governors and mayors.[5] In some states, the gubernatorial elections permitted the emergence of new political leaderships distinct from those of AD and the Comité de Organización Política Electoral Independiente (COPEI). Revealing the extent of popular rejection of the government party, its neoliberal policies, and its management of the Caracazo, AD saw its statewide victories shrink from nineteen (won in the national elections of 1988) to eleven. The Movimiento al Socialismo (MAS), which had never occupied executive offices, captured the governorship in the state of Aragua. The state of Bolívar witnessed the surprising victory of a union leader belonging to an organization on the margins of the political system: Andrés Velásquez of Causa R.

A second round of regional elections occurred in November 1992, following the two abortive military coups of that year against President Pérez. Governors of the opposition who had maintained a distance from the national government were generally rewarded at the polls. In 1993, these governors played a significant role during the difficult months prior to Pérez's impeachment on May 20, 1993. During these months, a convention of governors held in the city of Valencia demonstrated administrative continuity at the regional level, projecting an image of regional stability and autonomy in the midst of the crisis of the central government. The meeting boosted the legitimacy of these leaders and their parties, strengthening the political commitment to decentralization. In the following years, governors, mayors, and organizations (such as Causa R in 1993 and Proyecto Venezuela in 1998) engaged in important political work at the local level, providing the new faces and ideas in the arena of the sociopolitical transition.

In the barracks the repression carried out against a poor and defenseless civilian population during the Caracazo began to influence behavior in a critical manner. Some of the Bolivarianos, having exercised control of troops at the time, felt shame, indignation, and a sense of having defended the wrong side (Gott, 2000: 48; Zago, 1992: 51–53). If the idea of rising up in arms had already jelled, now plans accelerated and contacts with civilians, particularly with the PRV and Causa R, became more constant. Moreover, the military base of the movement expanded, as members of different forces approached the group. Chávez relates that on beginning work at Miraflores Palace some weeks after the Caracazo, presidential guards approached him to demonstrate their desire to join the group (Gott, 2000: 47–49). Similarly, leftist groups came alive with the popular revolt and began to develop contacts and alliances (Gott, 2000: 62–63). The PRV began to meet frequently with the MBR-200, sharing ideas and some strategies (Bravo and Melet, 1991: 159–174; former guerrilla Francisco Prada, interviewed in *El Nacional,* February 25, 2001, www.el-nacional.com). Continuous ties to some Causa R leaders, such as Pablo Medina and Alí Rodríguez, were also established.

With the expansion of the civilian base, tension between members of the military and civilians—as has manifested itself in the MBR-200 and the MVR ever since—became visible. The civilians believed that their participation in the attempt should be equal to that of their military companions, and Douglas Bravo, a former guerrilla, even argued that the civilian action should precede that of the military (Gott, 2000: 62–63). Nevertheless, according to declarations by different civilians involved with the coup, the rebel officers never shared this perception. Because of this, Bravo separated from Chávez shortly before the coup attempt (Arvelo Ramos, 1998: 40–45). Kléber Ramírez of the PRV, who was in charge of drafting the decrees that were to be emitted by the provisional government, would also sense the military officers' distrust of civilian capabilities and accordingly left the movement. Pablo Medina affirmed years later that due to distrust, Chávez and his military companions never turned over the promised arms to the civilians on the eve of the coup (personal conversation with Pablo Medina, New York, March 15, 1997). The rifts at this time between the Bolivarianos and Causa R leaders set the tone for the tense relations that have prevailed between them ever since.

The coup of February 4, 1992, failed militarily, as the rebellious soldiers were unable to capture the president and subdue strategic military sites in Caracas. Nevertheless, in the state of Zulia the military rebels led by Franciso Arias Cárdenas obtained rapid success, and on the morning of the February 4 they controlled the state government, the oil fields, and the airport (López Maya, 1994: 40–49). In the states of Carabobo and Aragua, the rebels succeeded in taking over important positions, and in the city of Valencia they even distributed weapons to civilians. Yet by nine o'clock in the morning, having failed to achieve the principal objective of seizing the president, Chávez surrendered and asked to speak on television to his companions in arms to ask that they do the same in order to avoid a massacre. As is now well known, this appearance of less than one minute gave a face to the insurrection and captured the collective imagination of broad sectors of the population. Although the Peréz government survived, it was left mortally wounded. Chávez and a large number of the coup participants were imprisoned.

The coup attempt deepened the crisis of legitimacy, demonstrating that neoliberal policies had produced a fracture within the bloc of social and political forces that sustained the regime. It showed that the armed forces were divided in their loyalties to the political system of 1958. Speeches delivered in Congress by Rafael Caldera and Aristóbulo Istúriz of Causa R, as well as declarations of governors of different parties including COPEI and the future Proyecto Venezuela, attributed the coup to the errors of recent political leaders and to the desperation of poor people confronting a crisis without any easy solution. These statements revealed the extent of President Pérez's isolation. The abortive coup of November 27 of the same year, which unlike its predecessor included high-ranking officers of the air force and navy, convinced many political actors that Pérez's fall was inevitable. It was then that the search for a peaceful solution began.

President Pérez and his administration committed the error of thinking that they could apply a program of macroeconomic adjustment in Venezuela without internal political support, even from the governing party. Furthermore, the Pérez administration spurned traditional channels for constructing consensus and failed to explain to the general population the necessity of such a drastic economic turnaround. Despite the enormous popular rejection expressed in the Caracazo and the street protests of the following years, the government failed to implement substantial political or economic changes between 1989 and 1992. The concessions after the first coup attempt of 1992, in the form of cabinet changes and the constitution of an advisory commission consisting of renowned independent figures, did not convince Venezuelans that needed changes were in store. On November 27 a second failed coup took place, after which Pérez and his government never recovered. The macroeconomic adjustment program did yield some positive macroeconomic results after 1990, but social indicators continued to fall, while the gap between the incomes of the poorest and wealthiest continued to increase (Rey, 1993; López Maya and Lander, 2000a). The disintegration of society continued its inexorable course. The general population rejected the political parties of the establishment because of their incapacity to alter the course of these events, not just because they resisted the internal democratization that the society had demanded since the prior decade. The change of attitudes gave rise to the distancing of the electorate from the institutionalized political system. The 1993 elections produced a break in the two-party system and Rafael Caldera's triumph, achieved through an antiadjustment platform and an electoral movement called Convergencia, which avoided identification with the traditional parties.

In the elections of 1993 the Causa R party, also with an antiparty and anti-neoliberal discourse, went from the margins of the political system to center stage. It became the third largest party in the country and its presidential candidate, Andrés Velásquez, came in fourth place just slightly behind AD and COPEI candidates. Causa R denounced the official results as fraudulent and accused the AD-COPEI–dominated National Electoral Commission of having perpetuated fraud.

In these years of intense political turbulence, the jailed Bolivarianos continually received visits from representatives of different social and political sectors, communicating their solidarity and support. The MBR-200 swelled with the addition of civilians from all ideological backgrounds. The rebel officers also took advantage of this time to study and plan their next actions. The relationships with those civilians who would become key to the Bolivarianos' ascent to power dated back to this period: Luis Miquilena, José Vicente Rangel, José Rafael Nuñez Tenorio, Jorge Giordani, and Pedro Duno, among many others.

From Liberty to Power

After being freed by President Caldera in March 1994, the Bolivarianos sought to convert their movement into a national political organization (*El Universal,* March 27, 1994, sec. 1, p. 1; MBR-200, 1994c). For this purpose, they traveled throughout the country and began establishing organizational structures and internal procedures to differentiate themselves from the establishment parties and to avoid sliding toward rigidity or authoritarianism (personal conversation with Jorge Giordani, Caracas, January 21, 1995). They also disseminated more extensively the ideological positions they had been developing since the 1980s, laid out political strategies, and elaborated the framework of a long-term political program that they called the "Simón Bolívar" national project.

Nevertheless, the organizational structures of the MBR-200 were not particularly original when compared with those of other Venezuelan parties. The primary organizational base, which they called "Bolivarian Circles," was composed of small local groups very similar to the committees or cells of other organizations. They did have as a peculiarity, however, the requirement that those who wished to join the groups had to make a "Bolivarian" commitment, specifically an oath to be "hard working, honest, and humble, and exercise solidarity" (MBR-200, 1994e). The circles were coordinated at the municipal level by the so-called municipal Bolivarian coordinators. By 1996, there were also regional Bolivarian coordinators in all the states throughout the country.

The fourth structural level (above the circles and the municipal and regional coordinators) was the national directorate, which made all final decisions for the organization. In 1996, this directorate was composed of two former officers of the armed forces, one of whom was Chávez, and the other the future foreign minister Luis Dávila; Freddy Bernal; a former police officer and future mayor of the Libertador municipality in the capital; and two civilians, one of whom—Leticia Barrios—was a woman. The members of the directorate formed secretariats that functioned as support teams for different internal areas. The composition of the directorate reflected the efforts that had been made to give the organization a civil-military balance, and to represent its base of support (personal interview with Hugo Chávez, Caracas, March 25, 1996).

The circles frequently organized local assemblies to discuss politics. The MBR-200 considered it important to carry out additional activities to train members, such as study circles and courses to examine national and international history. In these meetings, the disagreements between civilians and military officers arising from, for example, political style and interpersonal relations became evident, producing friction and tensions. However, these encounters were pursued because the movement's leaders believed that frequent political discussions and getting to know one another personally would help overcome military rigidity and political inexperience as well as civilian prejudice against officers. These advances, in turn, would strengthen democratic attitudes and horizontal relations. Furthermore, by 1996, the Bolivarianos had managed to carry out regional assemblies in some states, such as Miranda and Carabobo, where the movement was expanding rapidly. Similar to Causa R and other leftist parties, the procedure for making decisions was to engage in discussion until consensus was achieved. The decision not to participate in the 1995 elections was made in this way. Nevertheless, this was not a rigid position, and the voting process was recognized as a possible option in some circumstances, such as the selection of representatives for internal positions (personal interview with Hugo Chávez, Caracas, March 25, 1996; personal interview with Maigualida Barrera, MBR-200 member, Caracas, January 18, 1996).

The Bolivarian discourse reflected the influence of the PRV. The symbol of the tree with three roots has been used to represent the doctrine of Chávez's party, with each root corresponding to the thought of a Venezuelan figure of the nineteenth century. This harkens back to discussions held about Ezequiel Zamora, Simón Rodríguez, and Simón Bolívar in the PRV since at least the 1970s (Bravo and Melet, 1991: 1–37; Gott, 2000: 30–31). Nevertheless, the Bolivarianos, especially Chávez, achieved a command of the symbols and images of nationality and applied them to political propositions in a way that was novel, and that became one of the keys to their political success (López Maya and Lander, 1999, 2000b).

Since 1992, the MBR-200 called for a national constituent assembly as a means of achieving the profound political changes that society demanded through nonviolent methods (MBR-200, 1994a, 1994b, 1994d). The MBR-200 shared this position with other organizations of civil society during this period, such as the Frente Patriótico and the Centro Gumilla. In the MBR-

200, this request was closely related to the organization's support for elec-toral abstention at all levels, since the Bolivarianos maintained that the elections of recent years had been fraudulent and incapable of expressing the popular will. In 1993, the position of abstention motivated Francisco Arias Cárdenas's separation from the movement when he accepted Causa R's nomination as candidate for governor of Zulia.

In 1997 the MBR-200 changed its position and decided to compete in the electoral campaign of 1998. This decision resulted from an evaluation of the nature of those elections, in which the national vote was to occur on the same date as the regional and municipal races. The organization believed that too much was at stake in these elections and that not partici-pating in them would probably weaken the organization (personal interview with Hugo Chávez, Caracas, March 25, 1996). Furthermore, some leaders argued that even if they did not win, the effort would nonetheless leave them with a solid national structure and broad representation in Congress. In such an event they could dissolve Congress and convoke a constituent assembly, either alone or in alliance with other political organizations (per-sonal interview with José Rafael Núñez Tenorio, founding MVR member, Caracas, August 18, 1997). Following this resolution approved at the party's national assembly, other decisions about strategy that would prove essential to achieving electoral victory but that would create unexpected change in the organization were taken.[6]

The MBR-200 created an electoral structure that it called the Movimiento Quinta República as part of the general strategy of participat-ing in the elections. The new organization was designed to protect the still fragile structure of the MBR-200 from the vicissitudes of the electoral cam-paign. Some movement leaders feared that upon entering the electoral race, a new flood of party members and sympathizers who did not share the ideals or interests of the Bolivarianos would join the organization. This process ran the risk of blurring the movement's ideological orientation. The structure of the new organization was to be flexible and capable of handling all the activities connected with the campaign. This would spare the MBR-200 of the tensions arising from the construction of political alliances and decisions related to the electoral platform and other campaign issues. The MVR was thus conceived as a tool of the party to incorporate independent personalities and other groups with distinct ideologies and political posi-tions, whose only commonality with the MBR-200 was their support of Hugo Chávez's presidential candidacy (personal interview with José Rafael Nuñez Tenorio, Caracas, August 18, 1997). The party took the name of "Fifth Republic" because Venezuela legally prohibits using the name of Bolívar to register a political organization in the National Electoral Commission (CNE). Nevertheless, when abbreviated, "MVR" approximat-ed "MBR" phonetically, thus facilitating the transfer of identity. The movement's leaders were always careful about the symbolism of each political action, and the name they chose for the new organization was no exception. The name pointed to the "refounding" of the Venezuelan republic, taking into consideration that what they called the "Fourth Republic" had begun with Venezuela's separation from Gran Colombia in 1830 and had endured since then. This so-called Fourth Republic had always been dominated by oligarchies detached from the interests of the people.

Thus the MVR was not conceived to be a party, but rather an electoral front controlled by the MBR-200. Its creators did not see as its function the promotion of internal discussions or the training of members, nor did they endow the organization with democratic structures and procedures. They felt that the MVR should instead serve to make sound and rapid decisions related to the elections, having in its central leadership people in whom the candidate placed his greatest confidence, and whom he had himself selected. However, the successes achieved by this new organization in constructing alliances, planning strategies, and winning seven electoral processes in little more than three years left the MBR-200 without a role, thus causing it to disappear. This development fed into the separation of an important group of military companions of Chávez who backed Francisco Arias Cárdenas as a presidential alternative for the elections in 2000. Upon separating, this group claimed to be the "authentic" part of the Bolivarian movement.

In April 1997, Chávez and his movement announced their decision to compete in the December 1998 electoral campaign. The surprising and unstoppable growth of Chávez's presidential candidacy beginning in the early months of 1998 was related to a convergence of factors. On the one hand, toward the end of 1997, an economic recession set in, unleashed by the abrupt fall of international oil prices. This recession led to the further impoverishment of the population and, above all, to Venezuelans' pessimistic and critical perception of the Caldera government's economic performance. Caldera had won in 1993 using an antiliberal discourse critical of President Pérez's economic policies. Nevertheless, in 1996 Caldera's government began to apply the so-called Venezuela Agenda, a program of macroeconomic adjustment very similar to Pérez's "economic package." Once again the costs of the economic crisis appeared to have been placed on the shoulders of the poorest people. On the other hand, political-institutional deterioration continued during the Caldera years. This process manifested itself in the deterioration of state institutions and public services, as well as in the traditional parties' efforts to neutralize initiatives for political change that were being proposed by emerging actors since the 1980s.

Another factor explaining Chávez's rise was the reversed stand of the Causa R party. Along with Caldera and the parties that supported him, Causa R capitalized on popular discontent by putting forth anti-neoliberal positions in the 1993 elections. But following Caldera's election, Causa R dropped its intransigent stands and antiparty discourse at the same time that it supported certain neoliberal policies. As a result the party split in two. The more moderate faction, which kept the party name, adopted even more conciliatory positions and was thus no longer perceived as representing a true alternative.

During the presidential campaign, Chávez and the MVR developed a discourse of antiliberalism and rupture with the past. This discourse was given credibility by his refusal to be contaminated by alliances with traditional parties, as well as by his inclination to construct a wide alliance of alternative forces, known as the Polo Patriótico (PP; Patriotic Pole). One of Chávez's most valuable weapons was his incorporation of the term *el pueblo* ("the people") into his political discourse and relating it to the audience he addressed. The concept of *el pueblo* is a source of historical identity for low-income Venezuelans, providing them with a sense of self-esteem and hope. The discourse of the Bolivarianos, and that of Chávez in particular, greatly appealed to this *pueblo*. They linked the people to the great achievements of the nineteenth century, particularly independence and the Federal War, and repeatedly depicted the *el pueblo* as brave, noble, beautiful, and valiant—the main actor of history.[7]

The results of the congressional, gubernatorial, and presidential elections of 1998 opened up a new political spectrum for the society, more so than in 1993. AD and COPEI witnessed their congressional representation diminish drastically. The performance of emerging actors, including populists (MVR and PPT) and others (Proyecto Venezuela), brought new faces to the scene as new generations finally began to dominate the political leadership. At the eleventh hour of the December presidential elections, the traditional parties abandoned their own presidential candidates to embrace Henrique Salas Römer of Proyecto Venezuela, whom they had opposed only days before. This decision, a product of the panic that Chávez's imminent victory provoked among the top leaders of these parties, made it evident that the two-party system was nearing its end. At this time, the patterns of electoral behavior emerged that have been maintained until the present, including five further elections.

In contrast to the past, the electoral processes from 1998 to 2000 revealed a tendency to vote along the lines of social positions. While Chávez captured the vote of the poor and lower-middle sectors of the country by a wide margin, his opponents attracted those sectors with the greatest resources. This tendency toward social polarization was especially evident in Caracas, whose three wealthier municipalities—Chacao, Baruta, and El Hatillo—defeated MVR mayoral candidates, in contrast to the more predominately low-income Libertador and Sucre, which elected MVR mayors.

The Fifth Republic

Chávez's presidency was inaugurated on February 2, 1999. Consistent with what had been his electoral platform, Chávez decreed in his inaugural speech the holding of a popular referendum that would open the way for elections for a constituent assembly. Chávez's constitutional proposal was approved in a referendum held in April. Then, in elections based on a first-past-the-post system in July, the governmental alliance obtained 125 deputies, in contrast to only 6 seats won by the opposition. With this comfortable majority, the assembly was able to draft a new constitution in just over three months, which was approved in a national referendum held in December of the same year.

The constitutional process monopolized the Chávez government's efforts throughout 1999. It was a difficult year, full of tensions characterized by street mobilizations and other actions promoted by political parties, civil organizations, and different interest groups, all seeking to have their visions and demands incorporated in the new Magna Carta (López Maya, Smilde, and Stephany, 2001: 11–24).

Furthermore, the president and his alliance found themselves pressed to finish the process, conscious that with time political support for the constitution could begin weakening. This haste in dealing with such complex and delicate concerns generated ambiguities in the final text and resulted in dissatisfaction and tensions. The new national constitution has among its strengths the updating of human rights coverage, the incorporation of indigenous and environmental rights, the establishment of new guidelines for restructuring the judiciary, and the deepening of political democracy through the incorporation of various forms of direct participation. At the same time, it increased the branches of government based on checks and balances from three to five by creating the "Citizen Power" and the "Electoral Power." Both concepts had been discussed in the documents of the MBR-200 in the 1990s (Chávez, 1993; MBR-200, 1994d). Also reflecting the *chavista* movement's political base, the constitution granted the military the right to vote and stripped Congress of its ability to interfere with military promotions. A point of honor for the president was changing the name of the republic, which due to his insistence was incorporated into the constitutional text at the last minute, after the assembly had discarded this option. Venezuela became the República Bolivariana de Venezuela, or Bolivarian Republic of Venezuela.

The weaknesses of the constitution undoubtedly will come to the fore. Among the major criticisms of the new document are: the increased concentration of power in the presidency, which can now legislate on any matter once the national congress (now called the National Assembly) passes a special enabling law (Articles 203 and 236); the elimination of public financing of political parties, which weakens the ability of political organizations representative of sectors without resources to compete with more powerful interest groups (Article 67); and the excessive detail in many articles that produces a cumbersome rigidity. Critics also consider the decentralization embodied in the constitution to be insufficient and state intervention in various areas of social life (guaranteeing such rights as housing, free education at all levels, and free hospital services) to be excessive. In general, the constitution reflects fundamental aspects of the Bolivarian project, such as the expansion of direct democracy, the extension of public powers, and the military vote. The constitution's weaknesses and vagueness also reflect unclear aspects of the *chavista* project, as is the case with political decentralization.

The government's economic performance during Chávez's first two and a half years was mixed. The year 1999 closed with negative macroeconomic indicators, reflecting the continuation of the economic recession and the deterioration in the living conditions of the popular sectors. Nevertheless, in that year, Venezuela resumed an active role in the Organization of Petroleum-Exporting Countries (OPEC) from which it had distanced itself during the governments of Pérez and Caldera, and began to comply strictly with its assigned quotas, which it had flagrantly violated during previous years (Lander, 2001). At the same time, the Ministry of Energy and Mines undertook to recuperate its role in the formulation of petroleum policy, a function that in recent years was carried out by the state oil company, Petróleos de Venezuela, Sociedad Anónima (PDVSA) (see Chapter 7). Chávez restored the nationalist and statist content that Venezuelan oil policy had throughout most of the twentieth century. In practice, the new oil policy has been one of the most important successes of the Chávez government in that it had a direct impact on strengthening international petroleum prices. By 2001, in recognition of his support in strengthening OPEC, Minister of Mines Alí Rodríguez was designated secretary-general of that organization, the second Venezuelan to occupy that position.

The economic results for the year 2000 were more positive (see Chapter 6). Thanks to the increase in public revenue and improved fiscal discipline, the negative macroeconomic indicators were reversed: the Central Bank of Venezuela reported growth of 3.2 percent in the gross domestic product (GDP); inflation declined to 14.2 percent, the lowest in fifteen years; the current account obtained a surplus; and international reserves increased to U.S.$21.647 billion (BCV, 2001). At the same time, the fiscal deficit shrank from 2.6 percent of the GDP in 1999 to 1.8 percent in 2000. This reduction is particularly impressive, taking into account the extraordinary government expenditures due to the disastrous floods in the heavily populated coastal state of Vargas in December 1999 (BCV, 2001). There was reason to be optimistic that oil prices would be high and stable in 2001, promoting growth, but economic difficulties and a deficit of investment continued to challenge the government and threaten its base of support.

Although the MVR's political platform put forward some general strategies to overcome the problems that have characterized Venezuela's economic evolution in the last twenty years, there was much uncertainty about future economic policy. This naturally generated a lack of confidence among investors both at home and abroad. The MBR-200 rejected neoliberalism and criticized unrestrained economic globalization (MBR-200, 1996). By 2001 the MVR and the Chávez government had somewhat shifted from this position. Saying it was looking for a "third way," the government favored establishing a permanent regulatory and supervisory role for the state in the economy, placing a priority on agriculture, breaking up the concentration of capital by stimulating small and medium-size businesses, supporting national capital, retaining state ownership of the petroleum industry, and encouraging various forms of communal and participatory ownership. These notions are embodied in some of the articles of the 1999 constitution and have been reaffirmed by Chávez in numerous speeches and interviews (see, e.g., Gott, 2000: 179–189). Nevertheless, this announced direction needs to be concretized in the form of specific laws, institutions, and policies that can overcome the economic stagnation of the last decades and produce a sustainable national economy in the global world (as Julia Buxton discusses in Chapter 6). Designing and implementing an alternative economic model for Venezuela continue to be a challenge.

In contrast, the picture on the social front could not be viewed as encouraging by any means, even though important efforts were made to reverse the pressing situation of the past decades (López Maya and Lander, 2000a). In this sense, the expansion of social and family rights in the new constitutional text, compared with that of 1961, stands out (see Chapter V of the constitution). The new constitution incorporated housewives and workers of the informal economy into the social security system (Articles 86, 87, and 88) and made explicit the right to severance benefits calculated on the basis of seniority (Article 92) (see Chapter 9 for discussion of this controversy). Furthermore, lower inflation rates and social programs in education, health, and housing improved the living standards of vulnerable social sectors (Provea, 2000). The official activities carried out in 2000 in the state of Vargas after the floods stand out in this area. The three-year recovery plan, which included clean water service to 70 percent of the population, emergency educational programs, and housing set required investment for the year 2000 at 120 billion bolivars (approximately U.S.$167 million) (*Tal Cual,* December 12, 2000, p. 10).

Conclusion

The Bolivarian movement formed part of a larger group of social organizations that began to emerge and grow in Venezuela in the 1980s. Although it differed from other radical movements due to its clandestine nature, it was like the others given impetus by the complex challenges facing society following decades of uninterrupted growth and democracy. The humble origins of the original MBR-200 members, their physical proximity to the powerful elites, and their high level of public education gave them a distinct social awareness and made them receptive to nationalist and leftist ideas that came to constitute the ideological heart of the movement.

The Caracazo was an important milestone in the history of the MBR-200, as it has been for the general sociopolitical process of the country. For the Bolivarianos, it clearly demonstrated the antidemocratic and antipopular character of the civilian governments, and it served to consolidate their role as the exponents of an alternative political proposal. Following this popular revolt, a coup d'état became the group's clear objective, and the conspiracy acquired a more intense rhythm than before by incorporating broader civilian and military sectors.

Between 1989 and February 1992, the Pérez government continued its economic program without introducing substantial social reforms. The steady impoverishment of significant sectors of the middle classes, which had been under way since the end of the 1970s, was aggravated by the neoliberal policies of state abandonment of social and economic regulation and cuts in spending. For their part, the dominant political actors did not respond adequately to the demands for political reforms that different organizations of civil and political society clamored for. Thus even though the 1992 coups failed, they found a frustrated, impoverished citizenry that was ready to go along with whoever could crack open the petrified, isolated, and insensitive sphere of power.

Between 1992 and 1998, the Bolivarian movement experienced the dizzying ascent of its principal leader, Hugo Chávez Frías, from prison to power. The 1990s were characterized by political agitation, during which time emerging actors battled to occupy the space left by the traditional parties as a result of delegitimization and decomposition. During these years, Chávez's followers formed two substantially different organizations: the MBR-200, a political organization with internal structures, arenas for debate, and procedures for choosing members and making decisions; and the MVR, which was fundamentally an electoral structure created by the MBR-200 in order to compete in the electoral arena in 1998, and which came to take the place of its predecessor. The MVR's big challenge was to create internal structures of participation, which the MBR-200 had begun to develop. The MVR's electoral victory was the result of the continuing structural crisis of society and the growing perception that the Caldera government, which was elected as a "moderate" alternative to traditional power brokers, remained tied to the establishment. Causa R, which had represented an alternative to traditional parties in the early 1990s, dropped its intransigent stands, began to negotiate with other parties, and endorsed certain neoliberal positions along with the Caldera administration. To this general context was added the MVR and Chávez's ability to create a broad political alliance with alternative forces, and to develop a discourse based on inclusion of the vast majorities frustrated by twenty years of deterioration and unfulfilled promises.

Following the December 1998 triumph of Chávez, Venezuelan society began to construct a new hegemony, in which military sectors occupied a more visible and active position than in the past, new parties substituted traditional ones, and the popular sectors again became an object of official discourse and policies. Between 1998 and 2000, in addition to the definitive displacement of the old political elite through multiple electoral processes, a new constitution was written and significant changes in the orientation of economic and social policies took place. Among the most notable were the government's reforms in petroleum policy and the reintroduction of social policies into the political debate, which the prior pro-neoliberal governments had downplayed. Following this orientation, the constitution obliges the state to create a universal social security system, and the government has prioritized the poor in its efforts and expenditures in the area of public health, education, and housing in order to alleviate the conditions of poverty of the majority of Venezuelan families.

The process, however, was full of tensions, uncertainties, and obstacles. One of the most severe was political polarization, the result of two decades of economic recession and adjustment policies that reversed the social gains of the past and created growing social divisions. In 1997, 48.3 percent of families lived in poverty, and in 1998, 47.2 percent of the economically active population worked in the informal sector of the economy (IESA, 2001). At the same time, in 1997 the wealthiest 5 percent of the population had incomes that were 53.1 times greater than the poorest 5 percent; ten years earlier, the relationship—already bad—was only 42.6 times greater (Baptista, 1997: 149). After Chávez's election, this social polarization was expressed in the political arena through two blocs that showed little capacity for dialogue and consensus: on one side, the government's party and its political allies; on the other, a divided opposition, which was radicalized and counted on considerable economic resources and the means to promote its ideas.

The program and discourse of the MVR permitted it to capitalize on the social polarization within the society. After 1998 the upper- and middle-class municipalities of Caracas and other large cities continued to demonstrate electoral behavior opposite to the general tendency within the Venezuelan electorate. Although this was not itself a cause for alarm, it was accompanied by an additional, worrisome factor: the scarce inclination of emerging political actors—whether pro- or antigovernment—to stabilize political institutions of representation. This lack of interest in constructing strong and permanent organizational structures, capable of consolidating political identities and formulating middle- or long-term programs, encouraged the confrontational street mobilization that was permanently present in the cities, especially Caracas. With the lack of less disruptive, effective channels, social actors of various kinds interrupted the daily life of thousands of people, helping to maintain the deteriorated societal atmosphere and consequently contributing to the socioeconomic decline of the country. Through 2001, Chávez's speeches and the MVR's behavior spurned the benefits that could be gained from strong institutions for representation, mediation, and conflict resolution, making the nation extremely vulnerable to momentary political vicissitudes. The organizational weakness of the parties in the government coalition left Chávez and his movement extremely dependent on the president's charisma and his performance in the government. And this, as President Caldera's government showed, is not sufficient to guarantee political survival.

Nevertheless, the electoral triumph of Chávez and his Bolivarian movement meant the irreversible displacement of the political elites who led the country since 1958. At the same time, it implied the return of *el pueblo* as a political subject, one that had disappeared from public discourse during the 1980s and early 1990s, when neoliberal ideas exercised a significant influence on the political debate of leading actors. President Chávez and his political allies, as the axes of a new hegemony for Venezuelan society, reflected as much the profound socioeconomic changes that society had lived in the past decades as the efforts of impoverished sectors to be included in society's plan for the twenty-first century. In this sense, Chávez, his movement and his presidency, moved the Venezuelan ideological and political debate toward a position that was closer to the country's reality. In the future, those who seek to form roots in the Venezuelan political system—which continues to be under construction— should understand and pay attention to this singular imperative.

Notes

This chapter was translated from the Spanish by Deborah Norden.
    1. Among the most recent academic analyses, see Chapters 6 and 7 in this book, as well as the articles by Dick Parker (2001), Medófilo Medina (2001), Carlos Vilas (2001), and Kenneth Roberts (2001), published in the *Revista*

Venezolana de Economía y Ciencias Sociales, which present a relatively complete review of academic output up to the present.

2. The Samán of Güere is a tree under which Simón Bolívar is said to have slept with his troops before the Battle of Carabobo (1821), which sealed Venezuelan independence.

3. Chávez has claimed to have made contact not only with groups and individuals from the ideological left during this period, but also with people of the center and right (personal interview with Hugo Chávez, Caracas, March 25, 1996). Nevertheless, such individuals and groups failed to leave a significant mark on the subsequent evolution of the movement.

4. Nevertheless, Chávez notes how living conditions in the army deteriorated during the 1980s as a result of the state's fiscal crisis (Chávez, 1993).

5. For an overview of the political reforms of COPRE, see Gómez Calcaño and López Maya, 1990. For an overview of the impact of the political process of decentralization on the crisis of 1992, see López Maya, 1994. The successive discussion is extracted from the latter text.

6. Some party members who opposed abandoning the policy of abstention deferred to the will of the majority. Others, such as Domingo Alberto Rangel and Leticia Barrios (a member of the national directorate), resigned from the MBR-200.

7. For a more detailed discussion, see López Maya and Lander, 2000b.

5

Democracy in Uniform: Chávez and the Venezuelan Armed Forces

Deborah L. Norden

In February 1999, Lieutenant Colonel Hugo Chávez became Venezuela's newly elected president, seven years after he and his colleagues had launched a military coup d'état to overthrow the government. Venezuelan politics suddenly became entirely transformed. Simultaneously a populist in the style of Argentina's Juan Perón, the semidemocratic leader of a "delegative democracy," and a revolutionary, Chávez was, above all, what he had originally intended to be: the coup leader who would dramatically sweep away the leaders and institutions of Venezuela's long-term two-party democracy. That he did so predominantly *through* the rules and procedures of Venezuela's existing constitutional democracy made his reforms even more remarkable. Within the strongly liberal democratic environment of the post–Cold War era, this approach was probably also relatively more feasible, or at least less vulnerable to strong international sanctions. However, despite Chávez's democratic procedures, his constitutional coup still brought the same kinds of problems that tend to emerge in the aftermath of most military coups: the militarization of politics and the politicization of the military. As a consequence of this, on April 11, 2002, a short-lived coup briefly ousted Chávez himself from office. This chapter thus seeks to explain why the apparently democratic election of Chávez became so problematic for the Venezuelan armed forces and the elected president who emerged from their ranks. To do so, I explore the nature of Chávez's government and its parallels to military regimes, the military policies of the government, and the consequences of the government's foundations and forms for civil-military relations in Venezuela.

**Delegative Democracy,
Constitutional Coup, or Elected Revolution?**

In many respects, Chávez's early government resembled the "delegative democracies" that Guillermo O'Donnell had described just a few years ear-

93

lier in countries such as Argentina and Peru. As O'Donnell defined it, "Delegative democracies rest on the premise that whoever wins election to the presidency is thereby entitled to govern as he or she sees fit, constrained only by the hard facts of existing power relations and by a constitutionally limited term of office" (1994: 59). This strong leader is thus granted much more autonomy to independently design and direct policy than would normally be expected within an elected democracy. For example, President Carlos Menem (1989–2000) governed Argentina by issuing an unprecedented number of decree laws, often bypassing the Congress. President Alberto Fujimori went even further, forcing the Peruvian legislature to close in what has been described as an autogolpe (self-coup). Yet unlike Venezuela, Argentina and Peru had very recent histories of military authoritarianism, and were still in the process of consolidating their democracies. The recent authoritarian pasts emphasized a tendency to seek—and accept—strong leadership, even to the detriment of democratic processes. Thus O'Donnell writes that delegative democracy "implies weak institutionalization and, at best, is indifferent toward strengthening it" (1994: 62).

Venezuela, however, had no similar recent authoritarian past. Instead, Chávez's election followed more than four decades of constitutional rule, with political and democratic parties that were very strongly institutionalized (too institutionalized, some would argue) (see Martz, 1995). In this case, the concentration of authority arose as a new innovation, in part as a reaction to circumstances of economic decline and neoliberal reforms, in the context of a stagnant political party system. These were conditions that Chávez sought to eliminate, through the dramatic transformation of Venezuela's political system. Thus, rather than indicating weak institutionalization, Venezuela's tendency toward delegative democracy suggests a process of deliberately destroying previous institutions and politically eliminating the prior leadership or, at the very least, the dominant political parties of the latter 1900s (Acción Democrática [AD] and the Comité de Organización Política Electoral Independiente [COPEI]).

In what way does this constitute a coup d'état? According to Edward Luttwack, a "coup consists of the infiltration of a small but critical segment of the state apparatus, which is then used to displace the government from its control of the remainder" (1968: 27). Since at the time of Chávez's assumption of power he was retired and his cohort no longer constituted a segment of the state, technically, this act cannot be considered a coup. Perhaps even more important, in 1999 Chávez did not use violence as a means of taking over the government; it truly was a peaceful and democratic change of hands. However, both the government's approach to dealing with the military and its consequences for civil-military relations did bear a strong resemblance to the kind of regime that would result from a military takeover. Little difference can be found, in fact, between Chávez's government and Eric Nordlinger's description of "praetorian rulers," the most far-reaching form of military government:

> Ruler-type praetorians . . . not only control the government but dominate the regime, sometimes attempting to control large slices of political, economic, and social life through the creation of mobilization structures. The political and economic objectives of praetorian rulers are exceptionally ambitious, occasionally warranting their self-description as radical modernizers or revolutionaries. (1977: 26)

Chávez clearly sought to transform the political system, at least in part through mobilizing the people and the military, as will be discussed in this chapter. Furthermore, he frequently referred to his government and its goals as "revolutionary." On the one hand, the use of the term reflected his intention to go beyond change *within* the system to change *of* the system, an intention shared by a number of reactionary military regimes that have appropriated the term "revolution" in somewhat misguided ways. However, in Chávez's case, the revolutionary self-designation also signaled his political identification with the left, his sympathy with Venezuela's poor, and his interest in the solutions of socialist regimes such as Cuba.

Neither the progressive thrust of Chávez's politics nor the fact that he took office through democratic means prevented his government from suffering many of the consequences of military coups. Contrary to the expectations of many, most forms of military insurrection, including those that do not result in military rule, as well as strongly militarized regimes, tend to be quite detrimental and divisive for military organizations. Professional officers who may previously have been quite safe and successful simply following rules and orders suddenly find themselves forced to take sides politically. As Genaro Arriagada Herrera writes, "In a mature political system, and of course in a democracy, civilian control of the military apparatus requires that the chief of staff fulfill the function of highest authority of the armed forces. . . . A military dictatorship confuses these roles" (1986: 124). Modern military regimes, especially bureaucratic-authoritarian regimes (O'Donnell, 1973), complicate matters even further in that the military as an institution moves into the government, and significant numbers of military officers tend to find themselves occupying normally civilian posts. These officers may then be compelled, by virtue of their dual positions, to take on bureaucratic bargaining roles directly contrary to the clear lines of authority within the military itself. Postcoup militaries thus tend to become politicized and divided, and inclined to foster further insurrections.

The 1992 Coup Attempts

This military divisiveness was relatively new for Venezuela. For at least the couple of decades leading up to the 1990s, military factionalism and politicization had posed little problem for Venezuela, contrary to most Latin American countries. After a long history of caudillism, a brief experiment with incipient democracy (1945–1948), and a decade of renewed military rule, Venezuela embarked on its solidly democratic path in 1958. From the 1960s, after the interventionist tendencies in the Venezuelan military had been largely squelched, the military was gradually transformed to a staunch institutional ally (if not a true subordinate) of political democracy (Norden, 1998). To be sure, such loyalty does appear to have been partially obtained through such methods of "subjective control" as politically controlled promotions to ensure like-minded senior officers (Huntington, 1957). Nevertheless, until the late 1980s, the divisiveness of such measures appeared limited and Venezuela's elected governments had little to fear from the armed forces.

In 1989 a major social crisis brought the armed forces out of the barracks for the first time in years. Newly reelected president Carlos Andrés Pérez (Pérez governed previously in the 1970s) sought to boost Venezuela's faltering economy by instituting an economic reform program known as *el Paquete*, or "the package." The reforms included raising the price of gasoline, which in petroleum-producing Venezuela had traditionally been kept well below international prices. The consequent increase in the cost of public transportation served as a trigger for an angry public outburst. Violent riots ensued throughout Caracas, as discussed elsewhere in this book. With the police hopelessly overwhelmed, Pérez sought help from the armed forces. Pérez essentially turned over the reins of power to the minister of defense, General Italo del Valle Alliegro, leaving it to him and his troops to reestablish control. Alliegro not only brought out the national guard, the force most suited to domestic crises, but also called on the traditional armed forces. Men who had been trained and socialized to fight external enemies now found themselves pointing their guns at their own countrymen. Bloodshed was considerable, with hundreds—and perhaps even thousands—left dead (Trinkunas, 1998: 301).

The experience as repressors enraged many in the military, including Lieutenant Colonels Hugo Chávez Frías and Francisco Arias Cárdenas. A strong emphasis on civic action roles had brought military officers in close contact with poorer sectors of the population, as beneficiaries of the latter. Chávez's generation enjoyed further contact with civilians through a new educational plan—instituted during their military studies in the 1970s—that encouraged much broader studies and enrollment in civilian universities. Furthermore, members of the military had themselves suffered from the country's economic decline. Thus, many found themselves identifying more with the people they were called to repress than with their civilian and military superiors. In essence, the government's decision to use the military against the people empowered members of the armed forces, leading them to question the government's ability to act in the best interest of the people, and encouraging them to align themselves *with* the Venezuelan masses, *against* an apparently corrupt and oppressive regime.

By 1992, Venezuela's economy actually appeared to be somewhat on the upswing due to rising oil prices, but it was too late to stop the wheels that had been put into motion. On February 4, 1992, Chávez and Arias Cárdenas led a group of primarily army officers in an attempt to oust Carlos Andrés Pérez from power. They sought to call a constitutional assembly (which remained Chávez's major agenda item both during the campaign and immediately following his election), hoping to organize a new democratic order for Venezuela, after an indefinite period of transitional rule. The insurgents, known as the Movimiento Bolivariano Revolucionario 200 (MBR-200), were defeated, but not without gaining considerable recognition and support among the Venezuelan public. Without any recent military rule, the Venezuelan military had not been demystified as it had elsewhere in South America, and many Venezuelans apparently retained the hope that the armed forces could perhaps govern more efficaciously than elected officials. As the military movement faded, a new political movement began to take root.

The growing politicization of the armed forces became evident even more rapidly, however. In November 1992, Venezuela endured a second coup attempt, this time including officers of all four forces (army, navy, air force, and national guard). The senior insurgents in this attempt—now at the rank of general—belonged to the navy and the air force, with the vast majority of final participants emanating from the latter force. Again, the coup leaders planned to install a civil-military junta while redesigning Venezuelan democracy. The unavoidable violence of a coup attempt from the air prevented these leaders from gaining the kind of public acclaim that surrounded the earlier insurgents, however, and the lack of active rebel ground troops made a takeover virtually impossible.

Both coup attempts failed, arguably partly due to the loyalty of many senior officers (Agüero, 1995). However, the coups profoundly changed both the military and public perceptions of the military. Within the military, political activism became much more familiar, and consequently much more probable. Beyond that, the intramilitary divisions that precede insurgencies generally tend to deepen further following the actual events, whether rebellions or coup attempts (see Norden, 1996). In the Venezuelan military, these divisions became even more complex following Chávez's election, as evidenced by the April 2002 coup against Chávez. With respect to the Venezuelan public, the 1992 coup attempts presented the people with a new and highly visible alternative to the increasingly stagnant party-dominant political system. By 2002, many Venezuelans had come to see military insurrection as equally valid for displacing Chávez, the very man who had succeeded in obliterating the previous political system. For both civilians and the armed forces, military affairs and political affairs had ceased to exist in separate spheres.

From the Military Campaign to the 1998 Electoral Campaign

By 1998, Chávez had set aside military insurrection and popular revolt as paths to power, in practice if not in principle. The upcoming elections offered Chávez the option of pursuing his original goals via another path, utilizing the public support he had built over the past years. To be sure, the original target of the MBR's attempt—Carlos Andrés Pérez—had long since been impeached as president. However, the MBR's true target had been the entire *partidocracia*—the two political parties, AD and COPEI, that had dominated Venezuelan politics for decades. Economic concerns composed the second pillar of Chávez campaigns—both the 1992 political-military campaign as well as the 1998 electoral campaign.

Chávez merged his support for greater economic distribution and his opposition to the existing parties into a substantive interpretation of democracy. According to his interpretation, Venezuela could not be considered a democracy because of the extreme inequality, and the failure to address the basic needs of the poor. "The basic food basket in Venezuela is getting close to 60,000 *bolívares*. Most of those who work earn less than 20,000 *bolívares*. How do they eat, if it doesn't even cover enough to eat? Therefore there is no democracy here."[1] True democracy, in his terms, must not only be far more responsive to the people than Venezuela's stagnating party system, but should also be far more effective in feeding them.

The MBR—which became the MVR political party, or Movimiento Quinta República, during the electoral campaign—proposed that in order to overcome such inequities, the corrupt political leadership needed to be essentially banished from power. However, to attain this, the leaders of the MBR argued that it was necessary to transform the entire system on which the parties' authority had been based. Venezuela's democracy was founded through the Pact of Punto Fijo, a 1958 agreement between the leaders of three key political parties of the time—AD, COPEI, and the relatively politically moderate Unión Republicana Democrática (URD). This agreement set the terms for democracy, including both mild substantive agreements regarding economic policies and policies toward business and the church, as well as procedural agreements to respect elections, consult with opposition party leaders, and share responsibility. Shortly thereafter, a new constitution was written, signed in 1961 by some of the same political party leaders involved in writing the Pact of Punto Fijo.

Despite the fact that most provisions favoring the original political parties were embodied in the 1958 pact instead of the 1961 constitution, Chávez and other leaders of the 1992 coup attempts managed to turn the document into the symbol of the Punto Fijo *partidocracia*. Consequently, eliminating the constitution became the central aim of the movement, even before Chávez entered electoral politics. In 1994, Chávez argued that "the Constitution that they made in the year '61 is an illegitimate constitution, by origin and by process. When it was made, the dominant political parties made it. . . . Then they installed themselves as dictators here for practically all the time that they wanted."[2] Subsequently, the goal of holding a constitutional assembly to rewrite the constitution became the centerpiece of the MBR campaign, and the symbol of Chávez's determination to establish an entirely new political order—now through democratic means, but with the thoroughness of any praetorian ruler.

Militarizing Politics: Stage One of Chávez's Government

As promised, immediately upon taking office in February 1999, Chávez embarked on the task of convening a constitutional assembly, securing authorization through a popular referendum. By the end of the year, a new Venezuelan constitution was in place, and the country had been renamed the Bolivarian Republic of Venezuela. The 1999 constitution contributed significantly to expanding the military's role in Venezuelan politics. The extensive presence of military officers in the government and administration furthered this tendency.

Rewriting the Constitution

On the surface, the constitutional changes appeared minor; they were, nonetheless, quite significant. Venezuela's tradition of an apparently subordinate—or at least politically neutral—military institution came from the constitutional premise that "[t]he National Armed Forces form an apolitical, obedient and non-deliberating institution, organized by the State to ensure national defense, the stability of democratic institutions and respect for the Constitution and the laws" (Article 132 of the 1961 constitution). Although the MBR specifically sought to challenge the existing democratic institutions and constitution, most of the Venezuelan military appeared to have accepted the premise of abstaining from politics.

The 1999 constitution, however, lacks this requirement that the military remain apolitical. Instead, this version of the constitution proclaims that the military should be "without political militancy," and that "[its] fundamental pillars are discipline, obedience and subordination" (Article 328). The subtle differences in the phrasing were in part designed to more easily grant active-duty members of the military the right to vote (Article 330), a privilege not enjoyed by the Venezuelan military previously. Granting the military the right to vote in itself is not necessarily problematic. Voting is primarily an individual act, and a right enjoyed by most citizens; it does not, in itself, politicize the armed forces. However, the implications of replacing the term "apolitical" with "without political militancy" seem more significant. Given the vagueness of the phrase "political militancy," this wording would seem to allow space for a fair amount of political activism within the armed forces. As Anibal Romero (2000) points out, the constitution also "eliminates parliamentary control over promotions, leaving them in the hands of the military institution itself, with the exception of promotions to general (or admiral)," which the president himself oversees. This both helps concentrate presidential power and further limits broader political oversight of the armed forces.[3]

At the same time, the constitution appeared to lay the groundwork for expanding the role of the armed forces. For example, both the 1961 and 1999 constitutions granted the state (presumably the armed forces) the sole right to possess military weapons. However, unlike the 1961 document, the new constitution specifically assigned the military oversight over virtually all issues regarding weapons: "The National Armed Force will be the institution authorized to regulate and control, in accordance with the respective laws, the manufacturing, importation, exportation, storage, trafficking, registration, control, inspection, trade, possession and use of other weapons, munitions and explosives" (Article 324). This wide-ranging authority endowed the military with various responsibilities that might more naturally fall to other government officials, such as those in foreign relations or the customs office, since these duties involve broader issues of trade and foreign affairs.

Military in Politics and Administration

The considerable changes that occurred in the military's role during this period went well beyond those foreshadowed by the constitution. While the constitution expanded the military's administrative duties and political rights, Chávez more substantially expanded the military's political presence by actively bringing military personnel—primarily retired—into the government. Some entered through elections, while others joined the leadership of Chávez's MBR, participated in the 1999 Constitutional Assembly, and/or were appointed to positions in Chávez's new government.

The military's presence in elections, especially that of former coup conspirators, actually began prior to Chávez's election. Preceding Chávez into electoral politics was his former comrade in arms Francisco Arias Cárdenas, co-leader of the February 1992 coup attempt. After the 1993 impeachment of Carlos Andrés Pérez and the election of President Rafael Caldera (who now rejected his earlier ties with COPEI), Arias Cárdenas shifted away from the politics of force. Asserting that the MBR had already reached its primary goals, Arias became an active participant in Venezuela's constitutional democracy. Shortly after his release from prison in 1994, the former coup leader accepted a position in Caldera's administration as head of PAMI, a nutritional program for mothers and infants. The following year, Arias Cárdenas successfully ran for governor of the state of Zulia—the state from which he had exercised his coup leadership. Arias Cárdenas was reelected governor in the 1998 elections, and in the massive general elections of 2000—a consequence of the 1999 constitution—he mounted the most significant challenge to Chávez's campaign, coming in second in the presidential race.

By 1998, and again in 2000, increasing numbers of military officers—and especially former coup participants—threw their hats into the electoral ring. For example, in 1998, retired lieutenant colonel Yoel Acosta Chirinos, a participant in Chávez's February 4, 1992, coup attempt, was elected MVR deputy from the state of Falcón. Another veteran of the February 4 rebellion, retired captain Jesús Aguilarte, won a seat in the House of Deputies representing the state of Apure, also on the MVR ticket. At the same time, retired air force colonel Luis Alfonso Dávila, a member of the MVR directorate, became senator for the state of Anzoátegui. Another successful candidate to the House of Deputies (Federal District) for the MVR was Freddy Bernal, who participated in the November 1992 coup attempt with the elite police unit Grupo Ceta (Comando Especial Táctico de Apoyo).

However, almost immediately upon assuming the presidency, Chávez began making arrangements for the long-promised National Constitutional Assembly (ANC). According to the rules, candidates to the ANC could not simultaneously hold public office, and thus would need to resign their newly won seats and appointments. But Chávez supporters were even more successful in the elections for the constituent assembly than they had been in the 1998 congressional elections: "His candidates won 121 of the 131 seats in the ANC. Among them were his wife, a brother, five of his former ministers and various retired members of the military who accompanied him in an attempted coup d'etat in February 1992."[4] This new body—clearly strongly supportive of Chávez, as well as heavily influenced by military insurgents—

was endowed with the power to rewrite the Venezuelan constitution and, in the process, entirely restructure the Venezuelan political system.

In the process, Chávez and the ANC succeeded in entirely dismantling the Venezuelan Congress. For a time, the government even functioned without an elected legislature, legislating instead through an appointed body drawn from the ANC. This continued until the massive 2000 "mega-elections," responsible not only for choosing the new unicameral legislature, but also for electing the president, governors, and mayors; in other words, all elected offices in the country were subject to these elections.

This time, even more than in 1998, retired military officers showed up in significant numbers on the ballots. Notably, in the 2000 elections, many of these even ran in opposition to the MVR. As noted above, retired lieutenant colonel Francisco Arias Cárdenas became Chávez's principal opponent for the presidency. Freddy Bernal again ran successfully, this time for mayor of a Caracas municipality; notably, Bernal proved to be an important ally to Chávez following the April 2002 coup. The competitions for governorships demonstrated most clearly the growing military presence in electoral politics, as well as the increasing divisions among the former rebels. According to Steve Ellner, "at the outset of the campaign for the May elections, retired military officers sought MVR endorsements as gubernatorial candidates in as many as 18 of the nation's 23 states" (2000: 32). Retired lieutenant colonel Jesús Urdaneta now ran against the MVR candidate in Aragua, as did Yoel Acosta Chirinos—formerly national coordinator of the MVR—in the state of Falcón. Retired air force general Francisco Visconti, one of the principal leaders of the November 1992 coup attempt, challenged Chávez's father for the governorship of the state of Barinas. In sum, former military insurgents participated broadly in these elections, competing not only against the traditional parties, but even against each other.

Other military officers found their way into the political realm through appointments. For example, in the first phase of his presidency (following his 1998 election), Chávez appointed Lieutenant Colonel Jesús Urdaneta, one of the founding members of the MBR-200, to the position of director of DISIP, the state intelligence directorate. A classmate of Chávez's from the state military academy who had remained in the military, General Arévalo Méndez Romero, became private secretary to the new president.[5] Other military officers were appointed throughout the bureaucracy, abroad in consulates and embassies, as well as to local positions. Even a few active-duty military officers were given political appointments, especially in the state oil company, Petróleos de Venezuela, Sociedad Anónima (PDVSA).[6] One of the more interesting appointments was Chávez's choice of Admiral Hernán Gruber, one of the leaders of the November 1992 coup attempt, for governor of the Federal District of Caracas.[7]

By the time of Chávez's July 2000 reelection, some of these officers either had been removed from their positions or had come to oppose Chávez and resigned. However, the military presence in the government remained substantial. In early 2001, for example, Lieutenant Colonel Luis Dávila (retired since 1990, before the coup attempts) became the minister of foreign relations, after having acted as minister of the interior.[8] Next in line in the Ministry of Foreign Affairs was General Arévalo Méndez Romero. General Ismael Hurtado—formerly minister of defense—became minister of infrastructure in February 2001, replacing General Alberto Esqueda Torres. Chávez named Esqueda Torres ambassador to Brazil. These examples represent only the militarization at the very top levels of the administration.

The problems inherent in this increased military presence in politics became evident in a variety of ways, including problems with defining the "line of command." In October 2000 a crisis emerged due to the fact that the newly appointed deputy minister of foreign affairs, Arévalo Méndez Romero, a brigade general, held an inferior rank to one of his new subordinates, National Guard Division General Rafael Chirinos, then acting as head of the National Office of Borders. Chirinos, an active-duty officer, found it difficult to take orders from someone beneath him in the military hierarchy, and submitted his resignation.[9] Such problems are typical of military governments, when civilian and military hierarchies and practices frequently conflict, and can contribute to the fragmentation and eventual collapse of the regime.

In February 2001, however, Chávez made an important symbolic move to reduce the military's administrative power by placing a civilian as minister of defense. With the appointment of José Vicente Rangel, previously Chávez's minister of foreign relations, to the head of the Ministry of Defense, Chávez broke a long tradition of having active-duty military officers as defense ministers (usually serving for very short appointments). This followed changing practices throughout Latin America since the 1980s and 1990s. During this period, increasing numbers of defense ministries came to be led by civilians, emphasizing the shift from widespread military authoritarianism to democracy in the region.

Nevertheless, it was not clear how much authority the new civilian defense minister would actually have. At the same time as the change in the Ministry of Defense was announced, Chávez created a new position, a chief of staff of the armed forces.[10] As Rangel explained, "the minister is a spokesman for the administrative policy of the institution. While the direct command of military personnel should correspond to a general or an admiral."[11] This officer would respond directly to the president, thereby bypassing the defense minister and probably diminishing his true power. Rangel's limited popularity within the armed forces—due to his critiques and investigations of various officers—weakened his personal influence on defense matters. In fact, some interpreted the civilian appointment and planned restructuring as a sign of Chávez's diminishing control over the disgruntled and divided armed forces, rather than as an effort at demilitarizing the government. This suspicion seemed to be confirmed in April 2002, when Rangel appeared to hold little authority over the military.

Civilianizing the Military

As the government and administration became increasingly military during Chávez's presidency, the military appeared to become less so. Military roles progressively shifted toward less defense-oriented functions, or "operations other than war." These included both expanded police responsibilities and extensive civic action operations, many subsumed within broader civil-military projects.

Such roles were by no means new for the Venezuelan armed forces. In the early 1960s, Venezuela's newly established democracy faced a number of challenges from leftist guerrilla groups, similar to movements throughout the region during this period. The military thus became involved in fighting internally. At the same time, the government sought to lessen the revolutionary potential within the country by engaging the military in civic action projects geared toward improving infrastructure and the economy. This practice did not end once the guerrillas had been defeated. As Winfield Burggraaff and Richard Millett noted, "After the antiguerrilla campaigns ended in the mid-1960s, the Venezuelan military gradually moved in the direction of developmentalism and a modified national security doctrine. This resulted in a broader role for the military in frontier and border areas and in government agencies and companies" (1995: 57). The national guard—formally the fourth branch of the armed forces, along with the army, navy, and air force—has, in particular, functioned somewhere between defense and civilian police operations, since its primary function is internal security. Thus the national guard has been responsible for tasks ranging from riot control and border control to environmental protection, counternarcotics, counterterrorism, and customs.

Once the Chávez administration took office, the entire military was launched with much fanfare into an ambitious, far-reaching campaign to fight poverty and improve the national infrastructure. While the campaign appears to have attained only limited success in mobilizing the population, the initial program seemed to emulate Cuba's revolutionary campaigns of some thirty to forty years earlier. The original plan, PAIS (Plan for Sustainable Immediate Action), foresaw utilizing tens of thousands of members of the military, from all four forces, to attack various problem areas, including health, education, nutrition, and infrastructure.[12] The plan was inaugurated on February 27, 1999, deliberately marking the tenth anniversary of the 1989 riots, at which time the armed forces were unwillingly used to suppress impoverished *caraqueño* rioters.

Plan Bolívar 2000, as the civil-military development project came to be called, sought to place the military clearly on the side of the poor, in alliance with the Venezuelan masses, while also publicly demonstrating the inadequacy of the old regime's efforts in this respect. The deficiencies and corruption of the *partidocracia* occupied a central place in Chávez's discourse, as he consistently sought to differentiate the "Bolivarian revolution" from the regime of his predecessors. For example, in September 1999, Chávez redirected funds from the sale of fifteen airplanes owned by the state oil company toward projects such as constructing schools and thousands of homes. He described the action as part of "extracting those devils of corruption, inefficiency [and] waste that were the mark and norm of Venezuela's last 40 years."[13]

To emphasize the contrast between the two periods, Chávez put public works projects at center stage, with the military in the leading role. Thus Plan Bolívar programs included repairing schools and hospitals, setting up medical clinics, and various cleanup projects. Members of the military could also be found "selling meat and cheese out of the back of a truck at a weekend market," in an effort to provide low-cost food.[14] Civilians were also brought in alongside members of the military. Many were volunteers, especially activists from Chávez's political party, the MVR. Others included homeless and unemployed people, brought in as part of the effort to counter unemployment and poverty, who were then paid for their work in the program.

The new government also expanded the military's presence in police work, particularly that of the national guard. With the "National Plan for Citizen Security," instituted in May 1999, the guard acquired central responsibility for combating Venezuela's severe public safety problems.[15] The police component of the plan "consist[ed] of executing preventative and punitive operations against any sign of criminal activity."[16] In the process, the national guard essentially assumed control of the police.

The military's new roles did not entirely win them acclaim. Instead, corruption and abuses plagued the efforts to civilianize military roles, just as corruption had permeated the civilian bureaucracy in years past. Accusations of extensive fraud pervaded in the aftermath of Plan Bolívar. Millions of U.S. dollars were reportedly paid either to nonexistent companies or to businesses that actually provided no services.[17] Some members of the military reportedly had also become concerned about the excessive focus on civic action, and the possibly detrimental effects on security of shifting the armed forces too far away from traditional defense. On another front, following the disastrous floods of late December 1999, which swept

shanty homes down the precarious hillsides surrounding Caracas, devastated the state of Vargas, and left thousands of Venezuelans homeless, the military was called in for disaster assistance. Again, scandal followed. This
time, the military was accused of human rights violations, including illegal
executions supposedly carried out while imposing control in the flood
zones.[18] The government did seek to investigate the purported violations,
but the accusations nonetheless tainted both the armed forces and the
regime.

The problems accompanying the expanding roles of the Venezuelan
military are by no means unique. On the contrary, shifting militaries into
more internal roles tends to be problematic for military professionalism. At
the same time, extensive involvement in domestic activities—whether civic
action or policing action—generally has a tendency to politicize militaries.
The internal focus encourages members of the armed forces to consider the
underlying political causes of dissent, instability, and public violence. The
military's involvement with domestic, civic action functions during the latter half of the twentieth century, and most certainly its involvement in
repressing the 1989 riots, undoubtedly contributed to the growth of the
coup movements in 1992. Increasing such involvement seemed to augment
the problem of military politicization even further.

Military Politicization and Factionalism: Chávez's Fragmenting Coup Coalition

The combination of the military's extensive involvement in government
during the Chávez administration, the armed forces' growing internal roles,
and the substantial political success of Venezuela's premier coup leader all
contributed to increasing factionalism and dissent within the military. Even
though the military initially served as Chávez's primary support base, within a year of assuming power the new president not only faced challenges
from prior opponents within the armed forces, but had also begun to alien-
ate former allies. Rumors of coup plots abounded, proliferating in the
months leading up to the April 2002 coup attempt.

Among the most notable indicators of the fragmentation of Chávez's
political and military base was his loss of support from members of his former coup coalition. That Arias Cárdenas defected, and became Chávez's
major competition in the 2000 presidential race, was actually much less
surprising and significant than many portrayed. Chávez and Arias Cárdenas
had opted for different paths before, beginning shortly after the coup
attempt. The breach had its origins both in political competition inside the
movement and in alternate perspectives of the best path for the group in the
period following the coup attempts. With respect to internal competition,

according to Arias Cárdenas, Chávez's television appearances during the February 4, 1992, coup attempt converted him to a public "idol."[19] Partly as a consequence of this, the imprisoned MBR cohort voted to make Chávez the leader. This placed him above the more senior Arias Cárdenas, which was contrary both to military practices and to the previously more collegial traditions of the MBR.

At the same time, Arias Cárdenas also diverged from Chávez by embracing political options far before his former ally. During and immediately following his imprisonment, Chávez remained adamant in his rejection of electoral politics. Meanwhile, Arias Cárdenas argued that the MBR needed to "construct a political organization, a foundation, a type of organization that would allow the people to be united and would . . . direct people toward change, but leaving aside the military perspective. This was a very strong disagreement I had with Hugo in prison."[20] These differences evidenced themselves further following Rafael Caldera's December 1993 election to the presidency, and the subsequent release of the insurgents. Chávez remained an opponent of the regime, whereas Arias became a part of it— first accepting an appointment in Caldera's administration, and subsequently running successfully for the governorship of Zulia.

Given these differences, a smooth partnership between Chávez and Arias Cárdenas seemed unlikely. During the 1998 presidential campaign, Arias eventually did throw his support to his former coup partner, and remained an ally during the early months of Chávez's presidency. However, within a few months of Chávez's inauguration, the fragility of the alliance became evident. Tensions peaked in early 2000 in an episode that came to involve much of the February 4 coup leadership. In January of that year, Lieutenant Colonel Jesús Urdaneta resigned from his position as director of DISIP, following statements by the minister of foreign relations, José Vicente Rangel, along with past and present ministers of the interior, recognizing the possibility of human rights abuses by DISIP following the floods (Ellner, 2000). Staunchly defending the actions of the security forces, Urdaneta—who had already established himself as a strong critic of Chávez's civilian appointees—demanded instead that Minister of Foreign Relations José Vicente Rangel and Minister of Interior Ignacio Arcaya be ousted from the government.[21] President Chávez refused.

The episode served to galvanize opposition from much of the MBR leadership against Chávez. Arias Cárdenas and another member of the early MBR leadership, Yoel Acosta Chirinos, joined Urdaneta in critiquing the prominent roles of civilians Rangel, Arcaya, and Luis Miquilena (the former minister of the interior, who at the time acted as president of the National Legislative Committee).[22] In increasingly resolute tones, the group suggested that Chávez needed to distance himself from these leaders— especially longtime leftist Miquilena, one of Chávez's closest advisers.[23]

Some 200 additional retired coup veterans—led by Captain Luis Valderrama—joined their voices to those of the lieutenant colonels, critiquing Chávez for having strayed too far from the "Bolivarian project," or the initial goals of the military movement.[24] The movement culminated in Arias Cárdenas's challenge to Chávez during the 2000 presidential election. While Arias failed to defeat Chávez, he did manage to finish in second place. His challenge to Chávez continued following the elections, however, as he continued to critique his former partner and began designing his own political project.

Factionalism, furthermore, went well beyond the ranks of former coup participants. Chávez faced a number of uniformed opponents, ranging from those who had opposed him in his initial insurrection to others—both retired and active-duty—who questioned his policies (especially military policies) as president. For example, in March 2000 a group of retired officers announced the formation of the Frente Institucional Militar (FIM; Institutional Military Front), a purportedly nonpolitical organization strongly opposed to Chávez's military policies. Specifically, the FIM criticized Chávez for politicizing the military, using the armed forces as a personal instrument, immersing the armed forces in more appropriately civilian tasks (civic action), and overall, compromising military professionalism. In their initial "Declaration of Principles," the FIM also revealed their displeasure with Chávez's intended reincorporation into the armed forces of former coup participants, a particularly sensitive issue for militaries.[25]

The FIM's emergence was followed shortly by the more ominous announcement that another group—this one including both active-duty officers and civilians—had been formed clandestinely some months prior, and had now decided to make their existence public. Calling themselves the Junta Patriótica Militar (Patriotic Military Front), this new group proclaimed (in a forum sponsored by the FIM) that they sought President Chávez's resignation, although they declared that they would not pursue this through violent means.[26] Many of their critiques of Chávez's government echoed those of the FIM. However, given its mixed civil-military composition, this group appeared to have a broader span of concerns. In addition to raising objections about the civic action–oriented Plan Bolívar, the group also criticized Chávez for his undemocratic concentration of power. Religious, or more specifically, proclerical concerns also shaped the critiques of this group:

> The problem of the Church-State relationship in Venezuela stemmed from the tension between the demands made in the name of the political regime, and the requests made by the religious institution. Distrust was aggravated by the attitude of the president of the republic, who sometimes sought to discredit the Catholic Church.[27]

Not coincidentally, the spokesman for the Junta Patriótica Militar, Captain Luis García Morales, was a member of the national guard—the one branch of the military that remained entirely loyal to the government during the 1992 coup attempts.

By early 2001 it became less clear whether all Venezuelans had renounced force as an option for removing Chávez from office. In an amusing, albeit somewhat menacing demonstration of discontent, different-colored pairs of women's underwear were sent to 140 Venezuelan generals and admirals (see Chapter 2).[28] The act was widely interpreted as a provocation—a challenge to the masculinity of the senior officers, with the implication that "true men" would move to overthrow President Hugo Chávez. Over the following year, the danger signs intensified, as even a few high-ranking military officers began openly calling for the president's resignation.

The coup coalition that took power in the early morning hours of April 12, 2002, placing businessman Pedro Carmona in the presidency, endured less than two days before counterpressures forced the would-be executive to resign his ill-begotten office. Yet the events of those days underscored the extent to which both the armed forces and the general population had become divided. The immediate antecedent to the coup was a general strike, partially organized by Carmona. On April 11, as demonstrators converged on the central plaza in Caracas, violence erupted; several people died and many more were injured. While it remained unclear who precisely had fired the guns, the events seemed far too reminiscent of February 1989, when the armed forces had bloodily repressed rioters. The events of 1989 had convinced many—including Chávez and his allies in the MBR—that they would not support a government that forced them to turn on their own people. Given this history, the violence of April 11 convinced many in the armed forces that they could no longer remain loyal to Chávez.

Nevertheless, the rapid reversal of the coup demonstrated that Chávez may have lost much support, but he was not yet isolated. Within Venezuela, his supporters—both within and outside the armed forces—began to mobilize, demanding his return. Outside the country, the United States had been so unequivocal in its opposition to Chávez and so quick to welcome the new, unconstitutional leader that it seemed rather unlikely that the U.S. government would be cleared of culpability. However, in the meantime, the Latin American leaders proved much more committed to constitutional rule, and much more willing to call a coup by its name. The pressures against Carmona mounted so rapidly that the coup coalition barely had time to establish itself in power before that power was lost. On April 14, Hugo Chávez—onetime coup leader and temporary victim of a coup—returned to the presidency.

Consequences of the Venezuelan Military in the Government

In sum, despite the democratic initiation of Chávez's administration, the composition and consequences of the government in many ways paralleled those that would be expected from a military regime. Chávez tended to act just on the border between democracy and authoritarianism, finding mostly constitutional means to destroy the constitution itself, along with the party-dominant democracy it had sustained. Out of the ashes of Venezuela's dead party democracy, he built a new order, with power strongly concentrated in the presidency. Not only did the new uniformed president—and he continued to wear his military uniform until after the April 2002 coup—govern for a time without any legislature at all, but once a new assembly had been elected, he continued to rule quite independently. He also continued to look to the armed forces as the institution most capable of helping him achieve his objectives.

Yet the government could not be seen as a simple dictatorship. First, Chávez's charisma and populism, along with strong public distaste for the prior regime, helped him sustain a surprisingly high level of popularity, even as it became increasingly evident that he would be unable to provide instantaneous solutions for the country's profound socioeconomic problems. Second, Chávez did create new (albeit relatively weak) democratic institutions to replace those he had destroyed. Finally, to the extent this government resembled a military regime, the strongest parallel is with more modern military regimes, in which the military institution is directly involved in governing, rather than traditional dictatorships. While Chávez's presidency was not officially a military regime, members of the armed forces have had a substantial presence within the government. This trend toward militarization of the government was accompanied by civic action campaigns along the lines of civil-military campaigns in revolutionary regimes, which tend to further blur the distinction between civilian roles and military roles. The consequence of both tendencies has been an alarming increase in the politicization and factionalism of the armed forces. Chávez did, in the end, manage to take power without a military coup. He did not, however, succeed in avoiding the consequences of either his past military insurrection or his government's inclination to rely strongly on the armed forces. In April 2002, now the target of a coup, Chávez faced those consequences.

Notes

I would like to thank the editors of this volume, Steve Ellner and Dan Hellinger, for their extensive help with this chapter. Both were unusually generous not only in sharing their ideas and impressions with me, but also in forwarding to me a considerable amount of material to use for this project. The arguments and ideas in this article are nonetheless solely the responsibility of the author.

1. Personal interview with Lieutenant Colonel Hugo Chávez, Caracas, July 14, 1994. Author's translation.

2. Ibid.

3. Perhaps greater obstacles to civilian oversight have, however, emanated historically from the lack of either a civilian Ministry of Defense or congressional staff knowledgeable about military affairs. A few members of Congress have developed some level of expertise in this area, but this has not really been enough to allow effective oversight of the armed forces. Thus, while certainly unnecessarily expanding military autonomy and presidential authority, the elimination of congressional oversight may also have the positive consequence of reducing one source of political meddling and the resulting politicization.

4. *El Nacional,* 1999, www.el-nacional.com/especiales/Primer_año_Chavez/popularidad.asp.

5. "Curriculum del Vice-Canciller Arévalo E. Méndez Romero, Ministerio de Relaciones Exteriores," March 2, 2001, www.mre.gov.ve/arevalo_mendez.html.

6. Rafael Arráiz Lucca, "La militarización," *El Nacional,* February 12, 1999.

7. At the time of the November coup attempt, Chávez and the other February 4 leaders were in jail. During the coup attempt, however, supporters of Chávez replaced a video of the November coup leaders (all senior officers) with a fairly rough and provocative video of the imprisoned Chávez and some of his allies; the latter video appeared on national television. The November coup leaders—who had not met Chávez at the time—considered this one of the reasons for the failure of their insurrection. See Norden, 1998: 156–157.

8. "Curriculum del Canciller Luis Alfonso Dávila, Ministerio de Relaciones Exteriores," March 6, 2001, www.mre.gov.ve/davila_07.html.

9. "Jerarquía militar crea crisis gerencial en la Cancillería," *El Universal,* October 31, 2000, http://noticias.eluniversal.com/2000/10/31/31112DD.html.

10. Adlela Leal and Alonso Moleira, "El Presidente nombrará a un jefe de la FAN," *El Nacional,* February 2, 2001, p. 1.

11. Raquel Seijas, "El Ministro . . . ," *El Nacional,* February 6, 2001, pp. 1–2.

12. Javier Ignacio Mayorca, "50,000 efectivos irán a 26 regiones en el plan PAIS," *El Nacional,* February 13, 1999; Mireya Mata, "FAN y ministerios trabajarán en la coordinación del plan cívico-militar," *El Nacional,* February 21, 1999; "Ultiman detalles para el plan PAIS," *El Nacional,* February 2, 1999.

13. Yeneiza Delgado Mijares, "Chávez: Durante cierto tiempo conviveremos con vicios del pasado," *El Nacional,* September 15, 1999.

14. Larry Rohter, "In a New Role, Venezuelan Army Runs Clinics and Shops," *New York Times,* April 13, 1999, p. A15.

15. "La Guardia Nacional está en la calle para asumir responsabilidades policiales," *El Nacional,* May 10, 1999.

16. Ibid.

17. Willmer Poleo Zerpa, "Contraloría informó sobre fraude en el Plan Bolívar 2000 de Maturín," *El Nacional,* December 10, 1999. See also Larry Rohter, "Venezuela Military Bristles at Role Ordered by President," *New York Times,* April 16, 2001.

18. Edgar López, "Ministerio Público seguirá buscando evidencias," *El Nacional,* January 25, 2000.

19. Personal interview with Lieutenant Colonel Francisco Arias Cárdenas, Caracas, July 13, 1994. Author's translation.

20. Ibid.

21. According to an article in *El Nacional,* Urdaneta's request was signed by sixty other February 4 participants. "Chávez aceptó renuncia de Urdaneta Hernández," *El Nacional,* January 22, 2000.

22. Following the enactment of the new constitution, Chávez disbanded the existing bicameral legislature, pending elections for a new unicameral assembly. In the interim, however, Venezuela had no elected legislature; the National Legislative Committee—appointed from the ANC—took over these functions instead.

23. See "Los tres comandantes recomiendan a Chávez desprenderse de Rangel, Miquilena y Arcaya," *El Nacional,* February 5, 2000; José Marín, "Comandantes del 4-F le dan a Chávez 20 días para que responda los señalamientos," *El Nacional,* February 16, 2000.

24. "En el Gobierno no están los hombres más capaces y honestos," *El Nacional,* March 1, 2000.

25. FIM, "Declaración de principios," *Venezuela Analítica,* March 2000, www.analitica.com/bitblioteca/fim/principios.asp.

26. "Mensaje de la Junta Patriótica Venezolana," *Venezuela Analítica,* June 30, 2000, www.analitica.com/va/politica/tips/4946119.

27. Ibid.

28. Rodolfo Cardona Marrero, "Ministro Hurtado habló sobre Aure con generales de la Fuerza Armada," *El Universal,* January 30, 2001.

6

Economic Policy and the Rise of Hugo Chávez

Julia Buxton

Academic and media analysis of the collapse of Venezuela's Punto Fijo system has focused heavily on the political determinants of its deterioration. The pivotal question has been why an apparently consolidated democratic regime failed to prevent the rise of the "antisystem" actor Hugo Chávez. A core focus in this debate has been the institutional reform process of 1989, which introduced decentralization and changes to the electoral regime. The measures failed to arrest popular hostility toward the political system as evidenced in support nine years later for Chávez. During these years, many political analysts and actors formulated critiques of the institutional reforms enacted, focusing on the obstacles to their full realization (Buxton, 2001; Penfold-Becerra, 2001). However, while it is clear that Venezuelans viewed their political parties and system as unrepresentative, there is no evidence that a "successful" process of institutional reform would have avoided popular disaffection. Considering that by 1997, 67 percent of Venezuelans earned less than U.S.$2 per day, it is questionable whether institutional reform even mattered to the majority.

The issue of poverty raises a second aspect of the deterioration debate. The accession to power of Carlos Andrés Pérez in 1989 and his implementation of orthodox economic policies is viewed as a turning point for the Punto Fijo system. Pérez undermined the crude legitimacy equation institutionalized in 1958 under which a limited form of democracy was installed with a guarantee of economic distribution to all social classes. The Caracazo uprising of 1989 has been interpreted as a revolt against neoliberalism and as some form of primitive cultural resistance to the measures, informed by a history of artificial prosperity (Romero, 1997). But this popular reaction has to be placed in a historical context. By 1988, after thirty years of successive Acción Democrática (AD) and Comité de Organización Política Electoral Independiente (COPEI) governments, annual inflation was 40.3 percent, general poverty was 38.5 percent, unemployment was reaching double figures, and real salary levels had declined precipitously.

It is against this backdrop that Pérez unexpectedly imposed orthodox adjustment. The measures exacerbated structural and macroeconomic imbalances in the economy and had a critical impact on living standards, which had already witnessed a substantive deterioration. Economic policy under Pérez's successor, Rafael Caldera, accelerated this decline, with poverty levels rising to 66.7 percent in 1995. Without analysis of this gradual pauperization of Venezuelan society, it is difficult to comprehend the extensive popular support for Hugo Chávez that accompanied his rise to power and, despite falling popularity in the polls, brought people into the streets to defend his presidency after the coup of April 11, 2002.

Despite his depiction as a left-wing radical, Chávez did not immediately reverse measures taken by his predecessors to liberalize the economy. His first year in office demonstrated continuity with the orthodox approach followed during the latter part of the Caldera presidency. Even after he consolidated power in 2000, he failed to break sharply with the past on economic policy. Given this, it may seem surprising that the business elites and middle classes attempted to force him out of office and that the poor rallied to his defense in April 2002. The poor, however, viewed Chávez as a president cognizant of and working for their interests. His electoral success and political survival in April 2002 was indicative of class polarization in Venezuela, a country once noted for its multiclass, centrist tradition.

A Classless Society?

From the initiation of democracy in 1958 through the first administration of Carlos Andrés Pérez (1973–1978), Venezuela's economic performance was characterized by steady growth. Oil rents provided a stable flow of income, which was distributed by the state to promote national development and to meet the extensive welfare obligations established in the 1961 constitution. The strategy of achieving modernity through the "sowing" of oil revenues was underpinned by a tradition of state intervention (see Chapter 2). This approach allowed for major improvements in social indicators after democratization in 1958. The expanded public sector generated employment, while low rates of inflation facilitated real income growth. Between 1958 and 1973 the annual consumer price index averaged less than 3 percent. This economic scenario created a favorable political environment for the consolidation of the new regime. Popular support for the Punto Fijo system and the centrist parties that engineered it, AD, the Unión Republicana Democrática (URD), and COPEI, was pronounced. With rent distribution holding out the possibility for all to benefit materially, class cleavages were muted and not subject to politicization, despite the efforts of the revolutionary left.

There was a radical improvement in Venezuela's fortunes after 1973 as the Organization of Petroleum-Exporting Countries (OPEC) and turmoil in the Middle East combined to increase the oil price tenfold. These changes coincided with the nationalization of the Venezuelan oil industry in 1976, increasing central government revenues by an estimated 170 percent. The petrodollar boom, in addition to easy international borrowing conditions, prefigured a massive expansion of the state. This in turn created the twin benefits of an increase in employment opportunities and an extension of the network of subsidies. A minimum wage and legislation discouraging "unjustified layoffs" were introduced, the latter granting double severance pay to workers whose discharge was not sanctioned by tripartite commissions that represented the state, labor, and business. A public spending increase of 96.9 percent between 1973 and 1978 allowed for excellent public services and extensive job opportunities. It also led to a reduction in poverty. By 1978, 10 percent of the population lived in general poverty, and of this proportion just over 2 percent lived in extreme poverty.

Unsurprisingly, Venezuelans were optimistic during this period, with one survey finding that working-class people perceived themselves as middle class despite an incongruity with their actual financial position (Baloyra and Martz, 1979: 185). The raft of social measures helped to consolidate popular support for the centrist parties and their auxiliary apparatus. This was particularly the case with the main union confederation, the AD-dominated Confederación de Trabajadores de Venezuela (CTV; Confederation of Venezuelan Workers), which was privileged and nurtured by the state as the representative of working-class interests (McCoy, 1989). Elsewhere in Latin America, state-sponsored benefits for the working class typically came as a trade-off with those of the middle classes. This was not the case in Venezuela. Petrodollars financed a positive-sum game, with middle- and low-income groups enjoying blanket subsidies, low taxation, and generous welfare provision. The domestic private sector was not excluded from the distribution of benefits and enjoyed tariff protection, access to cheap credit, and other opportunities resulting from import substitution policies.

After 1980, a deterioration in previously favorable external factors, including a sustained decline in oil prices and a hike in international borrowing costs, undermined political and economic stability in Venezuela and presaged twenty years of recession. Policy decisions taken in response to the economic deterioration had a catastrophic effect on living standards and demonstrated the inequities implicit in the system of rent distribution. As such, they germinated socioeconomic conditions that ultimately bloomed into class polarization, increasing the receptiveness of the lower classes to the populist rhetoric of Chávez a decade later.

In the face of perceived government inaction, capital flight reached historic levels at the end of 1982 with U.S.$8 billion leaving the country.

The government forced the state oil company to repatriate foreign reserves in an attempt to shore up the domestic currency. Then in 1983, Luis Herrera Campíns imposed a tiered system of exchange controls with the cheapest rate—for the import of essential goods—set at 7 bolivars to the dollar. This represented devaluation from the rate of 4.3 bolivars that had prevailed throughout the 1970s, making debt repayments particularly onerous. The controls revealed the prevalence of corruption with political discretion enabling "clients" of the parties to obtain cheap dollars, siphoning an estimated U.S.$11 billion of hard-currency reserves. On the other side of the class spectrum, the corruption in the long term fueled perceptions of social injustice and claims that wealthy Venezuelans had "stolen" from their compatriots. As such, economic policy decisions during the 1980s, and their operation within the context of a clientelistic state and political structure, served to partition Venezuelan society between the politically connected and the politically unconnected, the "haves" and the "have nots."

Real salaries fell 20 percent during the six-year period the exchange regime was in operation. As fixed capital investment and public spending projects collapsed, unemployment rose, moving into double figures in 1983. This led to a growing informal labor sector and a sharp jump in households classified as living in poverty, as lower-income groups fell out of the "formal" framework of state distribution. The welfare system itself was segmented, politicized, and fragile and failed to provide an adequate safety net (Hellinger and Melcher, 1998: 2). Moreover, the rise of informal employment divorced workers from the "formal" representative structures of the Punto Fijo state, specifically the CTV. Despite a mounting social and economic crisis, policy reform incentives were dissipated by unexpected oil price increases, external borrowing, and a series of devaluations that relieved pressure on the fiscal accounts. The result was the near exhaustion of international reserves when Carlos Andrés Pérez took office for a second time in 1989.

Economic Crisis and Polarization

In the face of increased complexity of the national and international economy, the Venezuelan government lacked technical competence. No president considered himself a specialist in economic affairs, a critical problem given the absence of a trained civil service body and the concentration of power in the national executive. Although individuals with economic backgrounds were incorporated into the second Pérez cabinet, there was continuity in the insulated nature of policymaking. As ordinary Venezuelans experienced a profound deterioration in living standards, government remained divorced from the social impact of the policies implemented. This was linked to the failure of AD, COPEI, and their auxiliary apparatus, specifically the CTV, to act as effective channels of representation, debate, and policy evaluation (Villasmil, 2000). The notion that institutional reform in 1989 could relegitimize the political system obscures the fact that AD, COPEI, and the Punto Fijo state were "exhausted" well before the 1990s. Equally spent was the multiclass approach. The parties were no longer perceived as, or capable of, acting in the interests of all social classes.

Economic decline generated new political cleavages as AD and COPEI persevered with the myth that Venezuela was a classless, consensus-based country. Causa Radical (Causa R) emerged as a vehicle for working-class protests in industrial areas, while at the other end of the political spectrum proposals for free-market policies emanated from nascent lobby groups and think tanks, such as Roraima and the Centro de Divulgación del Conocimiento Económico. While Causa R flourished, it was difficult for promarket groups to build support, as the private sector was reluctant to eschew protectionism and the political parties viewed free-market reform as a threat to their role as the distributors of oil rent.

Growing class distinctions were also evident in the country's burgeoning civil-sector organizations. The neighborhood movement that crystallized in response to the collapse of public-sector provisions, particularly local government services, achieved a degree of autonomy and effectiveness in upper- and middle-class areas (Ellner, 1999d). While their concerns focused on garbage collection and security of private property, in the barrios weak but crucial social networks, encouraged by Jesuit priests, developed around vital issues of food distribution, personal security, and elementary education. An apartheid of social opportunities was also evident, particularly in the field of education. By the mid-1980s only 4 of every 100 students seeking entry into higher education came from families living in critical poverty, a sector that constituted 40 percent of the total population (Moros Ghersi, 1986). A more visible partition between rich and poor was the growth in private security, as the wealthy sealed their property in response to the breakdown in law and order and the rise in crime.

Carlos Andrés Pérez Returns: Preparing the Ground for Chávez

Venezuelans voted against free-market reform when they backed Carlos Andrés Pérez in the presidential election of 1988. Like Rafael Caldera after him, Pérez broke a preelection pledge to refrain from turning to international institutional lenders and within weeks of taking office he reached an agreement with the International Monetary Fund (IMF). Indicative of the limited level of policy debate and evaluation, the Pérez cabinet did not challenge the theoretical assumptions of economic orthodoxy and accepted the view that Venezuela's oil dependence was the root of its economic crisis. As such, the subsequent "reforms" sought to overturn the oil-financed, state-led model of development. A competitive, export-oriented economy driven by the private sector would replace import dependence and protectionist strategies. Macroeconomic policies were to be devised that would be conducive to growth in the nontraditional sector, with a surge of activity in this area designed to overcome oil export dependence. The administration prioritized privatization of the extensive state infrastructure, including proposals for opening the oil sector to private capital, until then exclusively reserved for the state oil company, Petróleos de Venezuela, Sociedad Anónima (PDVSA).

Public spending cuts and the freeing of prices, interest, and exchange rates marked the first stage of adjustment. This initial phase was successful in reducing imports, but at the cost of investment, job creation, and consumption. As the economy contracted by 8.6 percent, general poverty rose from 43.9 percent of the population in 1988 to 66.5 percent in 1989. Over the same period, extreme poverty jumped from 13.9 percent to 29.6 percent. This negative picture was reversed as higher oil prices following the Gulf War in 1991 and a strong performance in the nontraditional sector combined to produce economic growth of 6.5 percent, 9.7 percent, and 6.1 percent from 1990 to 1993. Curiously, the improvement in gross domestic product (GDP) indicators did not lead to any reversal in poverty. After a brief fall from 1991 to 1992, not only did general poverty continue to rise, but it was outstripped by increases in extreme poverty (Riutort, 1999). It is perhaps unsurprising that Venezuelans rejected neoliberalism. The trickle-down process clearly did not work.

The smallness of the private sector, preexisting levels of poverty and informality, and the separation of the oil sector from the rest of the economy exacerbated the negative impact of the orthodox measures. The fall in production that characterized the "corrective" phase of adjustment increased unemployment. This was not reversed by job creation in the weak private sector. Small and medium-size industries found it difficult to expand given the increase in interest rates and the slowdown in aggregate demand. When consumption did rise, notably with an increase in oil prices as a result of the Gulf War, this served only to increase import demand relative to bottlenecks in the domestic productive sector. Inflation remained an ongoing problem. It averaged 36 percent from 1990 to 1993 as domestic manufacturers passed on higher import costs to consumers. Further complicating this picture, Pérez was not immune to the temptation of expansionary policies when oil prices rose.

Neoliberalism works on the assumption that those located in the informal sector can "insert" themselves into the modern economy, a postulate undermined in Venezuela by low standards of education resulting from two decades of decline in social expenditures. The public spending cuts implemented by Pérez and maintained after him by Rafael Caldera ensured that levels of educational attainment continued to deteriorate. The social policy of the Pérez government was further informed by the view that economic growth would ultimately substitute for state intervention. As a result, the move from universal to targeted assistance was not based on a detailed analysis of social development or "human capital" needs. Instead it was conceived as a temporary palliative, which was in any case hamstrung by bureaucratic corruption and inefficiency.

The Pérez government failed to build a coalition of support for its neoliberal-inspired measures. This limited the administration's ability to pass legislation designed to increase ordinary fiscal revenues. However, the opposition of the parties in Congress, specifically the hostility of AD, was the result of clientelist imperatives, not ideological conviction. Concern that the party would lose access to oil revenues, in conjunction with a history of factional conflict between Pérez and the AD machine leadership, combined to isolate the president. Fedecámaras and other business associations were divided between pro- and anti-neoliberal interests. This further restricted support for Pérez, while demonstrating the limited ability of private-sector groups to articulate the increasingly fragmented interests of their members. This latter problem also pertained to the CTV, which was closely tied to the AD leadership and detached, as a result of politicization, from the interests of its members. The body offered only a weak challenge to Pérez's privatization policy and failed to transmit workers' concerns to the government. The CTV also faced stiff competition from the Nuevo Sindicalismo movement, pioneered by Causa R. As the CTV and AD grip on organized labor declined, traditional mechanisms of political control disintegrated.

Institutional changes introduced by Pérez compounded the complexity of this new political economy. Decentralization and electoral reform led to a pluralization of politics, but they also aggravated internal party conflict and the necessity for brokerage between parties in Congress. While there were some excellent initiatives at the local government level, these did not reverse a trend of growing poverty. As a result, the benefits of the reforms in terms of system legitimacy did not materialize. This was because the central concern of the majority of the population was the economic rather than the political situation.

Within this newly competitive political matrix, popular support coalesced around nontraditional political organizations that were opposed to Pérez's neoliberal program. After the February 1992 coup attempt, Rafael Caldera broke with the tendency to avoid open debate over economic orthodoxy. His solution to the unstable political scenario was posited in reactive terms—a return to the refuge of state interventionism. The notion that Venezuelan institutions were multiclass prevailed in the rhetoric of the elite. The reality was different and the class cleavages of the 1980s had hardened. This was revealed in the political fortunes of Causa R, which consolidated its support among the working class and marginalized urban sectors in the elections of 1993. The organization's claim that the wealthy had prospered at the expense of the poor struck a chord among those who saw themselves as bearing the cost of institutionalized corruption and neoliberal reform. Causa R also introduced a nationalist perspective into the rhetoric of opposition to orthodoxy, with the IMF and international investors posited as actors working against the national interest (Buxton, 2001: 157). In contrast, AD and COPEI moved rightward, at the same time that a new generation of politicians, elevated by the decentralization process, won the presidential candidacies of their parties.

Caught between the leftist-oriented and relatively unknown Causa R and the traditional parties AD and COPEI, the electorate went down the middle in the 1993 presidential election and backed the renegade Caldera. The contest saw an abstention rate of 39 percent, the highest ever recorded. Indicative of the persistent failure of Venezuelan politicians to inform and educate the electorate as to the country's economic realities, Caldera's economic manifesto, Carta de Intención con el Pueblo de Venezuela, emphasized abstract concepts with a multiclass appeal, such as social justice, rather than presenting concrete policy proposals. Like his predecessor, Caldera also promised never to turn to the IMF. The government's first economic policy, known as the Sosa Plan, was a mixture of spending cuts and tax increases. It was initially successful in closing the fiscal gap, but this was as far as Caldera got in actively defining his own economic direction. For the remainder of its term, the administration was compelled to react to events.

The End of the Fourth Republic: The Caldera Presidency

The first unexpected development was the banking crisis that broke just before Caldera took office in February 1994. A product of inadequate regulation and corruption, the country's financial services required stabilization, but this came at a cost, with the government spending 12 percent of 1994 GDP on intervention. The banking sector crisis triggered massive capital flight. In an attempt to shore up international reserves the currency was devalued, increasing inflation in 1994 to 70.8 percent. Strict price and exchange controls were subsequently imposed, reflecting the willingness of a Venezuelan government to fall back on tried and failed methods of economic management. The inevitable fiscal transfers and public spending cuts exacerbated the social cost of the banking crisis. By the end of 1994, official unemployment had risen to 8.5 percent and according to a congressional report published that year, 79 percent of families were poor, with one in every three families living in conditions of critical poverty. With the government incapable of maintaining investment ratios, the public infrastructure was increasingly subject to blackouts and shortages. Devoid of alternatives, Caldera announced an adjustment program backed by a U.S.$1.4 billion standby loan from the IMF in 1995.

The "Venezuela Agenda" was implemented in April 1996. It led to the removal of the price and exchange controls imposed in 1994. The bolivar floated freely before a system of exchange-rate bands was introduced. Its value fell to 290 to the dollar, while the lifting of price controls led to a further surge in inflation, which reached a record 103.2 percent in 1996. Consumption collapsed and poverty levels maintained their upward trend. By the end of 1996, generalized poverty afflicted 86 percent of the country. Of this total, 65 percent lived in extreme poverty (Pulido de Briceño, 1999).

While committing itself to the orthodox Agenda, the Caldera government rejected the Pérez administration's policy of diversifying the economic base and reverted to the strategy of increasing oil revenues to boost the economy. Under PDVSA president Luis Giusti, emphasis was placed on increasing export volumes at the cost of noncompliance with OPEC production quotas. A key component of this strategy was the legislation introduced in 1995 allowing operating rights in marginal fields to be auctioned to private investors. This boosted foreign direct investment, which rose to U.S.$5.5 billion in 1997. The inflow of foreign funds coincided with a hike in oil prices. Buoyed by the boom in the economy, the government opted not to accept the second tranche of the IMF loan and reverted back to expansionary efforts. These policies had vociferous critics, with Causa R vigorously opposed to the *apertura*. The party's energy spokesman, Alí Rodríguez, argued that the exclusion of domestic capital from the *apertura* inhibited the generation of forward and backward linkages in the economy (see Chapters 2 and 7). As such, the *apertura* served only to increase the profits of multinational companies at the expense of national interests. Causa R's critique was couched in nationalistic terms, tapping into popular opposition to privatization in general and the perceived "sale" of PDVSA in particular.

While foreign investment and higher oil prices allowed for GDP growth of 5.9 percent in 1997, they failed to arrest the growth of poverty or the deterioration of the public infrastructure. Moreover, there was inevitably a negative aspect to this economic policy. High levels of oil production, combined with a decline in international demand, had the effect of depreciating oil prices. Venezuela's basket of crude fell $6 between 1997 and 1998 to U.S.$10.57 per barrel and $5 below the projected average oil price in the 1998 budget. The slump, which continued into 1999, forced the government into a drastic revision of strategy and expenditures. Venezuela agreed to a reduction of production negotiated by OPEC, but these cuts had only a modest impact on prices, forcing Caldera into budget cuts of nearly U.S.$6 billion prior to the 1998 elections.

Protests against the government escalated in 1998, indicative of the collapse of institutionalized mechanisms for interest articulation. This was not a sudden burst of hostility. Opinion polls from 1994 onward reflected limited public confidence in Caldera, who was outstripped in poll surveys by the independent Irene Sáez, mayor of a wealthy Caracas-area municipality. The rise of political outsiders owed much to the failure of the parties to reverse negative public opinion about their performance. Even Causa R saw its credibility decline due to a mixture of organizational incoherence, internal divisions, and association with the Punto Fijo regime, into which it now seemed incorporated (Buxton, 2001). As party political alternatives to AD and COPEI declined, the system became increasingly vulnerable to populist, antiparty appeals.

The political atomization that characterized the Pérez period consequently accelerated under Caldera, as the majority in society, located in both the formal and the informal labor sectors, became completely detached from its "representatives." Continuing the previous administration's proprivatization policy, the Caldera government presided over the sale of state assets, including its remaining stake in the national telephone company, CANTV, and the steel sector, while preparing the legislative groundwork and opening tenders for the privatization of petrochemicals, electricity, and aluminum. Assets from the financial enterprises acquired in 1994 were privatized, and by 1997 foreign financial interests controlled 41 percent of Venezuelan banks. The CTV offered little resistance to the privatization process or the "rationalization" of the labor force that ensued (Ellner, 1999c: 116–119). The confederation was also party to a modification of the Labor Law in 1997. This ended retroactive severance payments for workers and established a framework for the privatization of the social security system based on the participation of public and private funds. Opponents of these measures, including Chávez, viewed them as nothing less than a betrayal of the working class. Not only did the amended law deprive workers of a critical welfare provision, but Caldera and the private sector failed to deliver the accumulated benefits promised in exchange for modification of the legislation. In addition, the revised law made no provision for workers in the informal economy (see Chapter 9).

The government's inability to explain or define its economic policy, combined with the mute compliance of the private sector with certain aspects of the new legislation, further eroded the legitimacy of Venezuela's political institutions. Caldera's flip-flop from heterodoxy to orthodoxy compounded perceptions that the government was incapable of handling the economy. A cogent example of the administration's tendency for ad hoc and belated policy responses was the proposal to create a macroeconomic stabilization fund (MSF). It was only when the oil price had fallen to an all-time low in 1999 that legislation was finally introduced to create the MSF, a device designed to put aside windfall revenues to cover periods when prices fell.

The Venezuelan political elite presided over a sustained decline of the economy, while facing no coherent opposition to the Punto Fijo system. Innovation, policy evaluation, and difficult decisions were constantly deferred or blocked in Congress, with the cost of policy lethargy born by those outside the clientelist framework. As a result, poverty increased more rapidly in Venezuela than in any country in the region (*El Universal,* June 20, 2001). The political establishment suffered a rude awakening in 1998, when a spokesman for the excluded emerged with the promise of strong leadership, radical political change, and an economic "third way" that promised to reverse the collapse in living standards.

The Economic Approach of Hugo Chávez

The 1998 presidential campaign was novel in demonstrating elements of class and racial polarization. It was perfectly "rational" for aspiring presidential candidates to mobilize on a class basis. Multiclass politics was seen to have failed and perceptions of class location showed a dramatic reversal from the optimism of the 1970s. By the 1990s, the poor identified themselves as poor, underlining both the adoption of a profoundly negative assessment of the country's future and a class consciousness (Consultores 21, 2000).

Chávez, of mixed race and from a lower-middle-class background, mocked his main opponent, Governor Henrique Salas Römer, the white, upper-class "oligarch." Salas Römer in turn played up his elite status by riding his horse, Frijolito, during campaigning. Chávez's colloquialisms stood in contrast to the technical language of the Yale-educated Salas, and the former's commitment to indigenous rights brought to the fore issues of race and poverty in a country upheld by a (white) elite as a model of racial equality. There was, however, a striking element of continuity with previous elections, with an anti- and a pro-neoliberal candidate pitted against each other in the electoral marketplace.

Chávez's opposition to "savage neoliberalism" is well known. His opponents attempted to make political capital through a simplistic interpretation of his argument by raising the specter of "statist" authoritarianism. Chávez's economic manifesto was more complex. While the private sector was initially concerned about his emphasis on traditionally "leftist" epithets such as national sovereignty and economic justice, it became clear in the campaign that a Chávez government would basically follow a social democratic trajectory in the economic sphere. Earlier claims that there would be no repayment of the country's "illegal" debt were downplayed during the latter part of the campaign when Chávez emphasized that foreign capital would be welcome, but on terms conducive to the national interest. The state had a role to play in reducing poverty and ensuring social welfare, but this would be a radically different type of state, one that was reformed, depoliticized, and devoid of corruption. As such, the focus of the Chávez campaign was the necessity of constitutional change. The message struck a responsive chord among the marginalized majority of Venezuelan society.

This was not the case with Salas Römer's promise of a 200-day program of shock therapy, embracing deregulation of prices, value-added taxation, fiscal austerity, reductions in the public bureaucracy, and a review of Venezuela's membership in OPEC. Salas advocated a harder, faster implementation of the unpopular orthodox policies pursued during the Pérez presidency on the hypothetical assumption that they would reap swifter economic dividends. The Venezuelan electorate was unconvinced.

On taking office in February 1999, Chávez's first speech to the nation was characterized by a firm emphasis on prudential economic management. Personifying this line of fiscal rectitude, Maritza Izaguirre, finance minister during the implementation of budget cuts in Caldera's final year in office, was retained. Continuity with the Caldera administration was also evident in macroeconomic policy management. The exchange-rate band was maintained and price and interest-rate controls were rejected. A series of measures was introduced to increase fiscal revenues. These included reforms of the tax superintendency, SENIAT, with the aim of increasing taxation revenues by 50 percent, and an anticorruption drive. The latter strategy led to a review of budget expenditures that revealed that over $1 million had been allotted to AD and COPEI think tanks and that $1.6 million was paid annually to a teachers union affiliated with AD.

There was no expropriation of foreign or domestic assets as the opposition claimed would happen. The administration began an immediate revision of the legislative framework for the privatization of electricity, aluminum, telecommunications, petrochemicals, and gas, but with an eye on defining rather than limiting investment opportunities. As such, the government neither reverted to the traditional left-wing policy of controlling strategic sectors nor opted for the wholesale privatization of state assets as recommended by neoliberals. Instead, there was a mixed approach, recognizing the role of private capital but ensuring it complied with national goals.

Constitutional reform dominated Chávez's agenda during his first year in office. The prioritization of the political over the economic was determined by two interrelated factors. For the Chávez administration, political reform was a prerequisite for economic reform. The link between the two was spelled out in the program of the Polo Patriótico (PP; Patriotic Pole), the interparty alliance that backed his candidacy. This looked to a "two-hand formula" of the "invisible hand of the market, in which competition and transparency exists and the visible hand of the state" counters the weakness and imperfections of the market. Chávez saw this as the embodiment of a Venezuelan "third way." As such, the country could develop endogenous solutions to its developmental crisis, beginning with institutional reform and the eradication of corrupt practices. The latter was a critical consideration given that tax evasion was higher than the fiscal deficit and that "fifteen per cent of the budget goes to corruption: bureaucratic spending, foundations, funding for the political parties . . . when the country is dying" (Hugo Chávez, cited in Blanco Muñoz, 1998: 609).

While the media and political opposition focused their attention on the election of the Constituent Assembly and its subsequent deliberations, there was a redefinition of the government's role in the economy. Oil policy was one of the first areas to feel the change. Under energy minister Alí Rodríguez, the strategy of increasing production was reversed, with the government prioritizing production cuts, a stronger role in OPEC, and diversification into downstream activities including petrochemicals. In addition, Rodríguez was able to act on his earlier critique of the *apertura* by advancing legislative reforms to reverse the negligible role afforded to domestic capital in the process (see Chapter 7). The role of PDVSA, condemned by Chávez as a "state within a state," was thus redefined in line with broader national interest.

Promotion of the national interest was revealed in other sectors, although the government's unorthodox solutions to the country's productive bottlenecks brought claims of protectionism and authoritarianism. Luisa Romero, minister for production and commerce, acknowledged that measures to promote economic development contradicted the trend of integration and free trade, both within the global economy and within the Community of Andean Nations. This was, however, justified on the basis that protectionism was a necessary and temporary requirement for reversing twenty years of industrial decline.

Cognizant of the weakness of the private sector, and in an attempt to overcome the oligopolistic profile of the economy, the government promoted small and medium-size industries through the introduction of credit facilities to be disbursed by a new banking entity, the Banco Popular, and adoption of a "Buy Venezuelan" policy. The government also sought to broker agreements with the financial sector to reduce interest rates and improve credit availability. In the rural sphere, where poverty stood at 84 percent of the population, the administration sought to tackle food import dependency, poverty, and one of the highest concentrations of landownership in Latin America. Initial measures aimed at improving agricultural productivity included the channeling of $15 million to create landholdings and the designation of "priority areas," including maize, palm oil, and forestry, which were awarded financial assistance and supported by special import tariffs.

The recognition afforded to problems in rural areas underlined Chávez's popularity among the poor, a heterogeneous mixture of people in different circumstances whom the administration sought to assist through diverse programs. A paradigmatic example of the government's social policy approach was recognition that women were subject to higher levels of poverty. To tackle this, credit facilities were provided to women through the Banco de la Mujer, a strategy that complemented the promotion of small and medium-size industries. Policies were devised to address two of the country's most pronounced problems in terms of social capital—education and informal-sector employment. Accepting the link between low standards of educational attainment, informal employment, and poverty, the government introduced a decree to improve educational standards at the end of 2000. Under Decree 1011, the Ministry of Education sent professionals to inspect schools in order to improve standards. This extended to the highly unregulated private education system, which had expanded as a result of the cut in public expenditures.

The government recognized that the traditional method of improving the living standards of workers—such as minimum-wage increases negotiated through tripartite structures—failed to include informal-sector workers. Not only were the tripartite commissions disbanded in 1999, but a revised version of the social security legislation, originally introduced under Caldera, was considered for approval. The proposed law established public pension and health protection rights for informal-economy workers.

A final noteworthy aspect of the government's social policy was Plan Bolívar 2000. This was conceived as a joint civil-military operation, which centered on programs to reverse the deterioration of the public infrastructure (see Chapter 5). Although the plan generated intense criticism that the country was being militarized, it reflected Chávez's concern regarding the state's extreme bureaucratization and its inability to confront the nation's pressing social problems. There was, of course, an ideological element to the military's new role, which extended to the appointment of military officers to senior cabinet positions. Chávez had conceived the Movimiento Quinta República (MVR; Fifth Republic Movement) party as a joint civil-military organization and he conceptualized the armed forces playing a vital role in national development. There was also a practical consideration.

The government could draw upon a limited pool of capable individuals who were not associated with AD or COPEI.

Chávez's first year in office was characterized by recession. Political uncertainty, fueled by concerns over the constitutional reform process and encouraged by the opposition, accelerated capital flight. This, in conjunction with a fall in foreign investment, low oil prices, and public spending cuts, led to an economic contraction of 7.2 percent in 1999 and a 24.9 percent decline in gross capital formation. In addition, the government had to contend with the economic and social costs of the devastating mudslides in December 1999. The social effects of the recession in the domestic economy were pronounced. Unemployment increased from 11.4 percent in 1998 to 15.4 percent in 1999, while consumption fell 4.8 percent. The only positive side effect of this harsh decline was a reduction in the rate of inflation to 20 percent and a balance of payments surplus as consumption and import demand fell. Chávez, however, remained popular through his first two years in office, with opinion polls demonstrating an approval rating of over 80 percent. This honeymoon owed as much to the weakness and discredited state of the political opposition as it did to Chávez's populist approach and policy innovations. Positive attitudes toward the administration were further sustained into 2000 by a reversal of the negative economic performance recorded in 1999. Consensus on production cuts within OPEC succeeded in lifting oil prices to an average of $26.3 per barrel in 2000, a $10 per barrel rise from 1999. This fed through into government spending, which increased 46 percent. Inflation fell to its lowest level since 1986 and, at $13 billion, the surplus on the current account was the highest since 1980.

Opposition and Policy Limitations

The "third way" approach of the government was institutionalized in the Bolivarian constitution of 1999. For one observer, the charter was "both democratic and consistent with good economic policy" (Kelly, 2000). The administration's commitment to maintaining a publicly funded welfare regime was explicitly echoed in the preamble to the constitution. This set out the right to "life, work, culture, education, social justice and equality." These rights were elaborated in Title III, wherein social security for the elderly, disability payments, housing, unemployment insurance, and public health care were guaranteed through obligatory financial contributions, forming the basis for an "integral and universal" social security system. An extensive revision of legislation was required for the state to meet these new obligations. Pertinent in this respect were the plans to reform the

Labor Law in line with Article 92 of the constitution, which marked the return of the retroactive system of severance payments abolished by Caldera in 1997. While government critics focused their concerns on how the state could possibly fund public welfare provisions (a questioning of both underlining ideology and fiscal capacity), the proposals were inevitably popular among Chávez's supporters. Not only had the government gone some way in addressing the need for an effective safety net, it was also seen to be prioritizing the neglected issue of social development. Pursuant to this, the measures responded to the popular view that Venezuelans should collectively enjoy the benefits stemming from the national oil industry.

Private-sector anxiety over the "statist" elements of the constitution also related to Article 303, which ruled out privatization of PDVSA, specifically the sale of its stock. Similarly, the constitution envisaged a sustained role for the state in the economy, which ran against the neoliberal mainstream, while reflecting Chávez's view that the market cannot be self-regulating. Typical in this respect are Articles 301 and 305–307, relating to tariffs and subsidies, cited as playing a necessary role in the economic and social development of the nation. While positing a seemingly heterodox approach to address the country's development needs, the constitution also embraced elements of orthodoxy. Complemented by legislative changes introduced under enabling legislation, the constitution reformed budgetary procedures and the fiscal management responsibilities of the Central Bank of Venezuela, while emphasizing the importance of the free market and recognizing private property.

Contrary to expectations, the constitution did not reflect a government seeking to re-create the Cuban regime, as claimed by the opposition, which used Chávez's amicable ties with Fidel Castro to incite fears of authoritarianism. Articles contained in the document, which was drawn up by an assembly composed overwhelmingly of members of the MVR, reflected Chávez's ideological emphasis on a middle course between capitalism and "failed" communism. Critically, and in stark contrast to previous governments, the "third way" approach viewed poverty and underdevelopment as a problem of distribution. This position led opponents of the government to perceive economic policy as a zero-sum game (as discussed in Chapter 1) and one that promoted the interests of one social class above another.

The initial series of reforms introduced by the government, ranging from Plan Bolívar to Education Decree 1011, was mired in controversy and interpreted as an attempt by the government to install an authoritarian, statist model. The Bolivarian constitution was subject to similar criticism, forging an unlikely and heterogeneous coalition of sectorial interests united against the government. Following the granting of enabling powers to Chávez in November 2000, speculation and rumor surrounded the contents of further legislative initiatives. A delay of nearly a year in the formulation of these measures spurred the opposition, which in turn drew the administration into day-to-day political conflicts. The heightened sense of political risk that persisted throughout 2001 accelerated capital flight. This, combined with a decline in oil prices, had a negative impact on the economy. Although inflation continued to fall, the balance of payments registered a deficit of $2.6 billion, while the central government budget deficit doubled between 2000 and 2001, representing 3.9 percent of GDP.

As the enabling powers came to an end in November 2001, forty-nine laws were decreed by the administration. They were far-reaching in content and covered a variety of policy areas, from insurance and banking to fishing, oil, and tourism. Informed by the view that state intervention and redistributive measures were a prerequisite for sustainable and equitable development, the legislation served to galvanize opponents of the government.

In order to tackle the second highest concentration of land in the region—with 70 percent of agricultural land in the hands of just 3 percent of proprietors—a radical land law, the Ley de Tierra, was introduced. The law set a maximum permissible hectarage of a farm (ranging from 100 to 5,000 hectares), determined by the level of agricultural productivity. Proprietors who failed to utilize more than 80 percent of their land were subject to an inactivity tax and, in exceptional circumstances, land could be assumed by the state. The legislation also sought to redistribute land, although squatters were not entitled to property rights and small farmers who were assigned land could not sell or mortgage the property. The Coasts, Fishery, and Aquaculture Laws were similarly conceived as a means of encouraging small-scale artisans. Coastal areas that had not been legally acquired passed into the public domain, and only traditional fishing techniques were permitted near the coastline. The redistributive nature of the proposals provoked intense opposition and generated claims that the government was following a statist strategy that violated the constitutional right to private property. The perception that the administration was acting against the interests of the private sector was echoed in criticisms of the Hydrocarbons Law. Although the law increased royalty payments from 16.7 percent to 30 percent (for conventional oil fields), it reduced the top bracket of income tax from 67.7 percent to 34 percent.

Although depicted as a leftist administration, throughout its first three years in office the government was slow in delivering promised benefits to the poorest sectors of the population. While there was economic growth, this did not translate into an immediate reduction in unemployment, poverty, crime, or informal-sector employment. There was also mounting evidence of an excessive centralization of power around the national executive, an unwillingness to build political consensus, and allegations of

corruption. Furthermore, the government demonstrated a troublesome tendency to bypass its own constitution and maintained the Venezuelan tradition of insulating economic policymaking from lobby group input.
Although this led to a significant erosion of the president's popularity in
late 2001 and 2002, it was the poor who rallied to the defense of Chávez in
April 2002.

While Chávez may have failed to deliver in the short term, his administration held out the possibility of benefits for the poor in the long term.
The defense of Chávez was predicated on the view that he both understood
and would strive to meet the needs of the poorest sectors. This contrasted
sharply with the interim administration of Pedro Carmona. Overwhelmingly white, elite, and pro–free market in composition, the junta represented a
step back, a return to the exclusion and inequality of the Fourth Republic.

Conclusion

In addressing his country's development crisis and vulnerability in a globalized economy, Chávez took a middle road, one imbued with nationalist
rhetoric but broadly resembling the ideological revisions and embrace of
capitalism seen on both the European and the Latin American left. In reject-
ing the intellectual hegemony of neoliberalism and focusing on the needs of
the marginalized sectors of the population, the Chávez government strug-
gled to deflect hostile criticism from a range of interests. These include the
opposition parties, unaccustomed to being out of power, the "clients" of the
Punto Fijo system, the private sector, and a wary U.S. Department of State.
While there were concerns over the style and direction of the Chávez government, understanding its survival requires recognition that the marginalized have a voice in contemporary democracies. Pursuant to this, a middle
ground can be chartered between state-led development and orthodoxy.
This is particularly the case in politically unstable countries where the costs
of adjustment come at an unacceptable social cost and with no guarantee of
success.

7

Subversive Oil

Bernard Mommer

Venezuela's Fourth Republic, as the political regime prior to 1998 has been posthumously baptized, was torn apart by two subversive movements, one in the military and the other in the national oil industry. The story of military subversion is well known, but not the story of subversion in the national oil company, Petróleos de Venezuela, Sociedad Anónima (PDVSA). After nationalization of the oil industry in 1976, PDVSA became something of a state within a state. Its Venezuelan executives shared the outlook of international oil companies, for whom they had worked for many years. Furthermore, successive governments of AD and the Comité de Organización Política Electoral Independiente (COPEI) during and after the boom period of the 1970s failed to create a new efficient fiscal and regulatory system, at the same time that they implemented disastrous developmental policies characterized by poor planning and waste. This ultimately led, after 1989, to the policy of opening the oil sector to foreign capital (the *apertura*), which put Venezuelan oil policy on a path toward reprivatization of the industry. It also put Venezuelan oil policy on a path toward minimization of fiscal oil revenues. President Hugo Chávez arrested the momentum, but the direction of oil policy remains very divisive not only in Venezuelan society but within the *chavista* movement as well.

There are some remarkable parallels between the ways each of these two subversive movements arose. Chávez founded his movement around 1982; PDVSA executives embarked on their strategy of internationalization in 1983. Internationalization was devised by PDVSA to create a conveyor belt to relocate profits out of the reach of the government through transfer pricing (i.e., the price charged by one affiliate to another affiliate in the accounts of the parent company). Both PDVSA executives and Chávez and his followers believed that the current political regime was beyond repair. In the judgment of both groups of conspirators, the squandering of oil revenues played a crucial role in this steady decline. Both the military and PDVSA took a moralizing approach, blaming corruption for the crisis. The military dreamt about saving the country; PDVSA executives dreamt about saving the oil industry from the country.

The Aftermath of Nationalization

Nationalization in Venezuela in 1976 was the outcome of a long-term policy of maximizing fiscal revenues collected from oil exports. For the last
two years prior to nationalization, for every dollar of oil exports, the government collected eighty cents in rents, royalties, and taxes. By 1970 the
government had asserted a right to levy export taxes at its sole discretion,
effectively leaving the companies with nothing but a regulated profit. The
foreign companies were losing control of their businesses. They could no
longer maximize their own profits because additional earnings were subject
to appropriation by the government via the export levy. They hardly resisted when President Carlos Andrés Pérez nationalized the industry on
January 1, 1976. However, only a few years after Pérez left office, his plans
to create "Great Venezuela" and develop the country through an overnight
program of industrialization had failed disastrously. PDVSA then began to
develop its own hidden agenda to break away from state control.

Nationalization changed ownership of the oil industry but not, for the
most part, management. Prior to nationalization, there were three major foreign companies operating concessions in Venezuela: Exxon, Shell, and
Gulf. Over the years, partly in response to political pressure, the companies
selected Venezuelan nationals for executive positions. These executives
accepted nationalization in 1976 only because they had no choice. Once
they were in charge of PDVSA, their prime objective was to displace the
Ministry of Energy and Mines (MEM), the traditional steward of the "land-
lord" state. The company certainly did not have in mind the maximization
of fiscal revenues (royalties, income taxes, and export levies). On the contrary, once the "Great Venezuela" of Pérez had crashed, PDVSA sought to
limit its own fiscal obligations. The failures of development policy only
reinforced the company's determination. Why generate fiscal revenues that
would be squandered anyway? Why maximize profits when the state would
inevitably siphon them into the treasury? Instead, the company concentrated on its own agenda: the development of the oil sector in real terms, maximizing volume, turnover, and sales (not profits) in all the segments of the
industry, both at a national and at an international level, at the same time
that fiscal revenues were disregarded.

PDVSA thus undermined nationalization and paved the way for the
return of private investors. By 1989, when Pérez was back in office and
implementing his "Great Turnabout," which included the *apertura* to foreign capital, an alliance emerged between the national oil company, on the
one hand, and the international oil companies and the consuming countries,
on the other. Contrary to what is widely believed, outright privatization was
not the top priority of this alliance. The international companies and the
consuming countries were primarily worried about dismantling the political

and institutional framework that had led to nationalization in the first place. That is, they wanted to reduce the power of the state to maximize its share of oil revenues and to control prices and supply. Their strategy was to put in place a new governance structure designed to prevent the government (in the form of MEM) from ever again pursuing a strategy of maximizing fiscal revenues. Only then would full-scale privatization move to the top of the agenda (Mommer, 2002a). In the meantime, foreign capital in association with PDVSA under the *apertura* arrangement became again a major producer in Venezuela. At present about 25 percent of Venezuelan oil is produced in this form. According to the contracts signed under the terms of the post-1989 period of *apertura,* this percentage will increase to over 40 percent by the year 2010 (Mommer, 1998).

When foreign companies controlled oil production and set prices, the state was naturally vigilant over their operations. After nationalization, vigilance seemed unnecessary. Worse, in response to the explosive growth of oil prices and hence fiscal revenues in 1973–1974, the newly elected Congress passed an enabling law that gave President Pérez complete liberty to spend the money at his discretion, in accordance with his vision of a "Great Venezuela." In other words, Congress shirked its most elementary and essential task: the control of public finances. Pérez then launched a series of huge investment projects, nationalized the iron industry, and forced foreign capital out of many other key economic areas, such as banking and retail commerce chains, while a system of state enterprises arose in the heart of the new economy. Simultaneously, private Venezuelan enterprise was marginalized. Fedecámaras, the peak organization of the business community, had grown on the eve of nationalization into a politically (even economically) relevant body. Once the foreign members of the organization left, among them the international oil companies, what remained was only a shadow of its former self.

During the postnationalization years, the government—or more precisely, the president—appeared to hold all the trump cards. Fiscal income from oil increased from U.S.$1.4 billion in 1970 (about 10 percent of gross domestic product [GDP]), to U.S.$9 billion in 1974 (a staggering 40 percent of GDP). Such an influx relative to the nation's productive structure was far beyond the absorptive capacity of the economy. Worse, in the rush to build his "Great Venezuela," the Pérez government contracted international loans, in effect spending future oil revenues on top of huge current earnings. With foreign enterprises leaving, the capacity of the economy to absorb capital was actually falling. The country did not need the money of foreign investors at the time, but it certainly needed their managerial skills in order to bring its ambitious investment plans to fruition.

Thus, at the end of the day, the government, isolated and helpless, was to drown in its financial wealth. Political clients, not citizens or business partners, surrounded the state, which was supposedly possessed of magical powers to develop the economy (Coronil, 1997). This was a recipe for disaster. Congress never recovered control over public finances; nor would the private sector ever recover its proper role. Only foreign creditors were eventually able to force the government and state enterprises to change policies, and then with their own particular agenda. After 1983 there was only one strong and working institution left standing within the national economy: PDVSA. The lack of checks and balances was to become of consequence for the company, as its virtually autonomous status allowed it to go ahead with its own particular agenda.

The Internationalization Policy of PDVSA and Transfer Pricing

PDVSA's first response to the implementation of exchange controls in 1983 was its internationalization policy (Boué, 1997). In a last-minute and unsuccessful effort to contain the developing foreign debt and currency crisis, the government has fallen back on the investment fund of the company, totaling about $5.5 billion, which it had been allowed to accumulate during the years of high prices. At the same time, however, oil price hikes led to sharply falling demand and to ever more restrictive quotas from the Organization of Petroleum-Exporting Countries (OPEC), which left the company no outlets for new investments in Venezuela. In order to prevent the government from appropriating its liquid assets again, PDVSA decided not to have any. As investing in the country was not feasible, accumulated profits had to be spent abroad. But where could the money be spent at a time when production was to be cut? The answer was PDVSA's internationalization policy. In 1983, PDVSA bought its first share of a foreign refinery (VEBA) in Germany. At the time, the company argued that this refinery would provide a market for Venezuela's heavy crude, which was difficult to market otherwise. To this very day, however, the German refinery has never processed heavy crude. Over the years, PDVSA has supplied VEBA with lighter crude oil that could have been easily placed on the world market anyway. Furthermore, PDVSA has sold the oil to its European interests at substantially discounted "transfer" prices, thereby shifting a portion of its profits beyond the reach of the Venezuelan government (Guevara, 1983).

Some politicians belonging to Acción Democrática (AD)—Rafael Guevara and Celestino Armas—became aware of the maneuver and raised the alarm in Congress, but to no avail. On the contrary, the issue of transfer pricing was settled entirely in favor of PDVSA when the government of President Jaime Lusinchi (1984–1989), himself a member of AD, decreed that the company would henceforth set its own prices. This decree gave the internationalization policy a new boost. Subsequently, PDVSA shifted its attention to the U.S. market, where it operates under the name of Citgo. Once again PDVSA bought systematically into refineries, signing long-term supply contracts and granting substantial discounts to its new affiliates for the purpose of transferring significant portions of its profits abroad. In order to ensure that this money was definitively beyond of the reach of the government, the contracts were used as collateral to secure foreign loans. Thus, before Chávez or any other future government can change the terms of the contracts between PDVSA and its own subsidiaries, it will have to pay off all of PDVSA's debts, which now total nearly $10 billion.

This goal of shifting profits abroad was the real motive for internationalization and explains the unchecked growth of PDVSA's international refinery network, presently capable of handling about 2 million barrels per day, and its retail business, consisting of over 14,000 gasoline stations in the United States. By the second half of the 1990s, PDVSA was remitting through transfer pricing an average of about $500 million annually from its domestic accounts to its foreign affiliates (Mendoza Potellá, 1995; Boué, 2002). For eighteen years after the beginning of internationalization, the foreign affiliates of PDVSA never paid dividends to the holding company in Caracas. But earning profits for the country was never the objective of the policy in the first place. In December 2001 the Chávez government obliged the foreign affiliates to pay dividends for the first time.

OPEC Quotas and PDVSA

In the early 1980s, after worldwide demand began to flag, OPEC created a quota system in an attempt to maintain high prices. Both PDVSA and the financially troubled Venezuelan government started to look for ways to minimize the impact of, or to bypass, these quotas. Thus, in 1983, Venezuela began to measure production subject to quotas at refinery gates and ports of export rather than in the storage tanks of the producing fields (as is usual everywhere in the world for calculating royalty payments). At the time, PDVSA promised MEM that it would install modern meters in the fields. This never happened, despite the repeated and formal protests of the ministry over the next fifteen years. As a result, MEM effectively lost its ability to monitor and control levels of production of crude oil and natural gas, giving PDVSA significant leeway to minimize its royalty payments.

PDVSA looked for other ways to manipulate the definition of crude oil subject to OPEC quotas: increasing production of the extra-heavy crude (i.e., heavier than water) of the Orinoco Belt, by far the largest reserve of its kind in the world. The company argued that Orinoco deposits—which are processed into a product called "Orimulsión"—did not fall under the definition of crude oil. (This assertion is technically correct, as these deposits do not constitute a liquid at normal temperatures.) Therefore, PDVSA argued, the Orinoco Belt should be classified as "bitumen" and hence not be subjected to OPEC quotas. In 2000, PDVSA produced approximately 100,000 barrels per day of Orimulsión derived from about 70,000 barrels per day of extra-heavy oil—and it planned to triple this figure in the near future.

After 1989, with the initiation of *apertura,* PDVSA entered into joint ventures with foreign companies in four integrated projects for the production of synthetic crude ("syncrude") from the same extra-heavy grades of oil. PDVSA planned to increase production of syncrude to 1.2 million barrels per day (requiring about 1.5 million barrels per day of extra-heavy crude) by the year 2010. Like Orimulsión, syncrude is subject to lower levels of taxation (1 percent royalty and 34 percent income tax). If this oil were included in Venezuela's OPEC quota, it would displace more highly taxed conventional crude from PDVSA's exports. Calculated on prices in the first half of 2001, the loss in revenue for the government would be as high as $10 per barrel.

The rush into the Orinoco Belt was justified during the years of *apertura* with the argument that it was not subject to OPEC quota. A more far-reaching purpose, however, was to force Venezuela into conflict with OPEC, possibly forcing it out of the organization, by committing the country once and for all to an oil policy predicated on high volumes and low prices. This strategy is consistent with goals of the International Energy Agency (IEA), which was founded by the consumer countries in the early 1970s in order to confront OPEC. Indeed, Andrés Sosa Pietri, PDVSA president in the early 1990s, has consistently advocated Venezuela's withdrawal from OPEC and its membership in the IEA.

The Chávez government had to confront this situation. The practical compromise has been to include syncrude in the OPEC quota, but not Orimulsión. Nevertheless, the recent cuts in production (2001) are causing very substantial and disproportionate losses in fiscal revenues. Lower prices, however, would even be worse. Leaving OPEC is not an option the Chávez government is about to consider.

Apertura *in the Context of Neoliberal Policy After 1989*

In 1988, Pérez was elected president for a second term, but he faced a totally different situation than fifteen years earlier. Notwithstanding the oil price collapse in 1986, the preceding administration of Jaime Lusinchi had carried on spending as usual. Thus, at the time Pérez took office in February 1989, the Central Bank of Venezuela was left without foreign reserves. Pérez immediately accepted agreements with the International Monetary Fund and the World Bank that included an increase in domestic gasoline prices. Pérez now promised a "Great Turnabout," which came as a surprise to the Venezuelan people, who had never been told that there was anything fundamentally wrong with the economy in the first place. Indeed, an increase in gasoline prices, reflected in higher transport fares, sparked the Caracazo of the week of February 27, 1989.

Pérez also began to allow private investors back into the Venezuelan oil industry. As part of the opening of the Venezuelan economy to the outside world, PDVSA was put in charge of the petroleum *apertura*. The role of MEM, which prior to nationalization had overseen contractual and fiscal relations with oil companies, was reduced to rubber-stamp status. PDVSA preached the gospel of competitiveness to the government, arguing that royalties and taxes would have to be lowered to attract foreign investors. The government followed its advice. In addition to the aforementioned joint ventures for extra-heavy oil, PDVSA opened "marginal" fields producing conventional grades to private investments (arrangements known as operating services agreements), which by 2001 accounted for about 500,000 barrels per day. The greater part of this oil is not subject to OPEC quotas, and is low-taxed. In the process, the higher-taxed production of PDVSA was cut. Moreover, in these agreements PDVSA acts as an umbrella shielding private capital from the state, guaranteeing that the state company will pay an indemnity to its "partners" if there is any "detrimental" legislative change. Contractual disputes were made subject to international arbitration, an arrangement Venezuela had never accepted before in its history. Last but not least, in case of disputes, PDVSA exports are subject to sequestration. Nevertheless, Congress approved all of these agreements.

Having acted on behalf of private foreign investors, PDVSA also insisted on lower taxation for itself. Its best opportunity came in the chaotic year of 1993. President Pérez was removed from office, mainly as a consequence of the two coup attempts in 1992. A very weak provisional government took over and accepted a new Income Tax Law with generous allowances for inflation costs. In addition, the government's power of discretion over the export levy, which had been created in 1970 to allow capture of extraordinary profits in periods of high prices, was phased out, and finally abolished in 1996. These measures contributed to a significant drop in fiscal revenue from oil.

Statistics put in evidence the government's declining share of oil income. In 1981, gross income from hydrocarbon production, including refining, peaked at $19.7 billion. In 2000, a new peak of $29.3 billion was reached. Nevertheless, in 1981 PDVSA paid $13.9 billion in fiscal revenues, but only $11.3 billion in 2000. In other words, for every dollar of gross income, PDVSA paid seventy-one cents to the government in rents, royalties, and taxes in 1981, but only thirty-nine cents in 2000 (see Figure 7.1). Moreover, government revenue derived from syncrude production

Figure 7.1   Fiscal Revenue from Oil as a Percentage of Gross Income from Oil, 1976–2000

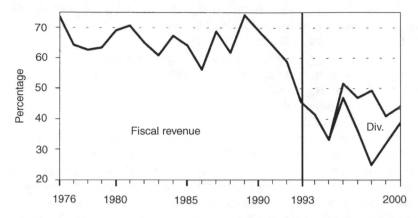

Source: Ministerio de Energía y Minas, *Petróleo y otros datos estadísticos* (Caracas: Ministerio de Energía y Minas, 2001).
    Note: Div. = dividends.

coming on-stream in the near future will be substantially lower. Thus the trend of falling fiscal revenue is bound to continue.

The End of the Fourth Republic

In the general elections of 1998, the two subversive movements—one led by PDVSA executives and the other by elements in the military—confronted each other (Arrioja, 1998; see also Chapter 2 in this volume). PDVSA had become powerful enough to play a high-profile political role, and its leadership was convinced that the time had come to implement fully its liberal agenda. Liberalism, in the context of international oil politics, is to be understood in its original revolutionary conception based on replacing the visible hand of the landlords with the invisible hand of the market. Like their forebears, today's liberals would reduce the power of "landlords" (i.e., sovereign nation-states) to restrict access of capital (i.e., international corporations). It is this restriction on access that is the basis for the landowner, private or public, to collect a rent. The goal for liberals is "land to the tiller," or to be more precise, "minerals to the miner." They want natural resources considered a free gift of nature, freely available to the producing companies and consumers. "Free" thus refers to elimination of the obligation to pay rent.

Is Venezuelan oil a free gift of nature to international producing companies and foreign consumers? PDVSA's liberal agenda answers this question with an unqualified "yes." This view is antithetical to everything that Venezuelan oil nationalism has ever achieved, including the founding of OPEC and nationalization. It is imperialism in its most ancient of definitions: the conquest of foreign land and its mineral resources.

Not surprisingly, PDVSA enjoyed strong backing from the governments of the developed consuming countries as well as international oil companies. Their experts designed the changes in Venezuela's fiscal system following the example of the British North Sea, the most liberal oil-producing region in the world in terms of allowing capital-free access to natural resources. PDVSA thus came to play an important role in bringing the country into a global world where the territorial state is supposed to have disappeared. Venezuela joined the World Trade Organization (WTO) without reserving any special rights regarding its oil (in contrast to Mexico). According to the vision adopted by PDVSA, natural resources are seen less as leverage to promote national development and more as advantages to attract foreign investment. In contrast to earlier periods, the nation no longer would require foreign investors to transfer technology or to purchase needed components from national producers.

PDVSA argued that any insistence upon measures to maximize oil revenue would obstruct the free flow of much-needed investment. If the paramount goal of the state as owner of natural resources is to attract foreign investment, then the more investment the better. Hence the lower the levels of taxation and the more flexible the fiscal regimes, the better. Consequently, the fiscal revenue maximization policy of the past was replaced with a policy of minimization. In February 1998 it seemed very likely that independent candidate Irene Sáez would easily win the elections and that PDVSA would play a central role in her government. Venezuela was on the brink of becoming Latin America's model pupil of natural resource liberalism and globalization. A nation that had played a key role in founding OPEC, the epitome of an organization dedicated to strengthening national sovereignty over exhaustible natural resources, was now to become a leader in dismantling what had been achieved within the OPEC framework.

Then, to spoil it all, Chávez turned up as a popular candidate. The small political groups that had opposed PDVSA's liberal oil policy supported Chávez, although he had no specific agenda for oil beyond a more or less vaguely formulated commitment to follow a nationalistic approach. He and his followers were still unaware of subversive oil, but one thing was certain: his victory would at the very least slow down the implementation of the liberal agenda. And there was nothing the PDVSA leadership and the traditional political parties could do about it. Desperate, AD and COPEI joined in a last-minute electoral front, but to no avail. During the electoral campaign Chávez moved steeply and inexorably upward in the opinion polls as world petroleum prices moved downward. PDVSA had been publicly boasting about never again cutting a single barrel of output. It was already no longer a question of extra-heavy oil not being subject to OPEC quotas, but to put an end to the quota system per se. Even the formidable public relations machinery of PDVSA—which contended that lower prices would secure more markets for Venezuela with the overall balance being positive—could not convince the country that falling prices were good news, try as hard as it might.

The Fifth Republic

Hugo Chávez took over the presidency in February 1999 in the middle of the worst price collapse in world petroleum markets in over fifty years. The situation, however, soon turned around radically and favorably, and there is no doubt that the Chávez government played a crucial role in the recovery. The last government of the ancien régime had come close to abandoning OPEC. PDVSA's publicly heralded policy to maximize volume in disregard of OPEC quotas and price objectives was a major cause of the 1998 oil price crisis. Even the Caldera government, which had shown little resistance to PDVSA initiatives, had to reverse its policy, and in its last months agreed to new OPEC quotas, but at home a weakened MEM was unable to impose them. Had it not been for the victory of Chávez, PDVSA would have been transformed into little more than a licensing agency, and the privatization of its subsidiaries would have been the inevitable outcome.

President Chávez and his oil minister, Alí Rodríguez Araque, reversed the policy of spurning OPEC quotas, and began to defend prices. Together with Mexico and Saudi Arabia, Venezuela successfully promoted a new understanding of quotas between OPEC members and other exporting countries. Venezuela also promoted and hosted in September 2000 the second summit meeting of OPEC heads of state. Prices recovered, with the gross proceeds from hydrocarbon exports peaking at $29.3 billion in 2000. However, price was only one aspect of oil problems confronting Chávez. His other task was to find a way to arrest the fall in fiscal revenues due to long-term structural and legal problems.

Regaining Control of the Nation's Natural Resources

As soon as Rodríguez Araque took over MEM in 1999, he began to implement a policy aimed at asserting control over natural resources and fiscal policy. Rodríguez Araque opposed the previous government's decision to leave the negotiation of upstream contracts to PDVSA. At the heart of the issue of formulation of fiscal policy is the question of royalty, which is the most secure form of revenue for the owners of natural resources (Mommer, 1999). The virtue of royalties is the ease with which they can be calculated, as there are only two variables involved: volumes and prices. Unlike in the case of income tax, royalties are immune to the manipulation of production costs. For that very reason PDVSA wanted the royalty scrapped; in its place it was willing to accept increased income tax rates on highly profitable fields (Espinasa, 1999). The problem with this proposal is that effective collection of income taxes is more difficult to achieve, especially for a state whose bureaucratic capabilities were declining. The Venezuelan government, as we have seen, was struggling just to measure and control volumes and prices. Although only partially successful, MEM, under the direction of Rodríguez Araque, began to monitor the volumes produced in some fields and rejected "transfer prices" (prices charged by PDVSA to its foreign affiliates) as the basis for calculating royalty payments. PDVSA was thus obliged to pay royalties on the basis of international market prices. However, the Ministry of Finance continued to accept transfer prices in calculating what the company had to pay in income taxes.

Under Rodríguez Araque, MEM also redesigned the terms of contracts for natural gas, which had been in preparation when the new government took over. A new Natural Gas Law, enacted in 1999, established a minimum royalty rate of 20 percent, and in practice rates reached as high as 32 percent. At the same time, this sector was completely opened up to private investors. A new Organic Law of Hydrocarbons, enacted in 2001—drafted by Álvaro Silva Calderón, who succeeded Rodríguez Araque as minister of energy and mines (Rodríguez Araque became secretary-general of OPEC)—establishes a minimum royalty rate of 30 percent for oil (with some downward flexibility to 20 percent for conventional oil, and to 16.5 percent in the case of extra-heavy oil). At the same time, the law lowers income tax on conventional crudes from 59 percent to 50 percent; for extra-heavy oil the tax rate remained at 32 percent. Overall, there is an increase in taxation based on the increase of royalty rates. The law also reserves for the state majority shareholding in any joint venture for exploration and production.

The new Hydrocarbons Law will apply only to new licenses, concessions, and contracts. Under existing arrangements, private companies will continue to pay less in royalties and taxes for access to Venezuela's highly profitable petroleum deposits than they pay for leases in marginal fields in the United States. Indeed, since 1993, even PDVSA pays less in royalties and taxes than do private oil companies in Alaska (Mommer, 2001a).

Controlling PDVSA

Under Rodríguez Araque and Silva Calderón, MEM hoped to force PDVSA to spend less and to pay more taxes. This goal was not easy to achieve. In late 2001, the ministry remained in the hands of officials belonging to two small parties, Patria Para Todos (PPT) and Movimiento Electoral del Pueblo (MEP). Their weak status was further eroded when both parties lost their small representation in the National Assembly in the general election of 2000. Hence the ministry lacked political support in the legislature, whereas PDVSA continued lobbying Chávez's Movimiento Quinta República (MVR; Fifth Republic Movement). In November 2000, PDVSA convinced the Committee of Energy and Mines of the National Assembly to declare publicly its intention to promote legislation in favor of lower royalty rates. This was the very day an enabling law was approved, according to which the government was authorized to do exactly the contrary—to raise royalties. The latter position prevailed at the governmental level, but it is unclear whether it will be defended in the National Assembly. PDVSA's president, General Guaicaipuro Lameda, publicly criticized the new Organic Law of Hydrocarbons for increasing royalties. In February 2002, President Chávez dismissed Lameda and appointed in his place Gastón Parra, a university professor with a strong nationalist background in line with MEM.

At first glance, the new constitution also appears to reinforce sovereign ownership of oil, but in reality the liberal agenda of PDVSA fared well in the Constituent Assembly. According to the new Bolivarian constitution, PDVSA, which is in reality a holding company, cannot be privatized, but this restriction does not apply to its affiliates. PDVSA, unlike its affiliates, does not produce a single barrel of oil. Most Venezuelans believe that the Bolivarian constitution has actually strengthened nationalization, but ironically it may have paved the road for the transformation of PDVSA into a liberal licensing agency for a private industry.

In the year 2000, costs and expenditures of the company increased by a staggering 44.6 percent as reported officially by PDVSA. This is mainly explained by the *apertura*'s operating services agreements with private companies, which were designed to be flexible enough to allow the company to produce very high-cost (and low-taxed) oil. PDVSA's costs now exceeded U.S.$10 per barrel. PDVSA also stuck to its old policy: whenever OPEC quotas discouraged investment of revenue in Venezuelan oil production, it was spent abroad. PDVSA continues to expand into the refining and retail business, but now all over Latin America and not just in the United States and Europe.

The two businesses of oil—the business of the investor, on the one hand, and the business of the natural resource owner, on the other—were easy to distinguish as long as the first was in the hands of foreign investors and the latter was vested in the government of the nation. Institutionally, MEM represented the latter. With nationalization in 1976 the two businesses became completely confused. If anything, nationalization required stricter and more clear-cut fiscal control on the part of the state, but the opposite happened. Fiscal control became more and more relaxed over the years, and control of the company by its single shareholder—the state— really never worked. The ministry wields no power of its own over the company because the president appoints all of its directors, who are peers of the minister of energy and mines. The only real shareholder is the president, with virtually no institutional or structural support.

PDVSA always advanced the same argument for relaxation of state control: the need to strengthen the national oil company, which was the pride of the nation, and to enhance its competitiveness. In fact, the company acted according to the maxim that it was always better to spend a dollar than to pay that dollar in taxes. Investment was a matter of principle, not a question of maximizing profits. Greater production at lower prices was always considered a better option than defending prices by limiting supply. Hence, PDVSA, contrary to its public claims, does not act as a commercial enterprise. It does not maximize profits (which might be converted into dividends for the government), but rather volumes all the way down the line, from production to refining, transport, and retail. Along the way it clears away profits from its Venezuelan accounts through the practice of "transfer pricing" (Boué, 2002).

To control PDVSA effectively again, the new Hydrocarbons Law requires the company to present accounts properly, separated according to its different activities. It should thus become evident where profits are made and where they are not, a sine qua non for any rational oil policy. PDVSA's opaque accounting methods are designed to hide discounts in transfer prices as well as deliberately inflated cost. For example, PDVSA transfers an important part of the costs of its internationalization program, including the service of its $10 billion debt, to its Caracas headquarters. In many ways PDVSA has even lost control over itself, most notably regarding its internationalization policy. The company has structured itself in the course of many years to prevent its shareholder (the state) from interfering. In doing so, it has made itself increasingly difficult to steer.

Conclusion

PDVSA turned its back on nationalization as early as 1983 with its policy of "internationalization." By 1989 it actually no longer claimed to be a national but a global company. Indeed, the gist of its message is that globalization requires elimination of national barriers to investments in the area of natural resources. As odd as it may seem, there is strong public support for this approach—whereby PDVSA aligns itself with the international oil companies and consumer countries—among Venezuelan professionals and the middle class in general. Until nationalization, it was clear to *all* Venezuelans that higher fiscal revenues in oil generated material well-being for the entire population. After nationalization, however, the validity of this thinking was questioned due to the appalling performance of the political and economic system. Hence, to bring PDVSA again under fiscal control may be much more difficult a task than one might imagine.

A large part of Venezuela's professional classes support PDVSA's reasoning that higher volumes are more important than defense of prices. Completely in the dark about oil policy (Baptista and Mommer, 1987), and under the influence of PDVSA's public relations department, these professionals are not likely to challenge the neoliberal logic. They seek a decent working environment in a modern (private) company and, of course, a decent salary, all of which the Fourth Republic was no longer able to offer. They do not believe that the Fifth Republic can offer it to them either. They thus believe that privatizing PDVSA would better their prospects. At a popular level, however, the outlook is quite different. The underprivileged sectors of the population fear that they will be excluded and left behind if the nation were to privatize the oil industry. Hence, oil policy has been caught up in the general process of polarization that characterized the country in early 2002.

The whole country has been spellbound since nationalization. One government after another has concentrated all of its attention on PDVSA and forgotten about the Ministry of Energy and Mines. One president after another has spent many hours in PDVSA; not one has set foot in MEM. The latter was progressively dismantled, and most of its best-qualified personnel were lured away to PDVSA. MEM has fallen prey to physical decay, its workers impoverished together with other public employees. PDVSA moved to fill the gap in the heyday of the petroleum *apertura* by paying a monthly bonus to employees of the ministry working in the hydro-carbon section (a continuing practice), effectively doubling their paltry salaries. Today the budget of PDVSA represents no less than 40 percent of public spending. PDVSA's financial leverage extends deep into the world of politics, journalism, and public opinion making in general, where people are easily convinced to work for PDVSA as part-time public relations consultants—not to speak of the international consultant companies that have established themselves in Caracas after the initiation of the petroleum *apertura* in 1989.

In short, PDVSA was transformed into a state within the state a long time ago, becoming more powerful the more the country became impoverished. Under the Chávez government this trend has been reversed; as a result, the country has made significant progress in recovering control over its most important natural resource. In achieving this goal, however, the government failed to win over PDVSA's top personnel. Today, company executives are no more willing to cooperate with the Fifth Republic than they were with the Fourth Republic.

These conclusions were fully confirmed by the April 2002 events in Venezuela. The failed coup left behind a highly fluid situation, and it left unsettled the ultimate fate of oil policy. Alí Rodríguez Araque, who at the time was serving as secretary-general of OPEC, agreed to take over the presidency of PDVSA as a candidate of a political consensus—at least as far as a political consensus was possible in Venezuela at that time. Rodríguez faced the task of carrying out a systematic reform of the oil sector for the first time since nationalization. The Chávez administration will have to demarcate the three roles of the state, politically and institutionally: the maximum representative of a sovereign nation, the owner of the natural resource, and the sole shareholder of the company. At the same time, it will have to define a new role for the private sector, national and foreign. Given the instability of Venezuelan politics, success remains very much in doubt.

8

State Reform Before and After Chávez's Election

Angel E. Alvarez

In 1999, President Hugo Chávez headed the effort to replace Venezuela's representative and party-based democracy shaped by the 1961 constitution with a new democratic political order defined as "social, just, participatory and protagonistic." In the final ten years of the Punto Fijo system the national political elite had experimented with political reform by attempting to decentralize political power and administration. However, decentralization failed to achieve the relegitimization of the old political system. Did the Chávez reforms promise to be more successful? What are the nature and long-term effects of the political changes introduced by the new constitution of the Bolivarian Republic of Venezuela? For some, the "Bolivarian revolution" was nothing more than a new type of Latin American populism (referred to as "neopopulism"), while others see it as a form of veiled "Castro-communism." Still others believe it to be more of a benevolent autocratic regime, with a strong and verbally populist leadership that is nonetheless neoliberal in practice. For Chávez himself, his government represented an innovative and unprecedented "process" of inventing a new democracy by creating new channels of popular participation in decision-making.

The principal fruit of the reform effort initiated in 1989 following the Caracazo was political decentralization, which permitted the political elite at state and local levels to formulate its own political agenda. This process had the potential to initiate even more profound changes in the party system and the state structure. Nevertheless, political decentralization failed to catapult local and state actors into a position of national authority where they would have had the power to challenge extreme centralization. Thus, in the 1993 elections, three major parties chose presidential candidates who became politically prominent as a result of their gubernatorial or mayoral administrations, namely Andrés Velásquez of Causa R, Claudio Fermín of Acción Democrática (AD), and Oswaldo Alvarez Paz of the Comité de Organización Política Electoral Independiente (COPEI). However, they did not succeed in defeating Rafael Caldera, one of the founding fathers of *puntofijista* democracy, whose triumph was due partly to the anti-neoliberal and antiparty thrust of his campaign. The same occurred in 1998, when Hugo Chávez, with an even more radically anti-neoliberal and antiparty discourse, defeated two candidates who had emerged from decentralization: Henrique Salas Römer (former governor of Carabobo) and Irene Sáez (former mayor of Chacao in Caracas). Finally, in the year 2000, Chávez confronted and defeated his former military ally, Francisco Arias Cárdenas, who had twice been elected governor of Zulia.

Under the Chávez presidency, Venezuela went from a representative democracy with strong party hegemony to a regime that sought to be innovative by creating new sources of decisionmaking power. This change occurred peacefully, with both popular and military backing, and through democratic and constitutional means. The transformations, however, certainly did not take place in the absence of acute conflict. Indeed, at times it appeared that Venezuelan democracy was on the verge of collapse, but it can be argued, as Daniel Levine and Brian Crisp have (1999), that such conflicts were part of the process of renovating the system.

Many efforts were made to ensure that the political system would evolve and not collapse. As president, Rafael Caldera attempted to alleviate the tensions created by the jailing of the leaders of the February 4, 1992, coup. Not only did his administration pardon coup leaders, restoring all their political rights and guaranteeing their state-paid retirement pensions, but it incorporated some of them into the government. Once Francisco Arias Cárdenas had his case dismissed in military court, Caldera appointed him president of the program for mother and infant nutrition (PAMI). From this position, he launched his candidacy for the governorship of Zulia, which he won in 1995 and again in 1998 with the backing of Causa R and COPEI.

The electoral triumph of Hugo Chávez in fair, open elections, as well as the subsequent bloodless sequence of political change, was largely possible thanks to a culture of conflict avoidance inherited from the Pact of Punto Fijo. Luis Miquelena and José Vicente Rangel, two members of the Chávez administration with broad experience in the style of political negotiation that made possible the 1958 democratic transition, were instrumental in the pacific process after 1998. President Chávez's discourse was aggressive, at times offensive (as was that of President Rómulo Betancourt, although the leader of AD was less colloquial), but during his first three years in office there was little sign of restricting public liberties or of political repression against the opposition. On the contrary, the government party, the Movimiento Quinta República (MVR; Fifth Republic Movement), established parliamentary pacts in order to augment governability, not only with allies on the left (the Movimiento al Socialismo [MAS] and the Patria Para

Todos [PPT]), but also with a party of the center-right (Proyecto Venezuela), in the style of the agreements between AD, COPEI, and smaller parliamentary forces that characterized the entire Punto Fijo period.

Contrary to what has occurred in other Latin American countries, the dilemma that confronted Venezuelan politics was not so much that of democracy versus authoritarianism. Rather the predominant issue was the type of democracy that should be constructed, while a near consensus existed at the national level over the validity of democracy, the necessity of carrying out institutional change, and the urgency of improving social equity. Nevertheless, as is common in situations in which new actors with unclear goals suddenly gain power, many political commentators did not discard the possibility that the end product of the Chávez "revolution" may be an authoritarian state.

Chávez's MVR maintained that the revolution it was spearheading was made necessary by the elites' failure to initiate institutional reforms. In order to examine the redesign of the state, I will concentrate on three dimensions that the MVR leadership considered key to the "political revolution": the "protagonistic," federal, and civil-military character of the nation's new democracy.

Critiques of Political Parties

The reduction of party influence in the political sphere and the establishment of new channels of direct participation in decisionmaking were banners that cut across the political spectrum before the rise of *chavismo* in 1998. Since the 1970s, the noncommunist left as represented by MAS had demanded more and better democracy in the form of participation from below. In the 1980s, various small but active social organizations (such as Queremos Elegir, Escuela de Vecinos, and Fiscales Electorales), as well as representatives of academic and business bodies tied to the economic elite (the Santa Lucía Group, the Roraima Group, and the Instituto de Estudios Superiores de Administración), called for limiting the role of political parties along with the nonpartisan supervision of elections and a single-member district electoral system at all levels.

In the 1990s, as demands for participation increased, academic and political experts formulated diverse proposals for political reform. Carlos Ayala Corao (1994: 108), for example, criticized Venezuela's representative democracy, and proposed extending the participatory arrangements of municipal government to the state and national levels. The practices he advocated included the legislative initiative, the consultative referendum, and the "sanctioning" or approval referendum for constitutional amendments. Shortly after the coup attempts of 1992, the president of the

Presidential Commission on State Reform (COPRE) wrote that the excesses of party interference in society and the state and the inadequacy of mechanisms for controlling elected officials had created a "political class" that was largely impervious to popular discontent (Blanco, 1993: 64–65). Ricardo Combellas, who was president of COPRE during the second Caldera administration (1994–1999) and who was later elected delegate to the National Constituent Assembly on the pro-Chávez ticket in 1999, put it this way:

> The Venezuelan constitutional system is formally representative. The challenge that confronts us is not only enforcing the constitution and making democracy more representative, but making it effectively participatory. The system's lack of representation can not be attributed to the Constitution, but rather political actors and parties. These actors had been widely accused of violating the principle of representation in order to further their interests. Their behavior is a perversion of the concept of the independence of the branches of public power. Extreme centralism and party discipline are expressions of their hegemonic control over civil society. (Combellas, 1994: 23)

According to one national survey carried out at the time of the two coup attempts of 1992, only 34 percent of the population actively defended political parties and believed they were essential for democracy and should take part in the accords to resolve the nation's political crisis. At the same time, 55 percent of Venezuelans believed that the best way to resolve the country's problems was to organize the population outside of the political party system. The vast majority of Venezuelans did not strongly identify with the party system (Njaim, Combellas, and Alvarez, 1998: 47–49).

The political elite failed to effectively confront this challenge (Combellas, 1994: 28–29). Congress thwarted or indefinitely postponed much proposed legislation that was designed to deepen the nation's democracy. Thus, for instance, the reform laws governing political parties and regulating campaign finance were tabled, as were two sets of all-encompassing reforms of the constitution. In sum, by the mid-1990s it became clear that political elites had stopped short of carrying out full-fledged state reform, even though they themselves had stressed its necessity over the previous ten years.

The *Partidocracia* in the 1961 Constitution

Some political scientists have characterized the Venezuelan democracy as essentially a party democracy, or *partidocracia* (Coppedge, 1993). The constitution of 1961 went a long way in promoting this model. Article 3 defined the Venezuelan government as "democratic, representative, responsible to the people and guaranteeing the rotation of elected public officials." Article 4 reinforced the purely representative character of democracy by confining the direct exercise of popular sovereignty mainly to suffrage. In short, with the exception of voting, all popular sovereignty was exercised at the intermediate level, with the party serving as an intermediary.

The 1961 constitution encouraged the formation of political parties and reserved them important areas of political activity. It established the principle of party equality before the law by ensuring the incorporation of all parties into the commissions that oversaw elections and avoiding their domination by any one party. The constitution stimulated the proliferation of parties by establishing proportional representation for all electoral organizations in both houses of Congress, as well as state legislatures and municipal councils.

The system established by the constitution for the appointment of high-level public functionaries reinforced the power of political parties. Congressional selection of Supreme Court justices, the attorney general, and the national comptroller was generally the product of high-level agreements between the major parties (AD and COPEI). During most of these years, AD and COPEI enjoyed an absolute majority in Congress and thus there was little need to consult smaller parties or the general populace. The judges of the Supreme Court were selected for nine years, three of them being chosen every three years. Thus the changes in the balance of power in the court corresponded to the balance of power in Congress. Congress also named the attorney general and the national comptroller every five years in the first thirty days of each constitutional period. The terms of these two functionaries coincided with those of the national executive and Congress; their appointments were among the first decisions made by each new legislature and were invariably the outcome of interparty negotiations.

In short, the *puntofijista* democracy was conducive to equilibrium and negotiation among the most important parties (AD, COPEI, and eventually MAS) at the national level. The system minimized competition among elites, and minimized popular participation even more.

"Protagonistic" Democracy in the 1999 Constitution

For large evils, large solutions. This was undoubtedly the motto of those who drafted the political chapters of the 1999 constitution. Venezuelan democracy appears to be have become less representative than that established by the 1961 constitution. The 1999 constitution defines Venezuelan democracy as "democratic, participatory, elective, decentralized, responsible to the people, pluralist, based on term limits for elected officials and with revocable mandates." The people *(el pueblo)* are the "protagonists" in public decisions through mechanisms of participation without the intermediation of elected representatives. This concept is embodied in the constitution's preamble, which calls for a "democratic, protagonist society."

In contrast to the party-dominated regime of the 1961 constitution, the new constitution stressed civil society and direct participation. The "Bolivarian" constitution even failed to make mention of political parties anywhere in the text. Instead, the document used the vague expression "associations with political ends," a phrase that lacks a tradition in Venezuelan politics and is without any theoretical basis in political science or public law. The use of the term undoubtedly revealed the aspiration of the *chavistas* to overcome political party hegemony.

The constitution reduced party influence in the naming of top public officials to the judicial branch, the "Citizen Power" (consisting of the attorney general, comptroller, and public defender), and the National Electoral Commission.[1] The constitution sought to keep these positions from being filled through the old arrangement of informal quotas among parties or other types of agreements, as occurred in the past at the congressional level. The quota system was replaced by a more complex system based on the participation of "civil society," which was to have an input in the newly created "Nominations Committees."

The twelve-year term established by the constitution for Supreme Court judges, which is greater than that of the National Assembly (five years) and of the president of the republic (six years), along with the elimination of reelection, reinforced the court's autonomy. The constitution called for the creation of a Judicial Nominations Committee to review judgeship candidates (some of whom were proposed by legal organizations) by taking into account "the opinion of the community" and then presenting a preliminary list to the Citizen Power for further consideration. A second selection was then to be presented to the National Assembly, which was to have the final say.

The system established by the constitution for designating judges and other top officials failed to get off to a good start. In 2000 a legislative committee of the Constituent Assembly known as the Congresillo, composed of members and sympathizers of Chávez's MVR, chose Supreme Court justices who were progovernment and who in many cases lacked the academic credentials and experience formally required by the constitution. A similar process occurred with the members of the National Electoral Commission. Following the suspension of the so-called megaelections in May 2000, the Congresillo briefly consulted the most important nongovernmental organizations (NGOs) in the country in order to make additional appointments in accordance with the spirit of the constitution, even though it did not adhere to the constitutional mechanisms for nominations.

The constitution called for the creation of a "Committee for Evaluating Nominations," composed of representatives of diverse social sectors, in order to provide for public scrutiny of the selection of the three positions of Citizen Power (attorney general, comptroller, and public defender). The committee was to submit a list of possible candidates to the National Assembly (the national congress) for final consideration. Ratification required the vote of two-thirds of the members of the National Assembly, and if this was not forthcoming the matter was to be decided upon in national elections.

None of this occurred, however, as the National Assembly opted for an alternative procedure. The constitution permitted the National Assembly to designate the members of the Citizen Power when the Evaluating Committee did not meet within a period determined by law. At the end of the year 2000, in the midst of an intense political and legal debate, the governing majority in the National Assembly proceeded to dictate the Nominations Law for the designation of the members of the Evaluating Committee. Considerable debate centered on the procedures for naming committee members. Congressmen belonging to the Justice-First Movement (Movimiento Primero Justicia) presented a bill in which the committee would be composed of representatives of different sectors of society,[2] but the National Assembly (with the support of the MVR, MAS, Proyecto Venezuela, and AD) ended up approving another proposal that was less participatory. In it, a Nominating Committee, consisting of fifteen national deputies and six civic representatives selected by the National Assembly itself, made selections on the basis of a simple majority. The committee was to engage in "consultations with the communities" through public forums known as "dialogue tables." This was the procedure used to choose the members of the Citizen Power as well as the Supreme Court in 2000. Thus the principle of direct participatory democracy was subordinated to that of representative democracy in the form of the National Assembly, considered in this case to be the vehicle of popular representation.

The Mechanisms of Popular "Protagonism"

The concept of the "protagonism" of the people was new and represented an essential part of the *chavista* doctrine. According to the 1999 constitution, "protagonism" manifests itself in various types of referendums (including one that allows for the removal of elected officials); public opinion polls; the legislative, constitutional, and constituent initiatives; the open municipal council *(cabildo abierto);* and the citizens assembly.[3] According to Giovanni Sartori (1997: 74–78), the use of polls and referendum in the formulation of policy is compatible with representative democracy. Nevertheless, the Constituent Assembly explicitly sought to go beyond that model and achieve a revolutionary transformation of the state that grants the people a "protagonistic" role. Indeed, President Chávez, on the day he presented his constitutional proposal to the Constituent Assembly, pointed out that his idea of participation was contrary to the logic of representative democracy, and that "protagonism" is an "eminently revolutionary concept" approaching direct democracy. Chávez added that in today's world democracy cannot be "absolutely direct," but "protagonistic" democracy is the form that comes closest to it (Asamblea Nacional Constituyente, 1999: 13).

In theory, the system of referendums to remove elected officials had two objectives: to force those who govern to respect the popular will, and to provide ways out of situations of extreme crisis of governability or legitimacy. Those who included the recall provision in the constitution sought to avoid two extremes. On the one hand, removal from office should not be so easy as to become a tool for political retaliation by the opposition, but on the other hand, its application should not be so difficult as to be unworkable in situations of crisis.

According to Article 72 of the new constitution, all popularly elected offices and judgeships are revocable in the second half of their electoral periods. The recall petition must have at least 20 percent of the registered voters in the electoral district and cannot be attempted more than once in the same term. Removal of the elected official requires an equal or greater number of votes than that which elected him in the first place and a turnout of at least 25 percent of registered voters. This requirement made officials who come to office in elections with a high rate of abstention especially susceptible to repeal. The stipulation protected the national government against the possibility of being easily removed as a result of political retaliation. Since abstention is historically higher at the local and state levels than at the national level (Molina and Pérez, 1999: 34–35), it would invariably be easier to repeal the election of a governor or mayor than that of the president. The latter would be susceptible to repeal only in situations of very intense crisis. Making it any easier to remove the national executive would have run the risk of undermining system stability.

Not only could the people remove elected officials, but gathered in an assembly, they could impose their will on the local, regional, and national governments. According to the constitution, the decisions reached by "assemblies of citizens" are binding. Legislation was required to define the specifics of this modality: the size of the assembly, its quorum, the procedures for convoking it, the location and time of its meeting, the decision-making rules, and the method of voting. At the same time that the system provided a mechanism for direct participation, it also ran the risk of facilitating elite manipulation of the decisionmaking process (Sartori, 1997: 75).

The intentions of some *chavistas* in making the proposal can be gleaned from public statements. Various leaders who belong to a left wing within the *chavista* movement (such as the former metropolitan police officer and mayor of Caracas, Freddy Bernal, and Iris Varela, national deputy from Táchira) favored modeling the assemblies after the Committees for the Defense of the Revolution in Cuba, even though both leaders stressed the "specificity of the Venezuelan process." This current within the MVR was at odds with a more institutional one headed by Minister of Interior Luis Miquilena, which favored working within existing structures. The opposition criticized the plan as part of an effort to monopolize all organizations in society in order to utilize them as instruments to achieve Chávez's political goals.

Finally, the constitution envisioned the "constituent power" as being supreme in that it overrode other branches of government. The people could convoke a national constituent assembly theoretically any time they judged it necessary, with the goal of transforming the state, creating a new legal order, and drafting a new constitution. Fifteen percent of registered voters sufficed for this initiative to be implemented. However, not only did the people, who were said to be its "trustees," have "constituent power," but various branches of the state did as well. The president could convoke a constituent assembly by issuing a decree in the Council of Ministers, while other branches had stiffer requirements. The National Assembly had to have the approval of two-thirds of its members and the municipal councils had to call a town meeting where two-thirds of those who attended voted in favor of the proposition. In short, the new constitution opened channels for direct participation at the same time that it enhanced the power of the national executive.

Federalism Versus Centralism

Political reforms in favor of decentralization in the late 1980s included the election of governors and the newly created figure of mayor. Decentralization provided political opportunities for parties that had previously never gone beyond being very small parliamentary minorities. MAS emerged as the primary political force in states such as Aragua, Lara, and Sucre, winning these governorships and strengthening its parliamentary representation. Causa R's most prominent leader, Andrés Velázquez, who barely received 2 percent of the votes in the 1988 presidential elections, went on to win the governorship of the state of Bolívar in 1989 and 1992. The following year he came close to winning the presidential elections. In fact, during this period the parliamentary representation of Causa R increased almost tenfold.

The direct election of mayors and governors stimulated the emergence of a new locally based "political class," which was more responsive to the voters than to national party leaders. From this class emerged nationally prominent politicians, including some who became important presidential candidates in the 1993, 1998, and 2000 elections. The performance of these leaders in local and state governments positioned them to run in national races. Decentralization, however, did not displace the coterie of national leaders who wielded overwhelming power in the political life of the nation.

One of the most important innovations of the 1999 constitution is the Consejo Federal del Gobierno (CFG), which was to plan and coordinate policies regarding decentralization. The CFG was presided over by the nation's vice president and consisted of all the ministers, governors, a mayor from each state, and representatives of civil society. The passage of legislation defining the CFG's powers was held up as a result of controversy, especially because of opposition from mayors and governors throughout the nation. The governors of the opposition led by Henrique Salas Feo of Carabobo sharply criticized the government's tendency to promote centralization.

The *chavistas* assumed two conflicting positions on the issue. On the one hand, National Deputy Alejandro de Armas, president of the National Assembly's Finance Committee, advocated tighter coordination between the legislative and executive branches and opposed centralized control of the budget assigned to local and statewide spheres. De Armas presented to the National Assembly a regional public finance bill that sought to confer financial autonomy to the states and grant them greater taxation powers. On the other hand, the nation's vice president, Adina Bastidas, presented an alternative CFG bill designed to reinforce the central government's control over expenditures.[4] This proposal would have rescinded legislation that both obliged the government to allocate a determined amount of money to state governments and stipulated that payments be made on a monthly basis. The Bastidas bill would have also eliminated the "Special Economic Allocations" laws in which the central government returns a percentage of the revenue derived from mining and petroleum activity to the respective states. Finally, the Bastidas bill intended to do away with the Fondo Intergubernamental para la Descentralización (FIDES), a government agency under the Ministry of the Interior that sets norms and negotiates projects designed by local and state governments. FIDES had promoted competition for resources based on projects formulated by local and regional governments that were independent of the central administration's plans for regional development. Over a period of time, the governors had attempted to strengthen FIDES, while the second Caldera and the Chávez presidencies pushed for greater national coordination of plans and projects. In short, the legislation on the CFG would likely determine whether the Chávez government would build on previous efforts of coordination between central, state, and municipal governments or would reverse the trend toward decentralization by creating new centralized structures.

Civilian-Military Relations

The failure of the nation's first democratic experiment led by AD between 1945 and 1948 was largely due to the failure to establish relations of subordination with the military officers who had been instrumental in allowing the regime to come to power. The ineffectiveness of the mechanisms used to resolve conflicts between AD and the military through negotiations led to the overthrow of President Rómulo Gallegos, even though his government enjoyed unprecedented popular support. A clandestine civilian-military coalition, which toppled the regime of General Marcos Pérez Jiménez on January 23, 1958, developed channels of communication and agreements that both parts could trust (Stambouli, 1980: 103–162). These understandings were later incorporated into the Pact of Punto Fijo and the 1961 constitution, and fed into the culture and style of political and military behavior that predominated until 1998 (Karl, 1996: 32–33).

Most important, the military after 1958 accepted the principle of the armed forces as an "apolitical, obedient, and non-deliberating institution." The military also agreed to a promotion system that obligated its members to regularly negotiate with the civilian elites. This arrangement, established in the 1961 constitution, granted the Senate the power to authorize the promotion of top military commanders (from the rank of colonel and naval captain up to general and admiral) whose names had been proposed by the president of the republic. As a consequence, the officers had to establish links of communication and usually demonstrate their loyalty to the nation's president, one of the major parties, and the members of the Senate's Defense Committee. The process included the elaboration of lists by the president and the senators and bargaining with officers, taking into account as much their professional merits as their commitment to democracy and the nation's main parties.

Civilians thus controlled the process of promotions. The principal advantage of the system was that it guaranteed regime stability at the same time that it encouraged a degree of professionalization of the armed forces. The most obvious drawback was the frequent exclusion of meritorious military officers who were not considered politically trustworthy or who had failed to cultivate the necessary personal relations. This defect in the system led to discontent within the institution, critiques, and even insubordination.

Chávez and his followers formulated three basic criticisms of military-civilian relations during this period: (1) a coterie of national party leaders along with the president disregarded the merits of individual officers in deciding promotions, in the process fomenting corruption and clientelism; (2) the nondeliberative role of the military and the denial of the military vote reduced political debate in the barracks to rumor and conspiracy; and (3) limiting the role of the military to national defense prevented many talented and capable officers from contributing to the tasks of national development. The new system established in the constitution granted the president the authority to promote officers above the rank of colonel or naval captain without congressional interference. President Chávez himself originally proposed this arrangement in his first constitutional draft presented to the Constituent Assembly.

The old system of negotiations among the major political parties, the armed forces, and the national executive was thus replaced by a system that enhanced the power of the president. As a result, new problems threatened to emerge:

1. Since the president was a party leader, military promotions ended up in the hands of a single political group. In this way, the system promoted alliances between the national executive and the armed forces that bypassed the minority parties in the National Assembly.
2. Officers seeking promotion were left to the mercy of superior officers without the possibility that representatives of other institutions would intervene on their behalf.
3. Military officers who were critical of the government were more easily excluded from promotion since Congress did not ratify the president's decisions.

Conclusion: The Revolution at the Crossroads

In the eyes of Venezuela's new political class and its followers, a revolutionary process was taking place in the nation. The "Bolivarian revolution," however, was not at all completely original, nor was the process of change linear. Indeed after three years in power, it faced risks.

The first of these was the precariousness of the legal order. Under the sway of the doctrine of "juridical transience," which allegedly prevailed while the new order awaited full implementation, the MVR-dominated Constituent Assembly, and the National Assembly after it, attempted to justify suspending aspects of the new legal system established by the constitution. This argument applied to the procedures to designate the members of the judicial, citizen, and electoral branches of government; the form in which certain electoral norms have been modified; and the way in which the parties, including the MVR itself, selected their own candidates in violation of the constitutionally established system of direct internal elections.

The legitimacy of the actions of the government and the Constituent Assembly rests not so much on the law but on the sovereign character of the people from whom the president allegedly received a mandate. The multiple elections carried out in Venezuela after 1998 took on a plebiscite-like character to the extent that they were perceived of as a vote in favor of or against President Chávez. Indeed, in each campaign, the president and his backers were at the center of debate. Even his adversaries contributed to this process. Few political actors based their arguments exclusively on the pros and cons of specific issues, but rather stressed their support for or opposition to Chávez.

The new constitution strengthened the position of the president, not only through the substantial powers it conferred on him, but through the provisional powers he could request from the National Assembly to allow him to legislate by decree on all matters for up to a year.[5] The president made use of this prerogative in order to approve decrees with legal standing in areas as diverse as finance and banking, landownership, and social security. Subsequently, Chávez announced the possibility of decreeing a state of emergency for socioeconomic reasons, which would have increased his powers even further.

President Chávez reached power with the backing of several parties and independents ranging from the moderate to radical left. This heterogeneous, if unstable, coalition continued during Chávez's first three years in office. The extent to which it survived was due to the emotional discourse that identified political corruption, represented by the traditional political parties, the Catholic Church, the union and business leaderships, and the communications media, as the cause of the moral, institutional, and economic degradation of the nation.

The MVR did not escape the tendency to become institutionalized. During the first three years of the Chávez government, the MVR's leadership at national, state, and local levels was strengthened, with Luis Miquilena playing a key role. As Steve Ellner discusses in Chapter 9, Miquilena favored MVR participation within existing structures, such as the Venezuelan Confederation of Workers. The institutionalization envisioned by Miquilena converted the MVR into a power broker, but recognized the right of other political parties to benefit from participation within the public sphere. Nevertheless, in 2001, Chávez denounced the bureaucra-

tization of the MVR and announced the decision to relaunch the
Movimiento Bolivariano Revolucionario 200 (MBR-200). These moves
pointed to the intention of impeding further institutionalization out of fear
that it would prevent the deepening of the revolution. Nevertheless, in the
medium term, a new form of political institutionalization was likely to
emerge leading to the routinization of Chávez's charisma and the surfacing
of new forms of political and social organization. But personalistic tendencies threatened to predominate, in which case what began as a revolution in
pursuit of a new form of democracy ran the risk of approximating autocra-
cy. With the exit of Miquilena from the MVR and the government in
January 2002, the incipient steps toward institutionalization evidently came
to a halt, thus placing in doubt the future direction of the movement.

Notes

This chapter was translated from the Spanish by Deborah Norden.

1. The 1999 constitution broke with the tripartite division of public powers by
creating two additional branches: the "Citizen Power" and the "Electoral Power"
(consisting of the National Electoral Commission and the Electoral Chamber of the
Supreme Court).

2. The proposed law provided the following sectors of civil society with input
into the selection process: the law schools of national universities; the presidents of
national business organizations; the presidents of trade union confederations; the
peasant federation; the presidents of organizations representing the media; the
National Council of Churches; members of the indigenous communities; the governors; the mayors; the cultural sector; the Venezuelan Teachers Federation; the
Federations of University Students; and NGOs concerned with legal activity.

3. Municipal legislation in 1989 established the consultative referendum, the
initiative, and the system of recall for mayors. The Bicameral Committee for the
Revision of the Constitution, presided over by Rafael Caldera in 1992, planned the
extension of these practices to all elected officials. The proposal for the system of
recall in 1992 was seen by some as an instrument to remove President Carlos
Andrés Pérez by constitutional means. This perception undoubtedly contributed to
the obstruction of Caldera's entire reform effort. The phrase "removal from office"
was not even used in the 1992 proposal, but rather the euphemism "evaluation of
mandate."

4. Vice President Bastidas introduced legislation in which the CFG consisted
of the vice president, the fourteen ministers, twenty-three governors, twenty-three
mayors (one from each state), and six representatives of civil society.

5. The 1961 constitution also made possible presidential assumption of
extraordinary powers in the areas of economic and financial legislation. However,
since 1974 almost all presidents have been granted this special authority, including
Chávez himself in 1999, on matters that went beyond the strictly economic sphere.

9

Organized Labor and the Challenge of *Chavismo*

Steve Ellner

Other chapters in this book trace the steady loss of credibility of Venezuela's political institutions and particularly political parties since 1980. Economic contraction combined with flagrant corruption to undermine regime legitimacy in the 1980s, a trend that was aggravated when Presidents Carlos Andrés Pérez (1989–1993) and Rafael Caldera (1994–1999) disregarded their electoral programs by embracing neoliberal formulas. Venezuela's political party system went from three decades of stability to volatility in the 1990s and then collapsed following the election of Hugo Chávez in 1998. This 180-degree change was unmatched in other Latin American nations, which lacked Venezuela's democratic longevity and tradition of well-institutionalized parties.

The loss of prestige of the Venezuelan labor movement over the same period is not surprising given its close ties with the nation's increasingly discredited traditional parties. Formerly, political analysts characterized the Confederación de Trabajadores de Venezuela (CTV; Confederation of Venezuelan Workers) as a major pillar of the political system since the organization's founding in 1936 and as an interlocutor, not only for organized workers, but also for popular sectors in general (Collier and Collier, 1991: 251–270; Ellner, 1993: 102). This historical behavior was demonstrated by the two most important strikes in the nation's history, both in the oil industry—the strike of 1936–1937, which unified the entire nation in opposition to the "imperialist" oil companies; and that of 1950, aimed at overthrowing the military government of Marcos Pérez Jiménez. In 1980 the CTV again went beyond the bread-and-butter concerns of its members with its proposal for the reorganization of society under the slogan of "Workers Participation" *(Cogestión)*. And in May 1989 the CTV linked up with the lower classes, which had taken part in the massive disturbances of the week of February 27, by calling a general strike against the neoliberal program of Carlos Andrés Pérez.

During the 1990s the CTV narrowed the focus of its concerns and moderated its positions related to social benefits and economic transformation. At the same time, its natural constituency shrank, and the informal economy, which was largely outside of the union fold, steadily grew (see Chapter 3). The CTV failed to reach beyond the organized working class by defending the interests of this lower stratum of the population. For instance, the CTV accepted the privatization of the health system, which essentially legalized the practice of providing the poor, who lacked insurance coverage or ability to pay, with second-class treatment in public hospitals. In another concession to neoliberal formulas, the CTV dropped its opposition to changes in the system of job severance payments and approved a reform that in effect reduced the large sums of money companies had to pay employees when they left their jobs. Finally, the CTV virtually abandoned its *Cogestión* proposal without replacing it with another all-encompassing strategy for change, thus putting in evidence the confederation's short-term approach and its loss of interest in societal transformation.

Given these retreats from defense of worker interests, the CTV could but timidly react to the hostile posture assumed by Hugo Chávez, who characterized it as a corrupted pillar of an undemocratic Punto Fijo system. In the face of threats including the confiscation of union property, the CTV leadership attempted to "cover its back" by drafting new statutes conceding many of the internal democratic reforms it had long resisted (personal interview with Alfredo Ramos, Causa R presidential candidate, Caracas, September 26, 2000). In December 1999, President Chávez sought a mandate via referendum for the radical restructuring of the labor movement. CTV leaders opposed the referendum on grounds that it was unconstitutional and violated internationally recognized norms. Even though the abstention rate was 77 percent, CTV leaders abided by the results and immediately stepped down from their posts.

Chavista union leaders, however, were unable to take advantage of the vulnerability of their CTV adversaries. As a result, the CTV regained the initiative in 2001 by promoting strikes among steel and oil workers, teachers, and public employees. At the same time the confederation organized internal elections to select members of its executive board and those of affiliate unions. The pro-*chavista* labor leaders failed to strengthen their position in the electoral process by organizing large numbers of workers who were outside the union fold. This feeble response reflected the *chavista* movement's organizational weakness, which, as María Pilar García-Guadilla shows in Chapter 10, cut across the entire spectrum of civil society. Like other groups in civil society, the *chavista* labor movement was held back by the dilemma of whether to defend President Chávez unconditionally and reap benefits from his widespread popularity or to develop an autonomous movement and put forward critical positions.

The CTV's Response to Neoliberal Policies of the 1990s

Even though labor movements throughout the rest of the continent were forced on the defensive in the 1990s, many of them maintained critical positions toward government policy. In contrast, the CTV abandoned its traditional stands. At the outset of the decade, the behavior of the CTV invited comparisons among political analysts with Argentina's Confederación General de Trabajadores (CGT; General Confederation of Workers), which was also controlled by a pro–social democratic governing party. The CTV was initially more militant in its opposition to the market reforms of the Pérez administration than was the CGT to Carlos Menem's policies (Murillo, 1997). By 1996, however, the CTV had followed Acción Democrática (AD) into its tacit alliance with the pro-neoliberal Caldera administration without any significant or forceful objections on the part of top party labor leaders. The CGT leaders, on the other hand, became increasingly critical of the government's proposed labor reform, which included the sharp reduction of severance payments; eventually a sizable hard-line faction split off from the confederation. In Brazil, Uruguay, Chile, and Colombia, labor confederations with considerable worker backing also adamantly opposed neoliberal programs.

The AD-dominated CTV reacted to the neoliberal program unveiled by Carlos Andrés Pérez upon assuming the presidency by calling a general strike on May 18, 1989. The work stoppage was the first time since the overthrow of Pérez Jiménez in 1958 that labor completely paralyzed economic activity in order to make a political statement. CTV leaders pledged themselves to additional protests, and indeed organized a more limited one in February of the following year, but after that they avoided mobilizations. Pérez's defenders (Naím, 1993; Naím and Francés, 1995) blame the CTV, along with other neocorporatist institutions such as the business organization Fedecámaras, for blocking market reforms. In fact, the CTV's opposition to Pérez's economic program lost momentum and ended up as purely rhetorical. Thus shortly prior to Pérez's removal from office, AD labor congressmen closed ranks with other party members by voting against a proposed censure of the government's neoliberal policies. Only the more independent AD leader José Beltrán Vallejo of the CTV's executive committee walked out of the congressional session prior to the vote. President Pérez checked the efforts of Vallejo to preside over the CTV, and indeed in subsequent years he was isolated within the AD bloc of the confederation's executive committee.

During the succeeding period of President Caldera (1994–1999), AD fashioned an unofficial alliance with the government in support of its neoliberal "Venezuela Agenda," and the CTV largely followed suit. Many political commentators, including leftist ones, applauded the CTV's inclusion in a tripartite commission to draw up important labor legislation, since it provided labor with input and was thus contrary to Pérez's nonconsultative "shock treatment" approach to neoliberalism. The CTV, however, paid a heavy price for its participation in the commission. The CTV's critics, particularly Causa R and the *chavista* movement, assailed the confederation's leadership not only for having accepted unpopular measures related to the "Venezuela Agenda," but also for having helped draft them in the first place.

The two key pieces of legislation drawn up by the commission transformed the severance payment and social security systems. The laws, which were promulgated in 1997, prioritized wages over worker security and favored well-paid workers at the expense of low-income ones, including members of the informal economy. In essence, the severance pay reform undermined the system's fundamental objective of providing workers with a large sum of money to help them cope with lengthy periods without formal employment. Most important, the reform eliminated what was referred to as "retroactivity" (which had no equivalent anywhere on the continent), in which severance payment was determined by the worker's last salary and the number of years at work. In effect, retroactivity served as a hedge against inflation. In contrast, the 1997 reform calculated worker severance pay on the basis of each month's salary. Following the passage of the reform, employers began to pay employees their severance payments at the end of each year, rather than wait until workers left their jobs (a practice formerly limited to small, nonunion firms). The workers, all too eager to receive payments in order to complement their salaries and fearful that inflation would erode the value of their accumulated severance payments, gladly accepted the practice. In those cases in which the company set the worker's money aside to be drawn when he or she left the firm, the 1997 reform granted the employee the right to withdraw up to 75 percent at a time for certain contingencies. In practice, workers were given authorization to make these withdrawals on a regular basis and thus they were left with virtually nothing at the time of layoff. In short, by gutting severance payments of their retroactivity, the reform defeated the system's very purpose by converting it into a veritable annual bonus.

The nation's privately run social security system enacted under Caldera favored workers whose salary far exceeded minimum wage. All workers deposited a percentage of their salary in an "individual pension fund" in their own name as well as in a "solidarity fund" for those whose retirement benefits did not reach minimum standard. Nevertheless, unlike the "mixed system" as practiced in Uruguay and elsewhere, low-paid workers could not draw money from both funds simultaneously and thus were to receive the very minimum amount set by law. The term "solidarity" was also misleading, since workers of the informal economy (even better-paid ones) received little incentive to form part of the system.

The CTV's failure to defend viable alternatives to neoliberal policies, as shown by its positions on severance payment and social security, undermined the confederation's image during the 1990s. One survey, which measured public confidence in twelve major institutions, placed organized labor in tenth place, behind the military, the neighborhood movement, the police, the private sector, the courts, and the Catholic Church (Fundación Pensamiento y Acción, 1996). Six negative aspects of the behavior of CTV leaders contributed to the confederation's loss of prestige:

1. *Failure to consult the rank and file over key issues.* Causa R's demand that the proposed modifications in the severance payment system be submitted to workers in a referendum went unheeded. In addition, various labor leaders insisted that the tripartite commission be enlarged to include the church and professional organizations and that the CTV itself call a special general council to discuss the issue (Urquijo, 2000: 81). Some CTV leaders who defended the 1997 reform subsequently recognized that the confederation had committed a grave error in not opening a debate within the movement in order to win the workers over to the proposed changes (personal interview with Rodrigo Penso, CTV executive committee member, Caracas, July 11, 2001).

2. *Abandonment of mobilization strategy.* Following the initial protests against Pérez's economic program, occasional threats of CTV leaders to launch a nationwide work stoppage failed to go beyond words. The CTV, for instance, refused to support a nationwide *paro cívico* (civic strike) called on August 27, 1991, against the government's economic policies on grounds that it had not been formally invited to participate. Instead it announced that it was organizing demonstrations of its own on September 25, but the protests were never held.

3. *Acceptance of a series of concessions that whittled away historical worker benefits.* For years, the CTV leadership refused to even discuss modification of the retroactive feature of severance payment, even though the major parties, including AD, the Comité de Organización Política Electoral Independiente (COPEI), and the Movimiento al Socialismo (MAS), had favored changing the system since the early 1990s. The CTV reaffirmed its position at its 1995 congress, but by January of the following year the confederation reached a tentative agreement with Fedecámaras in the tripartite commission to eliminate retroactivity. The CTV placed three conditions on its abandonment of retroactivity: a cost-of-living clause for wages, the right of each worker to choose between the old and new severance pay system, and the implementation of an effective social security sys-

tem to replace the highly deficient one then in effect. Nevertheless, the final agreement of the tripartite commission made public in a nationally televised ceremony with President Caldera did not contain any of the three stipulations. CTV leaders expressed satisfaction at the promises of business spokesmen that elimination of retroactivity would lead to higher wages and more employment, but neither of the two proved forthcoming. The tripartite commission's agreement on social security did include a fundamental CTV demand: the establishment of a "solidarity fund" providing low-paid workers with more than the bare minimum established by law. Even though Congress weakened this provision by fixing solidarity contributions to very low sums, the CTV placed its stamp of approval on the new law anyway (personal interview with León Arismendi, secretary-general of the CTV's Junta de Conducción, Caracas, July 11, 2001).

    4. *Adherence to party dictates rather than developing an independent position on labor-related issues.* Katrina Burgess argues that in Latin America and Europe neoliberal policies implemented or endorsed by social democratic parties put the party loyalty of labor leaders to the test. Burgess (1999: 131) calls the CTV's position a "balancing act" in which the confederation tried to maintain credibility among the workers but at the same time "remain in the good graces of the party." Burgess and others (Murillo, 2000: 154; 2001: 52–91) posit a correlation between the degree to which the social democratic labor leaders such as those of AD vied with other forces for control of organized labor and their autonomy vis-à-vis their own party. According to these scholars, the more intense the rivalry within the labor movement, the more its leaders are inclined to be critical of neoliberal reforms. Although the CTV is often viewed as "pluralistic" with broad political party representation, in fact AD hegemony was never seriously threatened (Ellner, 1993: 54). At the 1995 CTV congress, for instance, AD's delegate strength declined slightly, but the party maintained its dominant position while providing smaller parties a few additional posts in the confederation's internal structure. In accordance with Burgess's thesis of interparty rivalry within organized labor, the comfortable control exercised by AD union leaders in the labor movement obviated the necessity of confronting the party over its neoliberal policies in order to retain worker support.

    5. *Lack of a consistent line or analysis of such all-encompassing policies and trends as neoliberalism and globalization.* In some instances, the CTV defended Venezuelan capital and insisted on stringent conditions for the foreign takeover of privatized companies. In 1998, for instance, the CTV insisted on freezing plans to privatize the aluminum industry in order to ensure that national metal-mechanic companies receive a steady supply of aluminum and that national interests in general be guaranteed. The CTV leaders, however, had previously met with representatives of the Inter-

national Monetary Fund (IMF) and publicly committed themselves to a Venezuelan-IMF agreement, which included plans for mass privatization. Subsequently, they discussed the matter with the president of the Venezuelan Investment Fund (FIV) in charge of privatization and called for lifting the freeze. In general, the CTV failed to speak out against foreign penetration of sectors such as retail, finance, cement, paint, restaurants, and gasoline stations, nor did it put forward a critical analysis of Caldera's "Venezuela Agenda."

6. *Resistance to internal reforms designed to strengthen and democratize the movement.* While the nation's democratic impulse led to the implementation after 1989 of reforms sponsored by the Presidential Commission on State Reform (COPRE), organized labor was left largely behind. AD leaders opposed the Law of Trade Union Democracy sponsored by COPEI and Causa R (and supported by MAS), which called for direct rank-and-file elections of the executive committee members of the CTV and its affiliate federations. AD theoretically accepted direct elections for the federations, but on the eve of the CTV's 1995 congress negotiated an agreement with Carlos Navarro (the confederation's future secretary-general and member of COPEI) to put off the process until 2000. Furthermore, even though the CTV's 1990 congress highlighted the need to overcome fragmentation by centralizing the trade union structure (a goal that was facilitated by the new Labor Law promulgated in the same year), ten years later no national unions existed outside the public employees sector.

Structural changes related to globalization further weakened the position of organized labor. Partial or total privatization of such sectors as telecommunications, ports, oil, steel, and airlines after 1989 reduced the size of the strategically located work force and transferred ownership to foreign capital. Following privatization, unions could no longer channel their demands and grievances through political parties, nor could they insist on union privileges that did not strictly conform to the law in the area of union hiring, special job security for union officials, check-off of union dues, and other privileges (Ellner, 1999c: 133–134). The practice of outsourcing, which became widespread in the oil, metal-mechanic, and textile industries, and the growth of the informal economy, whose workers were hard to organize, further weakened the position of organized labor.

The declining influence of organized labor reflected itself in the structural reorganization of political parties, and AD in particular. Previously AD's Labor Bureau and Peasant Bureau chose labor leaders for top positions in party slates at all levels on a regular basis. Beginning in the early 1990s, five other party bureaus, including several newly created ones designed to represent the emerging civil society, competed with labor in placing their members on slates. Due to the loss of their party prerogatives,

AD labor leaders failed to gain practically any representation in the national congress in the December 1993 elections for the first time in fifty years (Ellner, 1996b: 97). Simultaneously, Causa R replaced AD as the only party with a significant number of trade unionists in elected positions.

The Chávez Presidency and the CTV Elections

For the first two years of Chávez's presidency, the CTV was on the defensive. The government reduced state subsidies to organized labor to a bare minimum at the same time that it threatened to dissolve the existing union structure. The CTV reacted in April 1999 by calling its Fourth Extraordinary Congress in order to democratize its internal electoral process. The Congress approved new statutes that included such far-reaching measures as direct rank-and-file election for the CTV's executive committee, automatic affiliation of all unions legalized by the Ministry of Labor, incorporation of organizations of retired workers and professional associations, worker referendums to approve contracts and remove union officials, and the elimination of political party domination of the confederation's electoral commission. Later that year, CTV leaders stated they would consider the possibility that union elections be supervised by the state's National Electoral Commission (CNE) in order to guarantee impartiality. In another major move designed to improve labor's image, the Federation of Oil Workers (Fedepetrol) renounced the highly criticized practice of union hiring of 60 percent of all oil workers, which over the years had bred corruption and clientelism.

By 2001 the CTV leadership had consolidated itself, established accepted rules for the organization, and assumed a more aggressive posture toward the government. The flexibility of AD labor leaders and the concessions they granted made possible their reemergence as important actors in 2001 and the formidable challenge they posed to the government (personal interview with León Arismendi, Caracas, July 11, 2001). Immediately following the December 2000 national referendum, which forced federation and confederation leaders to temporarily step down from office, prominent CTV leaders belonging to AD withdrew from national politics and union affairs. Of particular importance was the resignation of CTV president Federico Ramírez León and César Gil, the head of the confederation's collective bargaining department, both of whom had long been accused of unethical conduct. AD leaders Carlos Ortega and Manuel Cova, who ran as CTV president and secretary-general respectively, had merits of their own, not merely party endorsement. Ortega, president of Fedepetrol, had forcefully insisted that oil workers' unions renounce hiring rights and then gained national prominence for leading a successful strike in early 2001 against the state oil company, Petróleos de Venezuela, Sociedad Anónima (PDVSA). He had also successfully opposed application of the new severance pay system to the oil workers. Cova, the president of the construction workers, had close ties with the rank and file. Cova, however, was also widely accused of corrupt dealings stemming from union hiring practices, and indeed his initial aspiration to run as CTV president was staunchly opposed by fellow party trade unionists. Ortega, Cova, and other AD trade unionists ran as candidates on the ticket of the allegedly nonpartisan Frente Unitario de Trabajadores (FUT; United Workers Front) in order to appeal beyond their party.

Over the decades, CTV leaders had generally asserted a degree of independence from AD whenever it was in the opposition, but now their survival depended upon the confederation distancing itself from the party. During the December 2000 municipal elections, held simultaneously with the referendum on organized labor, the CTV called on workers to abstain, in contrast to AD, which urged voters to go to the polls to defeat the proposition and vote for its candidates. Following the referendum, the established labor leadership set up "Juntas de Conducción" to run the CTV and its federations until new elections were held. These juntas generally excluded top AD and COPEI leaders closely linked to the party and widely accused of corrupt practices. Many juntas were led by non-AD members and, in some cases (as in the CTV itself), by someone who was on the fringes of the labor movement. Subsequently, the Juntas de Conducción incorporated representatives of many different parties, including the former guerrilla party Bandera Roja and Causa R, which until then had refused to form part of the CTV's leadership. Causa R leaders justified their change of policy on grounds that the CTV had accepted their party's long-standing demand for direct rank-and-file elections for the confederation's national leadership. Rodrigo Penso, who had represented MAS in the CTV's executive committee, stressed the broad representation of the juntas and the absence of party control, stating that "for the first time CTV pluralism is no longer a myth but a reality" (personal interview with Rodrigo Penso, Caracas, July 11, 2001).

A moderate current within the *chavista* movement, represented by Reina Sequera of the health workers and supported by Interior Minister Luis Miquilena, favored participation in the CTV elections. They argued that the confederation's concessions in favor of internal democracy opened up the possibility of gaining control of the organization by electoral means. They also pointed out that the CTV was the main national interlocutor of several million workers, and that AD had lost its absolute grip over the confederation (personal interview with Luis Miquilena, Caracas, March 29, 2000). Pro-Chávez labor leaders who defended this position entered into discussions with Causa R over support for a united slate headed by Alfredo

Ramos (that party's former presidential candidate) as CTV president. In an attempt to secure backing from the *chavistas,* Ramos pledged himself to changing the CTV's name, calling a national workers assembly to unify and transform the entire labor movement, and supporting the inclusion of all workers of the formal economy in CTV elections. In some unions (such as the oil workers' federation, Fedepetrol), Chávez's followers and Causa R supported common candidates in the CTV's elections of 2001.

Nicolás Maduro, head of the Bolivarian Workers Force (FBT), which grouped *chavista* labor leaders, defended a second line that pointed in the direction of forming parallel unions. At one point, Maduro argued that "either we construct a force for real transformation or we stay in the CTV" (*El Nacional,* April 30, 2001, www.el-nacional.com). He went on to claim that the CTV had inflated its membership statistics, which in fact were far under 1 million. The FBT accused CTV unions of drawing up electoral lists behind closed doors and insisted that the entire electoral process be supervised by the National Electoral Commission (CNE), as required by the nation's constitution (in its Article 293). FBT leaders also pointed out that the CTV failed to make good on its promise to open its doors to retired workers, and that (in opposition to the CNE's criteria) the confederation opted for the old electoral system based exclusively on slates. Maduro coincided with the Communist-led United Workers Confederation (CUTV) on the need to rely on the backing of the national congress and executive in order to revamp the labor movement. CUTV president Pedro Eusse described this strategy as "simultaneously counting on political support from above and the workers from below" (personal interview with Pedro Eusse, Caracas, July 10, 2001).

Maduro and other hard-liners at times considered the possibility of participating in the CTV elections should the nation's electoral authorities (the CNE) guarantee its fairness. Nevertheless, Maduro insisted that the goal of "returning the Confederation to its members" in the form of a national workers assembly (which the *chavistas* called a "Workers Constituent Assembly") take precedence over discussion of actual names of candidates (personal interview with José Khan, national labor leader of the Movimiento Quinta República [MVR; Fifth Republic Movement], Caracas, April 20, 1999).

The hard-liners, who favored passing over the existing CTV structure, were reacting to the confederation's declining prestige and influence over the previous decade. Unlike Causa R, with its working-class orientation, many *chavistas* (including Chávez himself) displayed a certain distrust of organized labor per se (Blanco Muñoz, 1998: 392). They spoke of the need to discipline the labor movement, a goal best achieved by replacing the entire CTV bureaucracy. The impulse to form separate labor organizations, rather than engage in the drudgery of working within unions controlled by adversaries, was also a reflection of inexperience. Indeed, while a number of *chavistas* were veteran politicians, this was not the case with the *chavista* worker movement. These relatively young labor leaders did not participate in the labor movement of the 1960s, when the decision of the left to form parallel unions isolated it from the vast majority of organized workers, who belonged to CTV organizations. On the other hand, the young *chavista* labor leaders assimilated the apparent lesson of the 1990s that intransigence paid off and that once a party began making deals and entering into alliances for the sake of gaining positions (as Causa R did after 1995), it lost popularity and credibility.

The FBT avoided creating a formal structure and instead placed a premium on continuous discussion and consensus, practices that the Bolivarian movement sought to initiate throughout its history (see Chapter 4). The FBT leadership consisted of a committee of coordinators who were allegedly chosen on the basis of experience and general recognition, but whose undisputed head was Nicolás Maduro. The FBT created organizations in each state known as "Regional Workers Councils," whose members were chosen in worker assemblies. Following the December 2000 referendum, some of these councils decided to occupy the headquarters of the CTV-affiliate federation in their respective states in order to provide it with leadership until new elections were held. Nevertheless, aware that these actions were widely repudiated for being anarchical and that the loose structure of the *chavista* movement had encouraged spontaneity, the FBT refused to approve the takeovers (personal interview with Rubén Molina, FBT international relations coordinator, Caracas, July 9, 2001).

The vacillations of *chavista* trade unionists with regard to their policy toward the CTV, as well as their lack of an ongoing strategy, explain their failure to capitalize on the defensive position of the CTVistas during the first two years of Chávez's rule. The *chavista* trade unionists who were delegates to the Constituent Assembly from the outset attempted to pass a resolution dissolving the CTV and convoking a national assembly of workers to "refound" the labor movement. The proposal sought to apply the above-mentioned strategy of combining political initiatives from above with rank-and-file actions from below. The Constituent Assembly, in its final weeks of existence, issued several decrees designed to revamp the labor movement. One ordered government authorities to investigate the income of union officials and another called for worker elections to replace labor representatives on the board of directors of state companies. Neither the government nor the FBT actively pursued these matters. Then in 2000, *chavista* labor leaders began collecting signatures for a referendum on the CTV, but falling short of the required number, they left the matter in the hands of Congress. *Chavista* labor leaders in Congress favored a referendum that would have dissolved the CTV, but the final wording approved in

Congress did not go beyond the temporary removal of federation and confederation officials. Following the referendum, the CTV's new leadership
agreed to participate with the FBT in a worker assembly to unify all labor
organizations into one new confederation, but the *chavistas* failed to hold
the CTVistas to their word. Pressure from abroad, particularly from the
International Labour Organization (ILO), which censured the Venezuelan
government for violating international agreements on labor liberty, forced
the *chavistas* to refrain from taking drastic measures against the CTV.

On October 25, 2001, the CTV carried out direct, rank-and-file elections for the confederation's national leadership, a system with few equivalents in the labor movement throughout the world. During the campaign,
the *chavista* candidates, headed by Aristóbulo Istúriz (former mayor of
Caracas and a member of the Patria Para Todos [PPT] party), pledged
themselves to defend the social reforms embodied in the 1999 constitution,
including return to the old system of state-run social security and severance
payments based on retroactivity. Carlos Navarro (former CTV secretary-
general who had recently resigned from COPEI) represented the opposite
extreme in that he stressed the advantages of globalization and "modernization." Other candidates for the CTV presidency included Alfredo Ramos
(of Causa R) and Carlos Ortega of the FUT (supported by AD, COPEI, the
far-leftist Bandera Roja, and the Union Party of Chávez's former ally
Francisco Arias Cárdenas).

The electoral contests were marred by widespread disturbances, accusations of fraud and other irregularities, and an abstention rate estimated at
between 50 and 70 percent. Indeed, the elections for the all-important
Fedepetrol were so disruptive that no definitive results were announced.
Furthermore, the elections for the CTV leadership were postponed in the
oil-producing states of Anzoátegui, Zulia, Monagas, and Amacuro, while
Causa R's Alfredo Ramos filed for a recount in several other states.

In the days following the election, only four of the eleven members of
the CTV's electoral commission were willing to place their signatures on
the final document confirming the results. Nevertheless, Ortega (AD's candidate) was proclaimed the winner, allegedly receiving 57 percent of the
vote, compared to Istúriz with 16 percent, Ramos with 11 percent, and
Navarro with 6 percent. The CNE certified the validity of the elections for
individual federations, but not for the CTV itself.

Much of the conflict revolved around the CTV's refusal to accept the
participation of recently formed pro-Chávez unions representing the informal economy, even though the Ministry of Labor had granted them legalized status. The traditional CTV leaders did not reject unionization of the
informal sector in principle, and indeed Ortega and Navarro included representatives of that sector on their respective slates. Nevertheless, they
claimed that the *chavistas* had created over 1,000 bogus unions consisting

of party members, many of whom belonged to the informal economy (Díaz, 2001: 253).

Thus the social polarization of Venezuelan society (a major theme of this book) reverberated within organized labor and played a major role in the conflict within the CTV. As the formally employed, organized working class shrunk in size, resolving the question of how to incorporate economically marginalized sectors became more crucial for the continued vitality of organized labor. However, this issue was politically charged, as FBT leaders had the most to gain from allowing retired and unemployed workers into the CTV fold, as well as members of the informal sector.

The extent to which the CTV had lost its mobilization capacity was put in evidence by the three-day general strike that led up to the April 2002 coup attempt. Unlike the general strike that had been called in May 1989, which was a complete success, the CTV requested the endorsement of Fedecámaras, thus risking being accused of allying with labor's traditional enemy. Since the companies that complied with Fedecámaras's decision to back the work stoppage offered their employees the day off with pay, the degree of worker support for the strike call was difficult to determine. Industrial sectors in the Guyana region, public employees, and transportation workers did not respond positively to the call. The powerful steelworker leadership broke with Causa R (which had formerly controlled the union) by criticizing the CTV for uniting with Fedecámaras and called on workers throughout the country to ignore the strike. Similarly, Fedepetrol (also under non-*chavista* leadership), supported by two smaller oil worker federations, also publicly exhorted workers to resume their jobs. Finally, in states throughout the country, the CTV-affiliated federations were unable to mobilize large numbers of workers in favor of the strike. This lukewarm response contrasted with the colossal march in Caracas on the day of Chávez's removal from office, consisting mainly of middle- and upper-class Venezuelans.

The Moderate and Radical Wings of the Chávez Movement: Sources of Conflict

Following the contests of October 25, 2001, FBT leaders debated among themselves two possible approaches: placing pressure on the CNE to organize new elections, or the immediate exit from the CTV of *chavista* trade unionists and the creation of a rival confederation. Attitudes toward the CNE also reflected differences within the *chavista* movement. Some of the MVR hard-liners blamed Miquilena's followers, who held important positions in the CNE, for the commission's failure to fulfill its constitutional obligation of supervising the electoral process in order to guarantee fairness. The labor-leader hard-liners called the CNE's role in the CTV elections that of "a spectator," since AD labor leaders at the local level supervised the contests "single-handedly and according to their convenience" (personal interview with Oscar García, national FBT leader, Caracas, February 19, 2002). The hard-liners argued that the CNE's failure to step in, as the constitution stipulates, was partly because traditional party militants dominate the commission's bureaucracy at lower levels. The hard-liners' support for a CNE purge was typical of their attitude in general in that they called for a total reorganization of the public administration to rid it of traditional party loyalists who were "sabotaging" the revolution.

In addition to different opinions regarding participation in CTV elections, other issues pitted the MVR's moderate wing against the party's labor leaders. Conflicts had manifested themselves at the Constituent Assembly in 1999 in discussion regarding social and labor issues. The four worker representatives elected delegates to the assembly defended an article of the original draft of the constitution that reduced the workweek from forty-four to forty hours and nighttime work from forty to thirty-five hours. After considerable debate, a majority of the delegates accepted maintaining the workweek at forty-four hours, although they also decided on thirty-five hours for nighttime work. As one of the worker delegates stated: "The top *chavista* leaders at the Assembly indicated the party line to the mass of delegates, sometimes by means of a mere gesture, and this is what happened in the case of the work week proposition, but many delegates voted in favor of the 40-hour week anyway" (personal interview with Froilán Barrios, president of the Frente Constituyente de Trabajadores, Caracas, August 1, 2001).

The new constitution restored the retroactivity of the severance pay system, which had been a banner of the *chavista* movement during the 1998 presidential campaign. However, some pro-Chávez delegates (including those belonging to MAS) felt uncomfortable with the restoration of retroactivity, touching off a dispute that left the constitution somewhat ambiguous on the issue. Constituent Assembly vice president Isaías Rodríguez (Venezuela's future vice president) argued that the wording left open the possibility of paying employees their severance payment on a yearly basis, thus virtually discarding the principle of retroactivity (personal interview with David De Lima, future governor of Anzoátegui, Lechería, February 14, 2000). By 2001 the government began granting public-sector employees benefits corresponding to the 1997 reform, thus leaving the impression that the retroactivity requirement would not be pushed. Indeed, some MVR leaders argued in private that just as in the case of privatization of strategic industries, the elimination of retroactivity in 1997 had been an error but at the same time a fait accompli, and the nation simply lacked the resources to go back to the old system. As a way out, some *chavistas* considered the possibility of discarding retroactivity but restoring the old system of double severance pay in cases of layoffs without just cause. (The 1997 reform had limited such payments to five months' salary.) Causa R supported this compromise arrangement, unlike most FBT trade unionists, who continued to defend retroactivity as a point of honor.

Similar conflicts within the *chavista* movement arose over the social security system at the Constituent Assembly in 1999. Differences centered on the role of the private sector in the health and pension plans. The worker representatives and members of a leftist current within the *chavista* movement succeeded in defining the social security system (in Article 86) as "administered under the direction of the state for only social purposes" and "free of profit or excessive profits" (*"de caracter no lucrativo"*). Nevertheless, as in the case of severance payment, the wording of the constitution was open to interpretation, as more conservative delegates argued that the clause allowed for private participation as long as the system was under the strict regulation of the state.

A presidential-appointed commission on social security headed by Vice President Isaías Rodríguez released its plan in March 2001 for a publicly run health system (which the business organization Fedecámaras harshly criticized) and a privately run pension system similar to the plan approved under the Caldera administration. Rodríguez pointed out that although the constitution (in Article 84) unequivocally prohibited private capital in the social security system's health program, it did not rule out private capital in the pension system as long as the state regulated profits and set standards. Chávez cabinet members in charge of social affairs heavily criticized the commission's pension proposal. They advocated the "mixed system" in which lower-paid workers would receive more than minimum coverage. These cabinet members as well as FBT labor leaders called the presidential commission's plan "marginal solidarity" in that the program for workers of the informal economy was separated from that for workers in the formal economy and amounted to nothing more than "social aid for the indigent" (Gabinete Social, 2001). Hard-liners known as "fundamentalists" in the FBT flatly ruled out privately run pension funds. In private, FBT leaders objected to the participation of representatives of private financial interests in the presidential commission's elaboration of the pension-system plan and to the lack of labor representation (personal interview with José Ignacio Arrieta, member of the Presidential Commission on Social Security, Caracas, July 24, 2001).

From the outset of Chávez's presidency, the moderate wing of the *chavista* movement cautioned against overreliance on the state in the reorganization of the labor movement. Thus the moderates watered down the wording of the referendum held in December 2000, which temporarily removed CTV leaders from office. According to the labor-leader hard-liners, by failing to dissolve the existing CTV structure, the referendum deprived the *chavistas* of a golden opportunity to deliver a fatal blow to the traditional labor leadership precisely when it was at its weakest. The error was allegedly aggravated by Miquilena's insistence that the Chávez labor movement participate in the CTV elections of October 2001 without guarantees that recently formed pro-*chavista* unions would be allowed to participate and that the CNE would play a supervisory role.

The issue of the relationship between *chavista* labor leaders and the MVR had been debated within the FBT's predecessor, the Frente Constituyente de Trabajadores, which in 2000 split from the party as a result of the critical positions assumed by some of its spokesmen. From the time of its founding, the FBT had attempted to refute the accusation that the organization was an appendix of the MVR, pointing out that it took in labor leaders of different party affiliations, including the PPT and the Communist Party. As the differences between the MVR's moderate wing and the FBT (over such issues as social security) became increasingly defined and solidified, *chavista* labor leaders realized the importance of asserting an independent position. The FBT, for instance, pointed out that during the three-week-long strike at the nation's steel plant, SIDOR, in 2001, the four *chavista* representatives on the union's executive committee backed the stoppage, even though they stopped short of accepting the conflict's escalation to other sectors of the economy (as proposed by Causa R, which controlled the union, and AD's Carlos Ortega). When the FBT finally decided to participate in CTV elections in mid-2001, it discarded the possibility of launching MVR leader Nicolás Maduro as presidential candidate and instead opted for PPT leader Aristóbulo Istúriz, even though that party had sharply clashed with President Chávez in the past. In spite of this recognition of the importance of autonomy, FBT leaders were grateful for the active endorsement of President Chávez in the CTV elections, which undoubtedly was their main drawing card.

Conclusion

Beginning with a seminal essay by Guillermo O'Donnell (1994), political scientists writing on contemporary Latin American democracy have noted the weakness of political parties, organized labor, and social movements and their failure to channel popular demands at the highest levels of decisionmaking. As a result, the national executive throughout the continent has become largely insulated from pressure groups and countervailing state institutions. Some political scientists were generally optimistic about this emerging model because it opened possibilities for a fluid and direct relationship between executive authorities and the people (Mettenheim and Malloy, 1998). Other writers, who considered mechanisms of sectorial representation in decisionmaking a sine qua non for well-functioning democracy, were naturally pessimistic about recent political developments on the continent.

Venezuela was certainly no exception to this pattern in the 1990s. Traditional intermediate organizations lost prestige, credibility, and effectiveness. Specifically in the case of organized labor, the CTV ceased to articulate the aspirations of the underprivileged sectors as a whole and became almost exclusively concerned with the monetary demands of its members. In addition, the neighborhood movement and other "new social movements," which proliferated and showed considerable promise in the 1980s, failed to develop a national leadership that was organically linked to the rank and file and thus had limited influence in the formulation of policy (Ellner, 1999d). Under the presidency of Chávez the weak linkage between policymakers and the people was aggravated. The government eliminated subsidies for political parties and labor unions at the same time that it removed the leadership of the CTV and its affiliate federations. Some political scientists characterized the government as caudillistic and authoritarian; others compared Venezuela under Chávez to the organizational barrenness of Alberto Fujimori's Peru.

This chapter adds to the picture presented by Angel Alvarez and María Pilar García-Guadilla in Chapters 8 and 10 regarding institutional weakness in Venezuela, which reached an extreme under the Chávez presidency. The revolution that Chávez proclaimed sought to replace the "moribund" institutions (a term Chávez himself popularized) of the so-called Fourth Republic with vibrant, autonomous ones particularly responsive to the underrepresented popular sectors. Nevertheless, radical social organizations identified with the "revolutionary process" did not emerge to the extent that they did, for instance, under the pro-leftist regime of General Juan Velasco Alvarado in Peru after 1968.

This shortcoming was particularly evident in the case of the labor movement. The revitalization of the CTV and the adeptness of its leaders in adjusting to the new situation demonstrated that organized labor as an institution was hardly "moribund." Indeed, the labor movement posed more of a challenge to the government than did the political parties of the opposition. Furthermore, creating a new trade union structure was no simple task. The FBT could not easily parlay Chávez's popularity among nonprivileged sectors into votes in union elections and organizational advances in general. Indeed, the moderate wing of the MVR criticized the strategy of *chavista* worker leaders of relying on state power to create a new labor movement without first building organizational links with the rank and file.

Nevertheless, the characterization of Chávez as a "caudillo" is exaggerated, if not deceptive, as the introductory and concluding chapters of this book argue. Even if Chávez suffered setbacks in his attempts to incorporate the unions into his movement, his challenge was responsible for fundamental changes in organized labor. This point is recognized by renovation currents in the CTV grouped in the "Primero de Mayo," the Frente Constituyente de Trabajadores, and Causa R factions of the confederation, which were highly critical of Chávez and which for the most part rejected alliances with the FBT (personal interviews with Rodrigo Penso, Froilán Barrios, and Alfredo Ramos). The CTV's statutes drawn up in 1999, which established direct rank-and-file elections for the CTV's executive committee and had few equivalents anywhere in the world, would not have been accepted by the AD labor leadership had it not been for the pressure exerted by the *chavista* movement and government. Other reforms, such as the elimination of union hiring of oil workers and the creation of a pluralistic electoral commission headed by a representative of Causa R, would have been unthinkable in the past. Furthermore, the most conspicuous symbols of party-dominated trade unionism, such as Federico Ramírez León, stepped down. The fact that AD labor leaders regrouped in the FUT and that COPEI's most prominent labor leader, Carlos Navarro, completely broke with his party pointed in the direction of a more autonomous relationship between labor leaders and their respective parties. In short, important steps toward the revitalization of organized labor were set in motion by *chavismo*—even though the Chávez movement did not lead the process. Furthermore, the Chávez government refrained from employing repressive measures against the CTV, even after traditional labor leaders regained control of the confederation. These developments rule out the application of the caudillo-masses model, employed by many political analysts writing on Chávez, which implies the complete absence of viable intermediary organizations between the state and the general populace.

10

Civil Society: Institutionalization, Fragmentation, Autonomy

María Pilar García-Guadilla

One of the most significant changes in Venezuela since 1958 has been the evolution of organized civil society. During this period, social organizations and movements with new identities, conceptions of citizenship, and social projects occupied political spaces and developed new strategies of interaction with the state. Their goal of gaining legitimacy as actors and interlocutors in the public sphere was achieved in the 1980s as part of the process of decentralization. They also succeeded in incorporating their fundamental demands into the public national agenda, particularly at the time of the National Constituent Assembly (ANC) in 1999.

From the outset of the democratic period in 1958, political parties and the other actors basic to the Pact of Punto Fijo (military, church, unions, business) facilitated the interaction between the state and society. But by 1999, space had opened for the participation of new actors, organizations, and social movements, which succeeded in "institutionalizing" their demands and proposals in the Bolivarian constitution. As a result, they became legitimate interlocutors insulated from the mediation of political parties.[1]

Indeed, the passage of the Bolivarian constitution changed the Venezuelan political system in fundamental ways. The election of the national congress (the National Assembly), the president, governors, and mayors in 2000 laid the bases for a new, more permanent legitimacy. The new constitutional framework defined the relations between the recently elected authorities and the rest of society. Most important, the Bolivarian constitution attempted to institutionalize direct democracy,[2] so that both forms of democracy (representative and participatory) would coexist and be underpinned by social organizations, more than by traditional political parties.

The transition to Venezuela's new democracy faced diverse challenges and obstacles, beginning with the need to formulate a precise definition of the term "participatory and protagonistic" democracy, which is basic to the

Bolivarian constitution. In addition, the relationship between these newly formed social movements, on the one hand, and the state and society, on the other, needed to be worked out (García-Guadilla, 2002). This task was particularly urgent because many of the new social organizations clashed with the Chávez government and its "Bolivarian Political Project."

This chapter will analyze four periods since the restoration of democracy in 1958: (1) the period of formation of social organizations and movements independent of the state, from 1958 until the end of the 1970s; (2) the period of their growth, consolidation, and diversification, beginning in the 1980s and including the political crisis in the 1990s, when constitutional solutions were proposed to transform the relations between these actors and the state; (3) the process of institutionalization of social organizations and movements that was set in motion by the Bolivarian constitution; and (4) the postconstitutional period beginning in 2001, when new critical dilemmas unfolded regarding the role of existing social organizations and movements and their interaction with the state. At the same time, these movements and organizations began to compete for political space with the state and with the incipient Bolivarian movement promoted by President Chávez.

Over the recent past, social organizations and movements, which had been excluded from the constitution of 1961, developed identities, achieved legitimacy, and eventually connected with the state and the public agenda through participatory-democratic mechanisms. The new relationship between the state and social movements was designed to avoid co-optation and maintain autonomy, at the same time allowing them to play an important political role in accordance with the Bolivarian constitution. This chapter also points to the downside of recent developments. The institutionalization of the demands of new organizations and their growing ideological diversification have contributed to their fragmentation. Furthermore, the challenges posed to the state as a result of divergent social projects generated conflict, which was aggravated by the state's support for new "Bolivarian" actors. This tension was further sharpened by the polarized political climate, which led to confrontations and encouraged the government and the government party to exclude social and political actors considered part of the "opposition."

The Broader Context of Venezuelan Social Movements

Beginning in the late 1970s, throughout Latin America new protest movements and organizations emerged that differed from older social organizations not only in their identities and strategies, but also in their objectives.

These more recently created organizations are clearly outside corporatist structures, including organized labor, and are distinct from formal social organizations that do not challenge the government in any way, such as nonprofit foundations and civil associations. These recent movements, which are based on the principles of participation, equity, and social solidarity, sometimes consist of well-structured organizations, but in other cases have but a rudimentary structure. They demand automatic participation in the decisionmaking processes on matters that concern them, whether on a local, regional, or national level. Furthermore, they are independent social actors in that they are separate from the state and political parties, and embrace projects based on new values and demands related to the environment, class matters, and human rights, among others. Nevertheless, these actors frequently mobilize their constituencies in order to influence political decisions.[3]

As in the rest of Latin America, beginning in the late 1970s, social organizations and movements in Venezuela united around general goals with high symbolic value, such as participatory democracy and decentralization, and skillfully used the media to promote these ends. This process was set off by legislation, beginning in 1979, that deepened democracy at municipal and state levels. Once their demands for political decentralization met certain successes in the late 1980s, many social organizations and movements returned to their specific goals; others demobilized, and still others were co-opted by political parties in search of members and legitimacy, as occurred with many neighborhood associations. In addition, state co-optation disarmed some organizations, which occurred to part of the cooperative movement as a result of certain social policies, specifically state assistance for the creation of new businesses. Nevertheless, in 1999 social organizations and movements again united around a general goal with great symbolic value, namely the drafting of a new constitution that embodied the concept of participatory democracy. Furthermore, in the 1990s they used successful strategies, such as joining formal networks, which contrasted with the informal ones created in the previous decade. At the same time, some organizations began to use the media as well as national and international electronic networks more effectively.

The impetus provided by the new constitution for the formulation of demands encouraged social organizations to define their identities, autonomous status, and reasons for interacting with the state. Scholars writing on social movements who exalt the emergence of new identities and motivations have stressed the importance of this process.

Another broader context explaining developments since the late 1980s is the social and ideological polarization in Venezuela as a consequence of the application of structural adjustment measures and the progressive impoverishment of the population. This polarization gave rise to struggles that placed in evidence social distinctions, while ideological polarization led to acute confrontations involving political and social actors, including street mobilizations. Such clashes threatened to become increasingly intense as social and ideological differences grew, partly as a result of President Chávez's discourse that blamed the "oligarchic" minority for poverty and other social problems.

The Formation and Consolidation of Social Organizations: 1960s–1980s

The 1961 constitution embodied "a minimal definition of democracy" (Rey, 1989) that was limited to electoral activity and the defense of individual rights from a liberal perspective. The constitution refrained from making reference to the role of organized civil society and the values associated with democracy and instead was mainly concerned with maintaining political stability, which at the time was threatened by sectors of the left and the military. A substantial number of formal social organizations in the 1960s, such as nonprofit foundations and civil associations, did not seek to participate in the political arena since they considered social and political spheres to be inherently separate (García-Guadilla and Roa Carrero, 1995). At the same time, corporatist organizations, such as organized labor, were strengthened by their participation as members of the Pact of Punto Fijo and by the modernization of the economy based on import substitution and government interventionism.

Nevertheless, by the 1980s the limitations of representative democracy as established in the 1961 constitution became evident due to the failure to consider the demands of new organizations of civil society. It is not surprising, then, that the paramount demand of these actors was the right of participation and, in general, "the deepening of democracy." This demand was principally raised by organizations that emerged in the late 1970s in the middle-class neighborhoods of Caracas as a reaction to the government's failure to consult them in the drafting of the Organic Law of the Municipal Regime (LORM) of 1979 (Santana, 1986). In contrast to the hierarchical structure of organized labor, these organizations had relatively flexible structures based to a certain degree on friendship and solidarity. The neighborhood organizations that emerged in the late 1970s acquired increasing political visibility due to their advocacy of decentralization and participatory democracy, which the middle class in general embraced. This vision was also shared by lesser-known organizations in the cooperative, environmentalist, and women's movements, among others.

The social movements began to attach multiple meanings to "participatory democracy." First, the term came to imply direct elections based on the majority electoral system for social organizations, political parties, and the government sphere, as well as practices related to direct democracy, such as various types of referendum (see Chapter 8). Second, it refers to mechanisms of civil society participation in decisionmaking and accountability of elected officials.

In accordance with his 1983 electoral platform, which called for a "new accord for social democracy," President Jaime Lusinchi created the Presidential Commission on State Reform (COPRE) with the explicit objective of modernizing the state, and the implicit objective of opening channels of communication and democratizing the relationship between the state and society (Gómez Calcaño and López Maya, 1990: 183). COPRE's "Comprehensive Reform of the State," presented to the national executive in 1988, prioritized the goal of citizen participation. Nevertheless, neoliberal thinking underpinned the proposal in that COPRE called for "relieving the state of certain functions and making the citizens assume responsibility for the solutions of their local problems including public services, without relying on state intervention, in order to extirpate paternalistic mentality" (Silva, 1999: 150). Furthermore, COPRE warned against excessive participation, since "hyper-participation fails to take into account those who do not have a great interest in actively participating" (COPRE, 1988: 103). As a result, the proposals advanced by COPRE sought to dampen representation in the existing system and not to promote democratic reform of institutions and greater participation by citizens (Silva, 1999).

The effectiveness of new social organizations in pressing for passage of the Organic Law of Decentralization (LOD) and the reform of the Organic Law of the Municipal Regime in late 1988 was undoubtedly due to the fact that they represented the only unified sector that had not reached agreements with the state and had not been penetrated by political parties. At the same time, with the deepening of the economic-political crisis and the steps taken toward decentralization, the new social organizations and movements became more ideologically heterogeneous. While some of them opposed the neoliberal model and the macroeconomic adjustment policies on grounds that they exacerbated social inequalities, other organizations continued to center their attention on political democracy and state reform. The former included the so-called eco-socialist environmental movement and the Christian base movement, while the latter took in the middle-class neighborhood associations and the offshoot organization Queremos Elegir ("We Want to Elect") (García-Guadilla, 1991; García-Guadilla and Silva Querales, 1999).

The 1990s: Ideological Heterogeneity, Institutionalization, and Participation

Political Reform: 1989–1998

Organizations of civil society presented constitutional proposals during three distinct time spans: between 1989 and the 1992 coup attempt; between 1992 and Caldera's presidential election in 1993; and in the early period of Caldera's administration. In contrast to the democratic reforms proposed in the late 1980s to achieve democratization and greater efficiency, the process of constitutional reform initiated in 1989 involved defining new rights and rules of the game that pointed in the direction of a new model of society.

In June 1989, following the violent demonstrations known as the Caracazo, the government of President Carlos Andrés Pérez decided to amend the 1961 constitution (Kornblith, 1992). These individual amendments were to improve democratic governability and increase consensus among different social actors (García-Guadilla and Roa Carrero, 1996), but the abortive coup of 1992 generated tensions and conflicts that required a more all-encompassing reform process. This crisis led to the search for other mechanisms capable of relegitimizing the democratic system, including the convocation of a National Constituent Assembly (ANC). Most of the nation's political parties opposed the ANC proposal, but various prominent political leaders and a large number of social organizations supported it as a means to open channels of participation to discuss a new model of society. Congress, however, rejected the ANC proposal and instead considered a "constitutional reform" (which was more all-encompassing than the individual amendments proposed during the 1989–1992 period, but less ambitious than the ANC proposal). The proposed reform, however, failed to define the mechanisms of communication between the state and society.

During the years 1989–1992, of the thirty-six proposals considered by the bicameral commission headed by Rafael Caldera, only eight had to do with civil society. Of these, only two were presented by three social organizations. Both of these proposals, however, were incorporated into the project submitted by the commission to Congress in March 1992.

Although the ANC proposal was vetoed by the major political parties following the February 1992 coup attempt, it was immediately taken up by diverse organizations of civil society. Of thirty-six social organizations whose positions are available from the press and communications with Congress, seventeen pronounced themselves in favor of convoking an ANC. Only one explicitly defended the proposed constitutional reform, which kept the process within the purview of the Congress, dominated by the nation's political parties. The seventeen organizations that supported the ANC viewed it as a viable vehicle to resolve the national crisis, encourage the emergence of a new political leadership, reform the state, and formulate a national project. Thus, for instance, the Centro al Servicio de la Acción Popular (CESAP; Center at the Service of Popular Action), a nongovernmental organization (NGO) devoted to education and support for grassroots economic and social projects, maintained that convening the ANC would allow needed changes without putting democratic stability in danger (CESAP, 1992a, 1992b). The pro-ANC social organizations rejected the congressional-sponsored constitutional reform, as they considered that institution unqualified to lead the process of far-reaching political change (Provea, 1992a, 1992b).

Following the 1992 coup attempt the bicameral commission drafted 128 articles, of which 28 were related to civil society. Of these 28, only 5 originated from civil society, while most of the rest were proposed by political actors. Five additional proposals were presented by organizations of civil society but were rejected by the commission. Thus although the number of articles related to civil society increased over the 1989–1992 period from 8 to 28, the number of those formulated by civil society continued to be low (5 in all).

The last period of constitutional reform began in July 1994 when President Caldera created a special Senate commission for that purpose, a task that he considered to be a national priority (*El Universal*, February 3, 1994, pp. 1–3). The government's expressed objective was to promote participatory democracy, reform the three branches of government, and put in motion decentralization. The commission, however, faced considerable resistance from the main opposition parties, namely AD and the Comité de Organización Política Electoral Independiente (COPEI). Furthermore, the majority of the social organizations indicated that the constitutional reform effort failed to point in the direction of "a national project" (García-Guadilla and Roa Carrero, 1996).

Social organizations in general viewed the reform process as merely palliative and objected to the lack of formal or effective mechanisms for consulting them or getting to know their proposals. As a corrective, Queremos Elegir recommended "a broad campaign of disseminating the Constitution and its proposed reforms and converting congressmen into channels of communication which tied in their respective regions to the process" (Queremos Elegir, 1994). In contrast to the months immediately following the 1992 coup attempt, when a wide number of organizations advocated an ANC to overcome the crisis, the social organizations during the Caldera presidency appeared to be skeptical. On the one hand, social leaders doubted that the political elite had the necessary commitment to see through necessary changes. On the other, many of these social leaders identified the ANC with the 1992 coup leaders, whom they also viewed with distrust.

The Constituent Assembly: Institutionalization of Demands

In contrast to the experience with constitutional reform over the previous ten years, the participation of civil society in the ANC was dynamic and, according to the organizations themselves, successful (GAU, 2000). Due to the crisis and loss of legitimacy by the traditional political parties, many viewed social organizations as ideal to provide input into the drafting of the new constitution. Indeed, they actively participated in the form of seminars, workshops, roundtables, commissions, and declarations to the media (Sinergia, 1999).[4]

A large number of organizations created formal and informal networks in order to facilitate the formulation of proposals and participation in ANC commissions. Frequently, networks with ideological affinity in areas such as human rights, the environment, and indigenous affairs supported each other's proposals. In general, the greater the number of organizations belonging to a network, the greater the thematic diversity of its proposals (GAU, 2000). This collaboration contrasted with the previous congressional deliberations on constitutional reform.[5]

Unlike the congressional discussion over constitutional reform in the years 1989 to 1994, social organizations in 1999 succeeded in persuading the ANC to include a high percentage of their proposals in the constitutional text. Of the 624 proposals they formulated, more than 50 percent were incorporated into the constitution, although sometimes with modifications in wording. These results contrasted with the limited success obtained by social organizations during the discussion of constitutional reform in the early 1990s.[6] Some of the organizations that participated in the ANC achieved a particularly high level of success, with two-thirds or more of their proposals incorporated in the final document.[7] The most successful proposals related to society, democracy, and citizenship were those that were new and different from proposals in the 1961 constitution. Another explanation for their success was the fact that demands formed part of the "Bolivarian Project" of President Chávez and as a consequence received the backing of the majority of ANC delegates, who were elected on the Chávez ticket. Organizations that publicized their propositions among their constituents and the public in general were also more successful, as were those whose proposals were designed to achieve fundamental organizational goals.

Many of the organizations relegated to a low level of success indicated that nevertheless they were satisfied with the results obtained.[8] They reacted this way because the themes that the organizations and networks succeeded in inserting into the new constitution were linked to the strategic interests and ideological principles they embraced. Most important in this respect, the constitution promoted new identities and conceptions of citizenship and democracy based on participation. The process of drafting the new constitution revealed that the heterogeneity of civil society and the diversity of concerns did not impede interorganizational cooperation and solidarity. Social organizations were enriched as a result of their experiences participating in the ANC in the form of elaborating proposals, lobbying, and negotiating with delegates.[9] In addition, they acquired public visibility through their exposure in the media.

Post-ANC Dilemmas and Participatory Democracy

A significant consequence of the Constituent Assembly process was that the various social organizations that participated and presented proposals found themselves having to define the kind of society they desired to construct. In addition, in order to establish alliances and identify opponents, they had to decide where they coincided and differed with the state and with other organizations. The incorporation of new mechanisms of participation into the Bolivarian constitution laid the foundation for a more pluralist democracy than embodied in the 1961 constitution, capable of embracing new values put forth by social organizations and movements whose fundamental claim was the "right to participate." Nevertheless, the new constitution's institutionalization of many of the demands of these actors raised fresh questions about their autonomy and their relationship to the state, which had ramifications within the organizations and movements themselves.

Given that the preamble of the Bolivarian constitution advanced the goal of constructing a "democratic, participatory and protagonistic society," defining the exact forms of participation for social and political organizations is of paramount importance (see Chapter 8). For the first time since the outset of democracy in 1958, the constitution recognized the importance of the organization and mobilization of citizens, but this participation fell into two distinct and even conflicting frameworks. In the first, civic participation was conceived as direct democracy in the form of popular assemblies called to make decisions on matters of public importance (as specified in Article 70). Haidée Machín, a popular leftist leader, called this idea "a distinctive Venezuelan version of democracy featuring popular sovereignty and direct participation" in a proposal she presented to the commission of the National Assembly that drafted the Organic Law on Citizen Participation (Machín, 2001: 4). The Machín project, which had the backing of at least sixty different organizations from a variety of sectors, argued that "the proposed law . . . is nothing other than direct and protagonistic participatory democracy in contrast to representative democracy" (p. 3). From this point of view, representation and participation are somewhat counterposed to each other. But Machín's proposal failed to define those organizations that ultimately would have the faculty to make decisions on public matters. Compounding the difficulty, the Machín proposal recognized the validity of the participation in this process of both "groups with a legal character as well as those that are not [legally] registered but have demonstrated influence in, or which spring from, community projects" (p. 6).

In the second, more liberal framework, direct participation appeared as a complement to representative democracy. This notion was expressed by Sinergia (2001), a network of organizations that embraces pluralism and liberalism, in its proposed Organic Law of Popular, Citizen, and Community Participation. The proposal stressed participation through the mediation of social organizations "with a legal character," although it recognized that those participating can vary depending on the types of issues involved.

Principles outlined in the constitution were supposed to underpin the legislative-legal framework (organic laws, ordinary laws, and regulations) governing interactions between state and society, but these relations became highly politicized. An example is the way that "civil society" was defined by the so-called Congresillo, a group of ANC members chosen by the national executive to act as a legislative body during the transition from the old to the new constitution. The Congresillo's criteria for participation excluded from official recognition those social organizations "that receive foreign financing," thus denying them the right to participate in the decisionmaking process as established in the Bolivarian constitution. This stipulation discriminated against many of the most consolidated and longest-existing social organizations, including the majority of human rights organizations and popular base organizations, such as CESAP. The measure against foreign financing was apparently designed to check the influence of international multilateral organizations such as the National Endowment for Democracy, which played an important role in the events leading up to the April 2002 coup.

Another issue of controversy that emerged following the ratification of the constitution involves the definition of civil society. The National Assembly as well as various social groups debated who would be allowed to participate in the nomination process for the two new branches of government known as "Citizen Power" and "Electoral Power." Social organizations, such as Queremos Elegir and Primero Justicia (First Justice), that had emerged in the 1990s were not taken into account. Indeed, President Chávez publicly accused them of being an elitist minority of "oligarchs who do not represent anybody." Eventually these appointments were decided by negotiation among political leaders and factions in the National Assembly, a style reminiscent of the practices of the old regime.

During Chávez's first three years in office, conflicts made evident a growing breach between the official discourse of the state, which legitimated its actions in accordance with principles and rights defined in the new constitution, and Chávez's tendency to harshly attack his opponents. The government sometimes resorted to mechanisms that violated the spirit of democracy in order to resolve conflicts with these groups. This practice took the form of threatening groups that assume a critical position with calling a referendum without specifying what bloc of voters would be allowed to participate. This occurred in the conflict over electric power lines to be constructed across the Gran Sabana to deliver energy to Brazil. Here the geopolitical and developmentalist orientation of President Chávez came into conflict with the interests of indigenous people and environmentalists who raised the banners of defense of ethnic identity and nature. The president characterized his opponents as "traitors, spies, and foreigners," and declared to the media that the issue was not negotiable since the power-line project was a fait accompli. At one point he proposed holding a referendum on the issue in Santa Elena de Uairén, the main region affected, but without defining who would have the right to participate. Evidently the organizations involved in the struggle were to have no input in the wording of the referendum proposition.

Regardless of how great their ideological heterogeneity or how closely their goals corresponded to those of the state, the co-optation of sociopolitical actors was a real possibility in the new political scenario, particularly because the government lacked a solid organizational base in civil society. Such was the case with the Bolivarian Women's Movement, created at the request of President Chávez. It was linked to the National Coordinator of Women's Organizations, which was founded in order to pursue a "feminist" agenda on such issues as legal equality, family and children's affairs, and the poverty that disproportionately affects women. Some of the leaders of the National Coordinator joined the Bolivarian Women's Movement, but overall the result was to weaken and fragment the women's movement ideologically. The movement prioritized the resolution of individual problems instead of concentrating on the goals of women as a whole. Co-optation was also a danger for the incipient indigenous movement, whose demands became polarized between "pro-power-line *chavistas*" and "anti-power-line *chavistas*," obscuring the larger issues involving economic development, identity, and the environment.

An additional dilemma was how the state and social organizations defined the concept of "participatory democracy," given the breadth of its meaning. In conflicts between the government and these organizations (e.g., in the power-line case), both sides brandished the term "participatory democracy" to favor their positions, despite the fact that each one interpreted it in a different manner according to their own values and strategies. As such, the issue of how to reconcile the competing value systems held by different actors in conflict constituted a major challenge for the nation's democracy, regardless of whether it was "representative" or "participatory."

One last observation regarding social movements and protests over the recent past is in order. The mobilizations in favor of and in opposition to President Chávez, which became nearly daily occurrences beginning in late 2001, put in evidence class cleavages. On December 10, 2001, for the first time business organizations openly protested against the policies of the Chávez government by calling a work stoppage in opposition to the recently promulgated agrarian reform and other legislation that allegedly jeopardized property rights. The protest was considered a success because it paralyzed major cities; even employees who did not approve of the action stayed home out of fear of possible street violence. In contrast, large numbers of poor people from the countryside went to gatherings in support of the agrarian reform, while many members of the informal economy defied the strike call by showing up to their workplaces that day. The mobilizations on January 23 and February 27, 2002 (in commemoration of the overthrow of Pérez Jiménez and the 1989 Caracazo respectively) also reflected class preferences. The antigovernment protests were dominated by the traditional political parties and middle-class-based social organizations with a neoliberal orientation (García-Guadilla and Silva Querales, 1999). Furthermore, while government supporters in Caracas gathered in the overwhelmingly poor western part of the city, the anti-Chávez protests took place in Altamira and other wealthy areas in the east.

Sovereignty and the Bolivarian Circles: Social or Political Actors?

The goal of reviving the Movimiento Bolivariano Revolucionario 200 (MBR-200) in the post-ANC era was to create a "countermovement" to confront preexisting political parties and social organizations. Chávez and other leaders proposed organizing "Bolivarian Circles" so that the people, *el soberano* ("the sovereign ones"), would no longer constitute a disorganized mass of individuals without ideology, tied to their charismatic leader (Chávez) only through clientelistic and populist mechanisms. In his discourse, Chávez stressed the growing consciousness of *el soberano* and its exclusion from social benefits, which he blamed on the "oligarchic and wretched" privileged sectors and the opposition (*los escuálidos,* i.e., "the squalid ones"). This discourse expressed class conflict and encouraged heightened social polarization. The poor actively demanded that the president, through personal and noninstitutional ties, control prices and deliver on promises of housing, land, employment, and wages. They identified their enemy as the middle class and the oligarchic class, which they defined along material lines. This attitude could legitimize land invasions or the use of violence, while on the other side middle-class citizens mobilized to demand respect for their rights.

With increasing frequency, *el soberano* and the middle class confronted each other on the street, thus raising the threat of violence during mobilizations. According to data from Cifras Encuestadora C.A., an average of 310 street demonstrations that required the intervention of public-order authorities were registered between April and May of 2000. *El Nacional* (July 17, 2001, http://archivo.eluniversal.com) warned that "the incendiary and contradictory discourse of President Hugo Chávez," on the one hand, and "the absence of an organized and effective opposition," on the other, have caused "the thermometer of social conflict to be in permanent ascent." This danger was evident, for example, in protests against "Cubanization" in front of the Cuban embassy in 2001, where pro and anti groups of demonstrators confronted each other and the police had to intervene.

Despite its lack of definition, the term *el soberano* constituted a major point of reference repeatedly mentioned both in the Bolivarian constitution and the discourse of the president. Chávez used it synonymously with the term *el pueblo* in a sense that seemed to exclude privileged sectors. The place of the working class in this schema was unclear. An attempt to reconstitute the union movement, one of the key actors incorporated into the Pact of Punto Fijo, and transform it into a "Bolivarian workers movement" through a referendum was unsuccessful (see Chapter 9). Indeed, President Chávez encountered resistance from a labor leadership that, although weakened, regrouped to occupy a space between society and the state. With regard to the marginalized poor, which is a much bigger sector, Chávez's use of the term *el soberano* as a socioeconomic category (as opposed to the "Venezuelan people," which embraces all social categories) was designed to allow him to reach out without the mediation of a political party or even social movements. The identity of *el soberano* was transformed into that of its leader, which permitted him to mobilize them at his request. Many members of the multitude linked themselves to the charismatic leader with the expectation of resolving problems of survival through populist mechanisms (García-Guadilla and Hurtado, 2000; García-Guadilla, 2002).

Upon the twentieth anniversary of the founding of the MBR-200, and on the occasion of Chávez's return from a lengthy trip abroad, the president made the surprise announcement of relaunching the MBR. Two months later, Guillermo García-Ponce, a leftist leader dating back to the 1940s, announced that "steps are being taken to form the Bolivarian Circles, which will strengthen the revolution and defend the Constitution" (*El Nacional,* June 4, 2001). In his June 10, 2001, broadcast of *¡Aló Presidente!* (his weekly radio-television program), Chávez called upon his supporters to form "Lists" or "Organizing Committees" of the Bolivarian revolution. The president defined the objective of this "organization of *el pueblo*" as the "strengthening of the revolutionary process with popular support, inserting the people into the administration of government" in order to "make participatory and protagonistic democracy effective." The call went out to women, peasants, students, the MBR-200, and "honest and patriotic workers without personal interests" to participate in the democratization of the nation.

García-Ponce responded to the accusation that such groups resemble the Committees for the Defense of the Revolution in Cuba by stating that "this project does not have anything to do with the Cuban model, but is rather the necessary process of organizing the forces that support [democracy]. If the neighbors, *el pueblo,* are not organized, it will not be possible to defend the Constitution" (*El Universal,* June 4, 2001). According to José Vicente Rangel, a former socialist presidential candidate named vice president in 2002, "a model is being imported or copied neither from Cuba nor any other country. . . . Popular organization forms part of all democratic societies" (Rangel, 2001). President Chávez proclaimed his objective as seeking to constitute a "popular force spread out in slums, towns, countryside and cities in order to consolidate, ideologize, and reinvigorate itself, thus contributing to the Bolivarian revolution" (*El Nacional,* April 25, 2001). The opposition questioned the use of government resources to promote and create the circles and branded support for them from the national executive "unconstitutional" (*El Universal,* June 12, 2001).

Rangel (2001) indicated that civilians, not military officers, would lead the Bolivarian Circles, but their political and social character was never made clear. The initiative was apparently an effort to augment regime legitimacy and subsume choices within the orbit of a particular political party. According to García-Ponce, "once the process of organization develops, the President will announce the role that the MBR-200 will play as a force for unity among revolutionaries, as a factor of support for the Bolivarian project and to give impetus to the country's progress" (*El Universal,* June 4, 2001). Considering the unstable participation of the Patria Para Todos (PPT) and the Movimiento al Socialismo (MAS) in the governing coalition, it would appear that the Bolivarian Circles were designed to strengthen the position of the government's "unconditional supporters"; these organizations may or may not have been meant to include parties allied to the government, or even the entire Movimiento Quinta República (MVR; Fifth Republic Movement).

Students, Peddlers, Pensioners, Homeless People: In Search of a Definition as Organized Actors

The role of recently created social groups in the political structure has not been defined. These organizations include groups of pensioners, ambulant merchants (or peddlers), and, of more recent creation, those displaced by natural disasters and the Bolivarian students (López Maya, 1999; Salamanca, 1999). Leaving aside the students, who constitute a special category, these groups tended to make narrow demands that could be resolved on an individual rather than collective basis and in a clientelistic and populist manner rather than through collective negotiation. Such demands often consisted of the right to occupy public and even private lands, pedestrian areas, and vacant lots in order to sell products, or the right to a minimum salary or social security benefits (in the case of members of the informal economy). In the case of displaced people and ambulant merchants, the satisfaction of their demands often entered into conflict with the rights of property owners, private organizations, or those traveling on public thoroughfares.

Given the predominately grievance-oriented character of these groups, their permanent integration into the political process is not easy. They may never transcend their narrow, material goals to constitute broader social organizations or movements. They may even disappear as groups once their needs are satisfied. On the other hand, if their demands are not met, they may move from unconditional to conditional support for Chávez, or even into outright opposition.

The attempts at creating a Bolivarian student movement found expression mainly in the occupations of rectors' offices at some state universities by small groups of students. In March 2001, students and employees took over the meeting room of the University Council of the Central University of Venezuela (UCV), demanding the installation of "a university constituent assembly" and refusing to recognize the institution's elected authorities. The rector, Giusepe Gianneto, warned that their intention was to "finish with institutionality" (*El Universal*, March 29, 2001). The takeover lasted for thirty-four days and was suspended once roundtable dialogues were installed in the different faculties of the UCV. The protesters called on the National Assembly to promulgate a constitutional reform that would allow university employees to participate in university elections. The protesters summarized their assessment of the takeover: "The first period has ended; we have broken with institutionality" (*El Universal*, May 2, 2001).

The occupation of the UCV council raised questions about the autonomous character (or lack thereof) of such groups and ultimately their potential as a social movement. It should be pointed out that the Young Fatherland Foundation (an organization tied to the government, formerly known as the Foundation for Youth and Change) played a major role in the takeover. The children of at least three important members of the national executive formed part of the leadership of the organization.[10] The Bolivarian student movement differed from other movements analyzed in this section in that it called for radical transformations. However, doubts remain regarding its capacity to act in an autonomous manner vis-à-vis the state. Although any prognosis is premature, rather than becoming a social movement, the Bolivarian student movement may embrace a political agenda and evolve into a kind of Bolivarian Circle for the defense of the revolution.

Representative, Delegative, or Participatory Democracy?

The adjective "participatory" that was attached to Venezuelan democracy left open the question as to whether liberal or radical democracy would be the main axis of orientation between civil society and the state. Which tendency emerged dominant depended on whether participation developed as a complement or a substitute for representation, on the type of criteria used to select the subjects or actors allowed to participate, on the extent to which the participation of minorities was permitted, and on whether the right to participate was defined by objective or partisan political criteria. The answers to these questions determined whether the state was likely to end up "kidnapping" preexisting sociopolitical actors and repeating a cycle of political exclusion familiar in Venezuelan history. Also unclear was the potential for political co-optation of new groups, such as the Bolivarian Circles, and whether they would replace preexisting organizations and social movements.

The process under way indicated that the government's promotion of participation sought to "win legitimacy without losing power." This posed challenges for the organizations and social movements that had already been constituted, as they had to deal with the possibility of co-optation, lack of recognition, confrontation with progovernment political parties, and competition with social forces that enjoy advantages as followers of the revolutionary project. One of the risks was that social spaces would be opened up not to encourage new forms of participation by social groups but to facilitate manipulation.

Notes

This chapter was translated from the Spanish by Deborah Norden. The author wishes to thank Rosangel Alvarez for comments on a preliminary version.

1. The importance of these organizations is enhanced by the scarce references made by the Bolivarian constitution (Article 67) to political parties, which are called "organizations and associations with political ends," in contrast to the very relevant role assigned to civil society. For a discussion of the distinction between "organized civil society," "social movements," and "social organizations," see García-Guadilla and Blauert, 1992: 5.

2. Political literature fails to define "participatory" democracy in precise terms. In Venezuela, it has generally been interpreted as the perfection of representative democracy through participatory mechanisms such as the referendum, participatory assemblies, or mechanisms of accountability. According to this view, for a democracy to be participatory, it should also be representative.

3. The much proclaimed goal of autonomy, however, has eluded organizations and social movements in Venezuela in recent years. Thus the mobilizations in opposition to President Chávez in late 2001 and early 2002 demonstrate the continued predominance of the political objectives formulated by corporatist organizations such as the Confederación de Trabajadores de Venezuela (CTV; Confederation of Venezuelan Workers) and Fedecámaras, Venezuela's main business confederation.

4. Organizations with concerns in the area of human rights, women's rights, education, neighborhood affairs, the environment, family planning, tax law, and local issues participated in the roundtable dialogues. There was also great heterogeneity in the proposals that these organizations formulated, which reflected their strategic interests as well as their individual identities.

5. In 48 percent of the cases, organizations (between two and sixty of them) grouped themselves in networks. These alliances presented a large number of proposals to the ANC, with the Foro por la Vida (Forum for Life) presenting 131 proposals and the Social Alliance for Justice presenting 112. In contrast, the Asociación Civil Muchachos de la Calle (Civil Association of Street Children), the Asociación Civil Voluntarios para Venezuela (Civil Association of Volunteers for Venezuela), and the Asociación de Planificación Familiar (PLAFAM; Association for Family Planning) only presented one proposal each. In some cases, however, organizations presented proposals individually and as part of a network. This was the case with PLAFAM, which made one proposal but at the same time supported various others of the Population and Sustainable Development Network (REDPOB), of which it formed part.

6. Five organizations are classified as having a high level of success: Alianza Social por la Justicia (Social Alliance for Justice), Escuela de Vecinos (School of Neighbors), Fundación Escuela Comunitaria Antimano (Antimano Communal School Foundation), the CESAP Social Group, and Provea. Eight organizations and/or networks are at the intermediate level, among which are the Fundación Vivienda Popular (Popular Housing Foundation), the Juventud Obrera Católica (Catholic Working Youth), Red de Apoyo por la Justicia y la Paz (Network of Support for Justice and Peace), Red Ambientalista ARA (ARA Environmentalist Network), Asamblea Nacional de Educación (National Assembly of Education), and Coordinadora de ONG's de Mujeres (Coordinator of Women's NGOs). Finally, sixteen organizations and/or networks are classified with a low level of success, including CEDICE, Acción Campesina (Farmworkers Action), and the REDPOB (Population and Sustainable Development Network).

7. If we classify those organizations that were most active throughout the process on the basis of their area of concern (human rights, neoliberal reforms, the environment, and women's issues), the most successful (as measured by the percentage of their proposals that were approved) were human rights organizations that proposed a radical transformation of democracy (65 percent). "Neoliberal organizations" (García-Guadilla and Silva Querales, 1999) that define democracy within a liberal framework had 33 percent of their proposals approved (García-Guadilla, 2000a).

8. The information on these attitudes was based on semistructured open

interviews carried out among organizations considered most significant in terms of the number of their proposals. See García-Guadilla, 2000b.

9. Throughout the constituent process, the social organizations participated with candidates, demands, proposals, and even all-encompassing projects for society. In fact, organizations such as Sinergia and Primero Justicia presented their own constitutional projects to the ANC. In general, social organizations had greater opportunity to have their demands and proposals incorporated into the new constitutional text than political parties and/or traditional political organizations.

10. The nation's vice president, Adina Bastidas, declared her support for the proposal of the occupiers to convoke a constituent assembly in the UCV (*El Universal,* April 2, 2001).

11

The Hugo Chávez Phenomenon: What Do "the People" Think?

Patricia Márquez

On December 6, 1998, 56 percent of the Venezuelan electorate voted for presidential candidate Hugo Chávez. His triumph represented the end of the reign of the two main political parties: the social democratic Acción Democrática (AD) and the social Christian Comité de Organización Política Electoral Independiente (COPEI), which had alternately governed and dominated most spheres of life and action since 1958. What brought about this dramatic political and social change? Why in a short span of time did such a large number of rank-and-file *adecos* and *copeyanos* shift loyalties and support Hugo Chávez, a man who verbally attacked the democratic system developed by these parties?[1]

While conducting fieldwork in Los Erasos, a Caracas barrio (shantytown), I asked a forty-year-old woman why she had voted for Chávez. All she said—despite my repeated efforts to get more information from her—was: "I support Chávez because he is a change. We need changes." After several more interviews with other people—young and old, poor and even poorer—who have lived for years along the steep, narrow streets and stairways of Los Erasos, I realized that most of their reasons for supporting Hugo Chávez revolved around the idea of change. Furthermore, most of them believed that at this point in Venezuelan history only Chávez could lead the changes.

In this chapter I will provide my own reflections, based on both personal experience and my work as an anthropologist in Caracas barrios, about the Venezuela of the last forty years. In doing so, I hope that a non-Venezuelan audience will better understand why Venezuelans from different social strata are desperately clinging to the idea of change. I will follow my anthropological imagination to convey the desperate need for change as people's everyday lives worsened, as the average annual salary dropped drastically over twenty years, crime rates soared, and the school and health system collapsed. Venezuelans shared a sense over the last four decades that the oil wealth has been kept in the hands of only a few, wasted by cor-

ruption and the bureaucratic inefficiencies associated with the rule of AD
and COPEI. Through testimonies and through an examination of certain
features in Venezuelan soap operas and common expressions, I will examine why people see Chávez as almost a supernatural agent of change and
how their perceptions stem from a particular Venezuelan political culture.
For many, Hugo Chávez represents hope and optimism in ways that people
from younger generations have never seen, but what do people see in this
leader that is so different from politicians of the past?

The Venezuela Where Everything Was Possible

I was born in 1965, seven years after the overthrow of military dictator
Marcos Pérez Jiménez. Like most people of my generation and younger, I
grew up understanding the political, social, and economic life of the country in relation to the ruling practices of the two alternating parties, AD and
COPEI, in the context of an oil-based economy. In my childhood, I had reason to believe that Venezuela was a wealthy, modernizing country. My earliest political memories were of the end of the first presidency of COPEI's
Rafael Caldera (1969–1974) and the campaign for president. I remember a
fairly young candidate, Carlos Andrés Pérez, on television, walking along
barrio streets while kissing old ladies and shaking hands, all choreographed
to the jingle, *"Ese hombre sí camina"* ("That man really moves"). Pérez
won the election promising a prosperous and modern Venezuela. I was in
grade school, but I retain many memories of that period. I had friends
whose families became suddenly very rich due to party connections or corruption; Venezuelans were known for their traveling and bad behavior
abroad; there was a large flow of immigration from Colombia and other
Latin American countries. Compared to the rest of Latin America, my
country was an example of a stable democracy.

In the Venezuela of the 1970s a new social class of wealthy *adecos*
emerged. Even in small towns in the interior, local politicians and entrepreneurs were benefiting from politics and oil wealth. This was the time of the
global oil price increase (1973–1974), when a large percentage of the
Venezuelan population, living under a democratic regime, found a variety
of opportunities to obtain a share of the wealth. A collective dream of
unlimited wealth and modernization emerged; for many Venezuelans in all
strata of society, the notion of progress involved the chance to travel at
least as far as Miami, which became a Mecca of consumerism. The nation
associated progress with the rapid flow of imported high technology and
goods, and there was both geographical and social mobility. Young people
could easily fathom going anywhere in the world to obtain a university
degree. President Pérez created the Fundación Gran Mariscal de Ayacucho,

an organization with great resources to provide scholarships to any student with either good grades or the right social connections. As writer Elisa Lerner puts it, this was a time when we all thought that we had a chance to prosper: "During the government of Carlos Andrés Pérez the equality equation within our society reached its most ambitious peak. We could see the intelligent son of Catia going to Harvard thanks to an Ayacucho scholarship" (1995: 11).[2] Unlike the 1990s, when the middle and lower classes got poorer, in the 1970s there was a trickle-down process in which the poor sectors of the population benefited.

By the time disco music and John Travolta posters began invading my room, another shift took place. Luis Herrera Campíns of COPEI won the 1978 election. All of the *adeco* officials, bureaucrats, and secretaries had to crate up their offices as the *copeyanos* replaced them. Although Herrera Campíns's campaign slogan was *"¿Dónde están los reales?"* ("Where is the money?"), his five years in power were also marked by a long list of corruption scandals. However, those becoming filthy rich were no longer *adecos* but *copeyanos*.

The administrations of Presidents Pérez and Herrera Campíns covered the period of the mid-1970s and early 1980s, which now seems more mythical than real and is known as "the 4.30 era" because 4.3 bolivars equaled 1 U.S. dollar.[3] We laughed about ourselves, the *"ta' baratos"* ("so cheap!"), people from the lower middle to upper classes who went crazy in Miami's malls repeating, "It's so cheap, give me two." However, the illusion of wealth began to falter on February 18, 1983, a day now popularly known as "Black Friday," when for the first time since the early 1960s the bolivar was devalued. Until then the existence of petrodollars had prevented serious social conflict by allowing the nation at least a superficial resolution of its many structural problems. It was at this time that some people, such as Elisa Lerner, began to wonder what would happen to a democratic system built upon the fantasy of endless oil wealth:

> The advantages of the "oil fairy" are almost gone. Before the devaluation of February 18, 1983, the oil fairy functioned as the "dollar princess" in the now forgotten central European operetta. Thus, we have to ask ourselves: could a national democratic project survive and mature in a nation where the budget suddenly has stopped being an overwhelming fantasy? Do we have enough strength to substitute the false brightness of the Miami sequin with a gentle passion useful to Venezuela? In the years to come, Venezuelans will have to speak, and above all they will have to act. (Lerner, 1995: 18)

If up until now many people had somehow benefited from the oil wealth, what would happen as oil prices dropped? It had suddenly become clear that democratic governments, no matter which party was in power, had failed to fulfill the promise of a modern Venezuela. The reality was that even in the 4.30 era the masses had a poor standard of living. True, in the early 1980s underneath the capital city, *caraqueños* could enjoy a new, efficient metro comparable to the most advanced systems in the world. Yet the barrios had increased in size. By then approximately 50 percent of the population lived in shantytowns and low-income housing. One study showed that already in 1982, 22.5 percent of the population lived under conditions of moderate poverty while 11 percent were critically poor (Riutort, 2001: 18–19). Still, expectations had risen for the poor during the 1970s; in the 1980s, everyday life for an increasing number of Venezuelans was increasingly one of enduring humiliations and long lines in order to gain access to basic services. This sense of inequality deepened, as the following government of *adeco* Jaime Lusinchi was riddled with excesses and corruption scandals (see Pérez Perdomo and Capriles, 1991; Pérez Perdomo, 1995).

The Collapse of the Illusion of Wealth

As in the rest of Latin America, in Venezuela the unequal distribution of income became acute throughout the 1980s: in 1989 the poorest 20 percent of households in Venezuela had 4.8 percent of the income, while the wealthiest 20 percent had 49.5 percent of the income (World Bank, 1994: 221). In the late 1980s the erosion of the oil economy became more evident to the general population: it was harder to obtain credit, to earn higher salaries, or to fund the universities properly. Those categorized as "middle class" decreased from 60.1 percent in 1982 to 34.4 percent in 1990 (Riutort, 2001: 18–19).

> For more than thirty years, Venezuela spent 10 to 14 percent of its GNP [gross national product] on so-called social programs. For instance, as data from the World Bank show, in the health sector, Venezuela spent *three times* more per capita in 1985 than Chile, Jamaica, or Panama. But in 1988, Venezuela's infant mortality was 200 percent higher than Jamaica's, 80 percent higher than Chile's, and 30 percent higher than Panama's. (Naím, 1993: 42–43)

In 1988 I returned to the country from studying abroad. I remember my two grandmothers and a large part of the voting population being excited about the candidacy of Carlos Andrés Pérez, who was seeking to return to the presidency. There was the illusion that if he won, Venezuela would go back to the days of the 4.30 era. One of my grandmothers simply hoped she could travel as often as she did in the past, while the other prayed that her life savings would be secure. Pérez was elected for a new term in December 1988, taking on a huge foreign debt (approximately U.S.$43 billion), the taint of moral scandals left by former president Jaime Lusinchi, and a population that expected and looked forward to the same wealth and distribution it had enjoyed during his first term.[4]

However, on February 27, 1989, only a few days after Pérez came to power and announced his intention to implement a structural adjustment program, *el paquete* ("the package"), popular violence broke out in Venezuela's major cities. Journalists in Caracas called it "the day the shantytowns came down from the hills." For five days, large crowds of people took over the streets, entering shops, looting, breaking windows, burning tires, and stealing cars. The poor and the marginalized residents of the shantytowns, as well as many considered middle class, were no longer passively accepting price inflation, food shortages, and the collapse of social services. The collective but unorganized and spontaneous rejection of rampant inequality translated into practices of overt, desperate, and surreal violence. Media images showed people from different strata of society running wildly out of shopping malls, pushing supermarket carts full of cartons of milk, television sets, and Coca-Cola bottles (Márquez, 1999: 16).

The February 27 riots were followed by two attempted military coups, on February 4 and November 27, 1992. The first one was led by Lieutenant Colonel Hugo Chávez. A *chavista* university professor (in a personal interview) explains why this was the beginning of Chávez's political popularity:

> The first support wave for Chávez stems from the fact that he led a coup. People liked the coup attempt. Let's be clear on that. The fact that somebody wanted to overthrow a government through a coup was a new thing for most Venezuelans. The truth is that the largest percentage of our population is very young. . . . For an eighteen-year-old it is sort of cool that a man takes up arms and tries to change the government. To that youngster today it doesn't seem a bad thing at all.[5]

In Search of Political Peace

In December 1993, Rafael Caldera was elected president on a platform offering to reverse the economic liberalization policies of Pérez. Caldera was the founder of COPEI and had been elected president on that party's ticket for the period 1969–1974, but now he was running as the candidate of an ad hoc alliance, Convergencia. Most people I interviewed during fieldwork in Caracas in 1993 said they voted for Caldera because he was the only person who could guarantee political peace and because he was an honest man. Their motives are understandable, considering that the previous presidential term was marked by the February 27 riots, the two failed military coups of 1992, and the impeachment of President Pérez in 1993.

As part of his attempt to restore stability, President Caldera released from prison the leaders of the 1992 coup attempts, including Chávez. In economic policy, Caldera's government imposed exchange and price controls, but ultimately he failed to reverse the economy's opening to market forces and momentum for privatization (see Chapter 6). He faced a major financial crisis in 1994, involving 60 percent of the Venezuelan banking system, resulting in losses equivalent to 20 percent of GNP. After two years of dismal economic performance, Caldera accepted the devaluation of the currency in 1995 and adopted in April 1996 a new set of liberalizing policies known as the "Venezuela Agenda" (Francés, 2001: 12).

By the end of Caldera's term, Venezuela was stricken with high rates of poverty. As the real salaries decreased over the years, so did the quality of life of most Venezuelans. In that context, issues such as the unequal and inefficient allocation of resources by the state came to the fore. In the late 1990s, there was a widespread feeling among the population that the traditional parties, as well as their politicians, were in large measure responsible for the terrible political, economic, and social crisis.

In this period, I was actively working with marginal young people living, working, or hanging out on the streets of Caracas. As Figure 11.1 indicates, poverty rates were climbing. Life was getting even harder for the great majority of citizens living in crowded barrios of the capital, where even running water was and is still lacking. Up in the hills surrounding the valley of Caracas, the people endured long lines to catch the Jeeps taking them down to their jobs; to get back to their ranchos, they walked up rickety steps so flimsy that they sometimes fell apart when it rained.

Figure 11.1   Percentage of Poor Households, 1980–1996

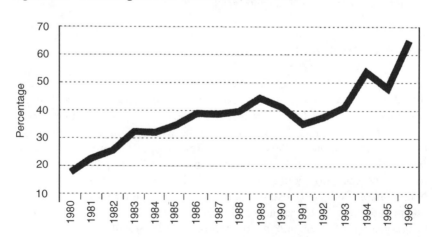

Source: Oficina Central de Estadísticas e Infomática, cited in Baena et al., 1998.

Young people in particular found their realistic options unacceptable, and reduced to few opportunities other than working, for example, as office boys for minimum wage. This feeling was particularly acute because they experienced abject poverty in the vicinity of a small but very visible elite with great wealth. For many of them, Hugo Chávez would be the hope for a better life. One individual I interviewed, twenty-two-year-old Jeilson, a motorcycle messenger for a company and an only son, stated the following:

> When I voted for Chávez, it was the first vote in my life. Why did I vote for him? There was so much anarchy within the old parties AD and COPEI. They had promised so many things and they never delivered. I trust that Chávez will do a better job. He wants equality for all Venezuelans. He wants neither rich nor poor people. For him we should all have the same.

Por estas calles . . .

Popular representations have provided a way for Venezuelans of different strata to further interpret the crisis that was becoming evident in the early 1990s. Songs, soap operas, and jokes offer a common language of characters, expressions, and representations that make it easier to understand or to make some sense of what has happened over the years.[6] In the 1990s, the soap opera *Por estas calles . . .* created idioms and characters that allowed the establishment of a dialogue between different members of society—a dialogue in which the boundaries between the real and the fictional in everyday life came together.[7] In its two-year run the series introduced a cast of characters who offered a vocabulary to converse about what was happening on the streets and in society at large. I discuss here four male characters: Don Chepe Orellana, Dr. Valerio, Eudomar Santos, and Rodilla, whose roles touched on four main areas where Venezuelans felt immediate transformations were needed: politics, corruption, violence, and impunity.[8]

Don Chepe, the governor, together with those who surrounded him, personified all the major political scandals of recent decades. The character of Don Chepe appeared to be based primarily on former president Jaime Lusinchi, who was manipulated by his private secretary (now wife), Blanca Ibañez (Lucha in the soap opera). Together, the characters Don Chepe and Lucha went through an election (at the same time as the actual national election of December 1993), developed all sorts of illegal schemes to gain more power, and eliminated political enemies by means of brute force. From Monday to Saturday, Don Chepe and his companions offered a tragicomic parody of real-life current politics, portraying the inefficiency, bureaucracy, and corruption that plagued the Venezuelan governments of recent decades.

The character Dr. Valerio was a caricature of the upper-middle-class scoundrel. He ran a private clinic and went through life developing schemes to obtain more money and power within the institution. Valerio had connections with groups who stole equipment from public hospitals and sold it to private clinics for less than market price. This very common practice in Venezuela underlies the deterioration of public hospitals. Dr. Valerio, like many well-known white-collar crooks, boasted about his cleverness in cheating the system.

Dr. Valerio was juxtaposed to Eudomar Santos in the soap opera, and in viewers' imagination these characters represented two versions of Venezuelans' *facilismo* ("easy way out"). They had in common the same two women and a desire for fast money with little effort. Eudomar Santos was a barrio man in his late twenties who, although he had more scruples than Dr. Valerio, also wanted to get rich the easy way. Dr. Valerio was educated and respected by society. Eudomar Santos was dark-skinned, and he was looked down upon by those in power as a petty crook. Santos was always looking for a *chamba,* an odd job often in the informal economy. Like Dr. Valerio, Santos was always in search of an opportunity to make money fast and easy. He represented those who as unproductive members of the economy reproduce the broader system of corruption. He popularized the slogan *"como vamos viendo, vamos yendo"* ("easy come, easy go"), symbolizing the short-term vision of many Venezuelans lacking viable options for stable employment. Most people live from day to day on wages that do not allow savings for the future, especially in a context of high political and economic uncertainty.

The most unexpected surprise of the series was Rodilla (whose name literally means "knee"), a fourteen-year-old boy who was a sort of *malandro* (a thug from the barrio). Rodilla appeared in the second year of the soap opera and brought the ratings back up. He was the next generation after Eudomar Santos, representing the new gangs who terrorized the barrio with their guns. Rodilla touched one of society's open wounds. He personalized the current degree of violence in the cities. He was indeed responsible for a great degree of individual violence (assaults and robberies), but every time he wanted to change, he argued he could not. Like many young people today, Rodilla felt that no matter what he did, he was always treated harshly by the state institutions, which were supposed to protect him.

This soap opera was a popular representation of the frustrations of many Venezuelans in the early 1990s. It is a metaphor for the crisis of democracy as actually lived at that time (for a discussion of the crisis of democracy, see Kornblith, 1998; Canache and Kuisheck, 1998; Alvarez, 1996a). By the 1993 election people were starting to seek change and they hoped that President Caldera would implement economic, political, and social policies to better the quality of life. However, during these years the quality of life worsened, crime rates soared (see Figure 11.2), and corruption continued to appear blatant. All this opened space for a political leader offering change in a very different fashion from formulas of the past.

Expressions of the Crisis

Popular expressions offer another way to get a sense of how everyday life was experienced in the 1990s. Obviously I can present only a sample of the terms that gained importance in conversations and interactions and that help make sense of the complex social fabric. I have chosen seven terms that reveal the deepening crisis for all strata of society and touch on a variety of themes—work dynamics, living arrangements, bureaucracy, violence, and access to basic services.

Matar tigre *(to kill a tiger).* As average annual salaries fell from U.S.$14,890 in 1978 to U.S.$6,421 in 1998, increasing numbers of professionals had to moonlight to maintain their standard of living (Baptista, 1997). For the lower classes, the term frequently used is *la chamba,* the occasional odd job found most often in the informal economy. Approximately 58 percent of the labor force worked in the informal sector. People increasingly searched for *chambas* as unemployment rates soared to 19 percent in the late 1990s.

Anexo *(room annex).* This term refers to how people from the middle and upper classes divided their houses either to obtain a rent in order to supple-

Figure 11.2 Declared Homicides, 1980–1996

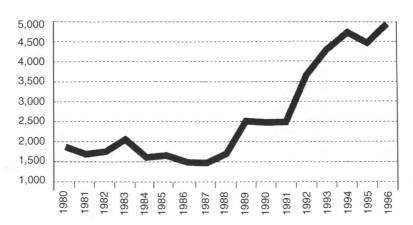

Source: Oficina Central de Estadísticas e Informática, cited in Baena et al., 1998.

ment their income or to solve the increasing difficulties their children faced in getting their own homes. In the barrios people use the term *planta* to refer to spaces used for the same purposes.

Conseguir cama *(to find a bed).*   Approximately 90 percent of the population use public hospitals. To undergo even simple surgical procedures people have to deal with the problem of "finding a bed." Since most hospitals are overcrowded, a patient might visit a hospital daily until he finds an available bed, where he can remain for a few days to months. The timing of the operation depends on a variety of factors, such as the availability of all the equipment and the ability to complete previous medical exams—which also entails patience and enduring long lines. While occupying the bed, people sometimes have to wait a long time; families need to provide all necessities, even drinking water. Having a friend as an employee at the hospital can help speed the procedure.

Cacerolazo *(banging on pots and pans).*   *Cacerolazos* emerged as a collective voice of protest in the 1990s. They started in the barrios after Chávez's coup attempt in 1992 as a way to express support. Throughout the decade, other social classes adopted the *cacerolazo* as a form of protest. Through the noise created, seemingly powerless people opened a dialogue with a deaf state.[9]

Encapuchado *(hooded).*   This term refers to increasing numbers of people protesting on the streets with T-shirts wrapped around their faces. Frequently, *encapuchados* are students protesting outside their university or high school over issues such as transportation fare increases or increased tuition costs at universities.

Gestor.   A profession born out of bureaucratic inefficiencies. With an increasingly inefficient state apparatus there has been a proliferation of *gestores,* whose job it is to help people navigate the bureaucracy to accomplish even the most menial administrative tasks. In Venezuela, getting a passport or a driver's license can be a harrowing experience. It is common to stand in line from five o'clock in the morning waiting for the office to open, only to find out that you might have to come back even earlier another day because only the first 100 people in line will be attended to, and unfortunately you are not one of them. Therefore, if you can afford it, you hire a *gestor,* a person who will get needed papers for a fee and will relieve you of having to stand in line.

Habilitar.   Although this is a legal term that implies the speeding of legal transactions, there is hardly a process involving a notary's office or judicial court where it is not used. Due to inefficiencies and corruption, state institutions have institutionalized the *habilitación*. If a person wants to avoid waiting for ridiculously long periods of time for a signature or a stamp, he or she will have to pay extra. There is almost no choice.

Supporting Chávez

In the 1990s, the majority of the people experienced economic hardships and a complete loss of faith in traditional politicians and political parties. A society sharing until that time a sense of "moving forward," as well as an illusion of wealth, faced a reality where social groups were moving in different directions. No longer did "the illusion of harmony" (to borrow the term from Naím and Piñango, 1985) hold true for Venezuelans. A large part of the population entered the informal sector. Those labeled as "middle class" increasingly despaired as their income diminished and opportunities for upward mobility waned. Bottled-up resentment against some groups identified as corrupt or easy to blame for the crisis—bankers and politicians—exploded into the open, leading to growing manifestations of resentment from people in the lower socioeconomic strata toward those they saw as the privileged sectors of society.

In this context of growing disenchantment and social polarization, Hugo Chávez emerged with a completely different political style and rhetoric. In the words of one professor:

> In creativity Chávez should get a score of 200 points. His political model embodies change. Upon examining the results of the elections, the conclusion is that his political strategy was brilliant. He followed the non-party model. His power lies in the masses' [*el pueblo*'s] support. He baptized the masses "the sovereign" and he was their leader. Remember that Venezuelans are poor; life is hard and they want change.

Hugo Chávez's emergence in political life brought an immediate and unprecedented wave of optimism among a large segment of the population.[10] Figure 11.3 illustrates how from 1989 until 1998 the only moment of optimism was a relatively low peak reached in 1993 during President Carlos Andrés Pérez's impeachment on the grounds of misuse of public funds. The graph dramatically shows that as soon as Chávez appeared in the political scene as a presidential candidate for the 1998 election, a widespread optimism appeared among people. How can a single person create such a wave of optimism?[11]

Hugo Chávez appealed to the discontented and the disillusioned, as well as the hopeful. That includes young people in the *barrios,* as represented by Eudomar Santos and Rodilla in the television series, the disgrun-

Figure 11.3   Evolution of the Nation's Climate

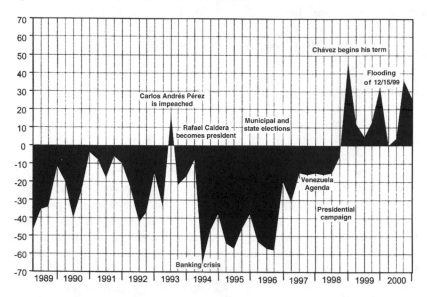

Source: Questionnaires designed and conducted by Consultores 21 every trimester since 1989.

Note: Vertically placed numbers refer to people's perception of their situation and that of the country as a whole, with extremes ranging from positive 100 to negative 100.

tled and shrinking middle classes facing pressing economic conditions, and the small-business entrepreneurs for whom things were getting tough. Unlike the distant, highly educated, and aged Dr. Caldera, Chávez was perceived to be a man of the people; he was young and expressed himself with energy, sounding almost like Eudomar Santos would in an everyday situation. He broke the traditional protocol followed by politicians who emulate the "high-culture" political style of the West. In fact, even today people of all kinds refer to him in everyday talk, as well as in public discussions, as "Chávez," not as "President Chávez," "Dr. Chávez," or anything else. For friends and enemies, he is simply "Chávez." I interviewed a sixty-seven-year-old woman named Selma who had been looking for work for five years and claimed that she had been unsuccessful because of her age and the fact that she had seven children: "I like how he speaks because it comes from his heart. When he is talking he always mentions first and foremost his *pueblo* [the people]. I like it when he says that he wants to move his country forward and that he wants equality for poor and rich people. That would be great. The problem is if others don't let him govern."

In popular imagination Chávez embodies many things, but more than anything else he is seen as the representative of a centralized power, visually embodied in the figure of president/caudillo. In his nationalistic style he repeatedly associates himself with the liberator Simón Bolívar. Like nineteenth-century caudillos of the past, such as Antonio Guzmán Blanco (1870–1888), Chávez continually builds on mythology surrounding Bolívar to legitimate his own actions and politics. Before and after being elected, his rhetoric became imbued with nationalism and a sense that his government would radically transform the order of things in the local and international spheres.

People in the barrios and those of the middle class who supported Chávez saw in him more simple virtues. He seemed to talk with them and was like them in many ways. Anyone hearing him in his weekly Sunday radio program *¡Aló Presidente!* could not help but be impressed by his communication skills. He entertained and informed the masses in unprecedented ways. In my interviews, the following were typical comments:

> I like the way he [Chávez] talks to people. He tells the truth. . . . If you think about the *cadenas* [mandatory national broadcasts] they are very good. What president has provided you with so much information?[12] (Tomás, thirty-eight years old, owns his own hot dog cart)
>
> All the politicians forgot about us after the elections. For Chávez we are still important because he says we are the sovercign. Can you imagine? We are the sovereign! (Alirio, twenty-eight years old, teacher at a public school with two sons)
>
> When he talks the first thing he says is "I'm here because the *pueblo* want me here, if they want me to stay then I stay." (Carmen, fifty-six years old, has a street stand in downtown Caracas and five children)

In most of the interviews I conducted in Los Erasos, people also voiced their deep belief that Chávez would fulfill the promises of the past. No longer would rampant corruption—a reified villain in popular consciousness—deter state resources from reaching them in the form of most basic services. Wilson, a thirty-year-old man I interviewed, confirms that Chávez after two years in power seemed to prioritize the needs of the poor:

> Chávez is a good man. He is helping all of us. You can see how this is the case with the Vargas tragedy.[13] Since then, many people have gotten new homes. There you can see change. Before him all we had were promises. All the stuff was for those high-up there, not for us from the barrios.

Yuleisi, thirty-five years old and a mother of four, had been a longtime *adeca*. When I asked her why she decided to support Chávez she said: "I was very *adeca,* my family is very *adeca,* but no government has given so much to poor people." When I asked her what Chávez had given to the people, she replied: "Attention. Besides, don't you see all the things he gave to people during the Vargas tragedy?" As she was going on about why she believed in Chávez's sincerity about improving the situation of the poor, we heard a gunshot in the distance, and she interrupted her previous statements to point out to me why people were desperate for change:

> This is the sort of thing that should change. We want to move out of here. Unfortunately I live here with my husband and my children. I have nowhere else to go. What do you see when you look out this window? It is hideous. You see that people are stealing or smoking. It is horrible. It is horrible. . . . We neighbors are angry at each other. Some are decent people, but many are not and can hurt you. How can you live watching your back all the time because you or any of your children can get killed any second? I'd move if I could.

From testimonies like these, it appears that people who were disappointed in politicians in general expected Chávez to deliver on his promises:

> People voted for him because they trust that he is going to fix our *barrio*. In the past we heard many promises: they are going to give jobs to people, they are going to deal with delinquents, you know. . . . Chávez is really going to move this forward. In a few months he is going to offer credits for the poor. (Pedro, forty-six years old, owns a small grocery store in the barrio and is a longtime *adeco*)

Venezuelans hardly were seeing themselves as active agents in the changes allegedly taking place. As in the previous forty years, the change they often want relates to distribution of the nation's wealth. Out of 1,000 people polled in 1998 by AKSA Partners, 92 percent said that Venezuela was a rich country; 82 percent answered that it was the government's job to distribute that wealth equally.[14] Newspaper accounts such as the following are examples of how people's expectations of the new regime continued to be based on the same rentier mentality of the past—the redistribution of oil wealth by the state:

> Thousands of petitions come pouring in every day. The petitions cover a wide range of expectations. Some ask for minor things, such as a piano or a meal for a sporting event, while in others people express more critical problems, such as the need for surgery, an organ transplant, or medicines. Other people write asking for money to buy an apartment. In Miraflores [the presidential palace] a million letters arrive every month and that does not include all the others that are addressed to La Casona [the president's residence], to the *Aló Presidente* program, or are given to him directly. (*El Nacional*, January 26, 2001, p. D-1)

The above account illustrates the sense of urgency and impotence people feel in a country where the quality of life has increasingly deteriorated.

It also speaks of a culture of paternalism. People expect to have a person or an organization solve their problems, whether these pertain to a musical instrument or a new roof for a family of ten. There have been populist presidents in the past, but the phenomenon of people inserting thousands of papers into Chávez's pockets while he is at an official event is new, suggesting the importance of his symbolic actions. In part, Chávez's support stemmed from his actions and his attention to specific cases. Any Sunday a man might call to tell the president that he can no longer work because his motorcycle broke down and he cannot afford the repairs. Chávez would tell him not to worry because he knows a mechanic where he should take the motorcycle and get it fixed at his expense. Then, during the program itself he would provide the exact address. Examples like this are typical. For the very first time, the socially excluded felt they were receiving continuous and direct attention from the powerful.

Hugo Chávez in the twenty-first century appeared to have a messianic appeal to the masses. That is not surprising for a culture accustomed to the presence of caudillos setting the course of the nation. In the end, a question that still remains unanswered is, how different a leader is Hugo Chávez? In some ways Chávez's many promises of welfare for a greater majority, as well as his dreams for an increasing international role for Venezuela, were reminiscent of those from past presidents. For instance, former president Carlos Andrés Pérez, amid the oil boom of the 1970s, promised greater social mobility, prosperity, and modernization, and to some degree he was able to deliver. His great charisma and similar promises, in the context of a very different economic and social situation, got him reelected in December 1988. After people realized that he would not act as promised, his government faced the 1989 Caracazo, two military coup attempts, and other forms of protest and resistance. If Chávez fails to deliver, eventually the reaction could be even stronger than that against Pérez.

In fact, the growing social polarization led to tragic and violent results when at least seventeen people died on April 11, 2002. On that day hundreds of thousands of people marched against Chávez and encountered a gathering of his followers, as well as the national guard. Shooting broke out. The episode points to the radicalization of differences: those in favor of and opposed to the Chávez administration increasingly protest in the open, and display their hatred and intolerance for those they consider to be "the Other." This polarization threatens Venezuela's social fabric, as family members and neighbors confront each other, and cities such as Caracas become even more spatially, politically, and emotionally divided.

Regardless of whether Chávez is a phenomenal communicator, a leader, an amazing politician, or a symbolic icon, he entered the presidency with the highest level of popularity in the last forty years of democracy. In the search for change, people endowed him with an enormous amount of political capital. Many Venezuelans believed that, unlike rulers of the past, Chávez was going to come through for them. However, the paternalism embodied in his rhetoric and actions ran contrary to the main principle of his so-called revolution, namely "participatory democracy." Unless Venezuelans are able to overcome the culture of paternalism reinforced over the last forty years by clientelistic practices, and transform a social order in which the majority are passive actors, participatory democracy will remain just another demagogical category or a political ruse.

Notes

I want to thank the people from the barrio Los Erasos who shared with me their views about Chávez, as well as their perceptions about what is happening in Venezuela. I also want to thank the following people, with whom I had long conversations that pushed the limits of my anthropological imagination: Carlos Jaramillo, Rogelio Pérez Perdomo, Federico Villanueva, Mariadela Villanueva, Iraima Camejo, and Janet Kelly. I am also grateful to Alfredo Keller of AKSA and Nicolás Toledo of Consultores 21 for sharing the results of the opinion polls they have conducted in the last decade.

1. The terms *adecos* and *copeyanos* refer to members of AD and COPEI and their sympathizers.

2. Catia is a low-income community in Caracas.

3. In February 2001, approximately 705 bolivars equaled 1 U.S. dollar.

4. Other chapters in this book deal with popular frustration with Pérez and his structural adjustment program, *el paquete*. These neoliberal reforms dealt with four areas: commercial reform, fiscal deficit, financial reform, and labor reform. However, the question of who would shoulder the program's social costs was largely ignored.

5. All interviewee names have either been changed or remain anonymous for the purpose of confidentiality.

6. In 1993, approximately 89 percent of all Venezuelan households had television sets. A popular soap opera might reach 50 percent of the population in a prime-time evening slot (Enright, Francés, and Saavedra, 1996: 75).

7. A more detailed discussion of the meaning of *Por estas calles . . .* appears in Márquez, 1999.

8. The soap opera began in June 1992 and was written to have only 250 episodes, to be shown from Monday to Saturday from 9:00 to 10:00 P.M. However, it was so successful, capturing about 70 percent of the viewers, that it was extended for over two years. As the series went on, new episodes merged real and fictional events, such as water shortages, homicides, and the 1993 national electoral campaign.

9. *Cacerolazos* were already popular in countries like Argentina, where people throughout the 1980s protested hyperinflation and economic instability by banging on pots and pans.

10. The degrees of optimism and negativism defining the nation's climate derive from the sum of the answers to a set of five questions asked by the organization Consultores 21 every trimester since 1989. The questionnaires are answered by 1,500 people from cities with a population of more than 20,000. People are asked to

respond to the following questions: (1) How do you see Venezuela's situation today? (2) How do you see your own personal and family situation today? (3) How do you see Venezuela's situation six months from now? (4) How do you see your own personal and family situation six months from now? (5) How do you see your own current situation compared to others? All of these questions provide the same set of possible answers: very good, good, regular-good, regular-bad, bad, or very bad.

11. Despite his popularity, Chávez also produced high levels of rejection, especially among the upper classes. His critics can be as passionate as his supporters. Criticisms included his personal appearance and traits: skin color, vulgarity, lack of education, and the like.

12. The term *cadena* refers to simultaneous broadcasts by television channels and radio stations. Chávez's *cadenas* lasted from one to four hours.

13. On December 15, 1999, in the biggest natural disaster in twentieth-century Venezuela, massive floods wiped out many areas along the northern coast. Thousands of people lost their lives and many others were left homeless.

14. "De como la cultura política se traduce en conducta electoral: El Caso Venezuela 1998," March 1999. Presentation prepared by Alfredo Keller based on results obtained from the AKSA poll.

12

Conclusion: The Democratic and Authoritarian Directions of the *Chavista* Movement

Steve Ellner and Daniel Hellinger

Determining the direction of the Venezuelan democratic system in the context of neoliberalism after 1989, and under the government of Hugo Chávez ten years later, has been the overriding concern of this book. Such a depiction and evaluation is not easy due to the extreme polarization that currently characterizes Venezuelan politics and society. Polarization has largely centered on the figure of one individual and thus detracts from an appreciation of broader political and socioeconomic developments. In addition, it has encouraged exaggerated and emotional responses that interfere with the objective analysis of a process whose end result, in the aftermath of the failed coup of April 12, 2002, is yet to be defined.

Democracy in the Context of
Extreme Social and Political Polarization

Venezuelan democracy has never been as sharply polarized as during the 1998 presidential campaign and the subsequent years of Hugo Chávez's presidency. Chávez's supporters were consistently pitted against his adversaries, who in effect united around his main rival in the presidential elections in 1998 and 2000. Nearly every major proposition advanced by the government generated intense opposition and debate, from drafting a new constitution to education policy. If Chávez often indulged in extreme rhetoric and accused the opposition of treasonous behavior, many of his opponents responded in kind. In doing so, they heavily relied on the mass media, much of which did not hide its antagonism to the government and even played an important role in the attempted overthrow of Chávez in April 2002. The opposition forcefully took its grievances to the international arena, such as the International Labour Organization and the Human

Rights Commission of the Organization of American States, which as a result became important actors in Venezuelan politics. Even in informal conversations in Venezuela, the name Chávez invariably evoked emotional reactions, thus leaving little room for a middle position. His adversaries frequently called him "crazy" and "irresponsible," while his admirers saw a man possessed of extensive knowledge, analytical capacity, and diverse interests. Indeed, it would appear that his followers and opponents were describing two completely different realities.

Perhaps the most striking aspect of the polarization of political organizations in Venezuela is the barrenness of a middle ground between *chavismo* and the hardened opposition. Although widely considered a leftist abroad and by his opponents at home, Chávez did not receive praise from pro-leftist groups and individuals outside his ruling coalition. For instance, parties such as Causa R and Izquierda Democrática (ID) lashed out at the government for breaking with established democratic norms, but they failed to balance their criticism with approval for those policies and actions (such as foreign, economic, and oil policies) that to a certain extent coincided with traditional leftist stands. Indeed, the ID dissolved itself in May 2001 to form part of the Unión para el Progreso, founded by Chávez's archrival Francisco Arias Cárdenas.

Polarization is also reflected in writing on Venezuela. Political analysts tend to pigeonhole Chávez as an "authoritarian nationalist" in the tradition of Egypt's Gamal Abdul Nasser, or a "neopopulist" similar to Alberto Fujimori. This tendency in favor of simplification, and comparisons without contrasts, is all too common among political essayists of all types (Caballero, 2000: 145–163; Kissinger, 2001: 87).

Writing in the aftermath of the failed April coup, we believe that the Chávez phenomenon is complex and that its direction remains to be defined. This uncertainty, combined with dramatic changes such as the collapse of the long-standing political party system and the empowerment of new actors, places Venezuela at a critical juncture. A unique set of characteristics militates against facile comparisons. Chávez's ascension to power through electoral means (and not through force as he originally attempted), and the new constitution, which sets in motion novel democratic practices, make comparisons with Nasser, Fidel Castro, and other leaders of nonliberal or nondemocratic states simplistic, if not misleading. Comparisons with Fujimori are also flawed. Fujimori displayed greater antiparty behavior than Chávez and indeed dissolved his own electoral organization practically after every election, at the same time that he failed to award party leaders government posts. Furthermore, Chávez's independent foreign policy, his radical discourse, and his failure to promote massive privatization distinguished him from Fujimori, who consequently did not face adamant opposition from the church, the state department, and business organizations, as did his Venezuelan counterpart.

Nevertheless, comparisons with Fujimori are not entirely unfounded. Chávez's followers failed to invigorate social movements in order to fill the vacuum created by the dissolution of the neocorporatist structures associated with the Punto Fijo regime. Chávez's own Movimiento Quinta República (MVR; Fifth Republic Movement) refrained from calling internal elections, which according to the new constitution are obligatory, and the party hardly broke with the hierarchical structure and clientelistic practices of the Acción Democrática (AD) and the Comité de Organización Política Electoral Independiente (COPEI). Like Fujimori, Chávez developed a special relationship with the military and appointed numerous officers to positions in the government and his party (as Deborah Norden discusses in Chapter 5).

Rather than placing Chávez in a ready-made category, we believe that a more nuanced approach is needed. A good starting point to understanding the impact of *chavismo* on the political system is its special appeal to the poorest and most marginalized strata of the population, which lack job security, social security, and influential interlocutors at any level. Indeed, the point of departure for this volume is the proposition that social polarization—more than the problem of extreme centralization that long characterized Venezuelan institutions—is the most fruitful place to begin in order to analyze the political crisis in Venezuela after 1989 and the concomitant rise of *chavismo*.

In Venezuela after 1958, as on the rest of the continent, social injustice was an important concern of the governing parties that came out of populist and prolabor traditions. As a result, the standard of living of nonprivileged sectors in Venezuela improved substantially. Indeed, in Latin America as a whole, economic disparities narrowed in the 1960s and 1970s, albeit in ever so moderate terms (Cornia, 1998). Several chapters in this volume, most notably those by Kenneth Roberts (Chapter 3) and Julia Buxton (Chapter 6), show how neoliberal policies in the context of globalization imperatives aggravated conditions of poverty at the same time that they increased the economic gap between rich and poor. The Venezuelan poor showed a notably higher preference for a return to state interventionist policies and opposition to neoliberal formulas than did privileged sectors (see Table 3.1).

Beginning in the 1980s, the discontent, alienation, and rebelliousness of the marginalized poor in Venezuela were at the root of the nation's political crisis. These social tensions were released during the February 27, 1989, disturbances, initiating what Margarita López Maya (1999) has called a five-year-long "cycle of protests," which included marches, street closings, and building takeovers by poor people. In addition, the disillusionment and cynicism of the marginal class helped generate high rates of electoral abstention (Buxton, 2001: 68; see also Table 2.3 in this volume), which also did much to undermine credibility in the democratic system. Finally, the prevailing sense of rebelliousness and outrage contributed to delinquency, which reached critical levels in the 1990s and led many Venezuelans to question the efficaciousness of the nation's democracy.

Throughout history, poverty-stricken sectors of the population who are not incorporated into fairly autonomous interest groups and movements have seldom constituted a solid political base for liberal democratic regimes. Very often they support demagogic leaders who move in an authoritarian direction. Nevertheless, the Chávez government diverged in various important ways from this pattern. First, during his first three years in office, Chávez displayed greater respect for democracy than many other leaders who have cultivated a charismatic relationship with the disenfranchised. The discourse of the *chavista* movement stressed the deepening of democracy and the role of civil society and was free of the technocratic vision embraced by Fujimori and other recent Latin American leaders with considerable lower-class backing. Although Chávez failed to develop new structures to deepen democracy, he did avoid state-sponsored repression against the communications media, which was extremely hostile to his government; nor did he consistently use force against demonstrations calling for his removal from office, and instead responded by mobilizing his own followers. Second, Chávez counted on the firm support of an important bloc within the armed forces—as demonstrated by the abortive coup of April 2002—which rejected authoritarian doctrines.

Furthermore, since the early 1990s, the marginalized poor in Venezuela have shown an outstanding capacity to engage in political and social action. They have at times occupied urban space, seized land, and marched in support of leaders and demands. In fact, by 2002, in response to large middle-class rallies in the wealthier, eastern districts of the Caracas metropolitan area, President Chávez found himself heavily relying upon marches through lower-class areas.

Nevertheless, these mobilizations did not translate themselves into organizational advances. Historically, the marginalized poor in Venezuela failed to create enduring autonomous organizations, nor were they integrated into influential neocorporatist structures, as was the Confederación de Trabajadores de Venezuela (CTV; Confederation of Venezuelan Workers) in the Punto Fijo era. For instance, the national leadership of the neighborhood movement, which includes slum areas, consisted of spokesmen who were not organically linked to individual associations. Furthermore, the associations of individual barrios were generally controlled by and dependent on political parties (Ellner, 1999d: 87–94). Thus the marginalized poor, although capable of important protest activities, lacked the particular organizational experience and skills needed to play the participatory role envisioned in the new constitution and to invigorate the MVR as a party independent of its main leader.

The difficulties in organizing the marginalized poor explain in large part the disparity between the MVR's declared intentions to deepen democracy, on the one hand, and the limited progress that was made, on the other. Undeniably, the *chavista* movement was committed to creating new institutions to overcome the hierarchical nature of the neocorporatist structures of the so-called Fourth Republic. Thus the *chavista* constitution embraced the concept of "participatory democracy" and incorporated organizations of civil society in the process of nominations for such key positions as judges (including those of the Supreme Court), the national controller, and members of the National Electoral Commission. In addition, the *chavista* MVR attempted to convert itself into a "movement" and not a "party" with the idea of systematically linking up with social struggles, rather than constituting an elitist vanguard. With that goal in mind, it set up party "fronts" and promoted the creation of neighborhood groups known as the "Bolivarian Circles" (discussed by María Pilar García-Guadilla in Chapter 10). *Chavista* leaders pledged themselves to a special relationship with social movements; indeed the MVR often spurned party allies on grounds that its only real commitment was with "civil society." In mid-2001, Chávez called for the creation of a new political organization that would constitute a "movement of movements" and coexist with the MVR.

Nevertheless, as various authors of this volume point out, throughout its first three years in power, the Chávez movement failed to move boldly toward institutionalizing participatory democracy. It certainly fell short of that ideal in early 2001 when the key role the constitution assigns to civil society in the nomination of Supreme Court judges and other crucial positions was minimized, though not completely discarded (as discussed by Angel Alvarez in Chapter 8). Organizational deficiencies also reflected themselves in the MVR, which lacked formal mechanisms linking higher and lower levels of the party and whose national executive committee failed to incorporate local leaders.

The paternalism and clientelism that characterized relations between MVR leaders and the rank and file represented a major obstacle to achieving participatory democracy. State paternalism permeated the entire Venezuelan society due in large part to the nation's status as an oil exporter, whose most profitable sector generated great revenue but employed few workers (Karl, 1997). Over the years, paternalistic behavior and mentality became especially rooted in the barrios as a result of the particularistic transactions that were the modus operandi of AD and other traditional parties in those areas (Santana, 1986). In Chapter 11, Patricia Márquez provides vivid examples of how Chávez's followers looked to the president for quick and easy solutions to their individual problems. She points out that each day President Chávez received thousands of petitions of this nature. In Chapter 10, García-Guadilla shows how a tendency to treat these petitions individually, rather than to address problems as collective demands, weakened the vitality of social organizations that are essential to the type of democracy envisioned by the new constitution.

A thumbnail comparison with classical populism puts in relief the MVR's institutional difficulties, partly the result of its class composition (Ellner, 2001; see also Chapter 3 in this volume). During the heyday of populism in the 1940s, Venezuela's AD, like other populist parties with considerable working-class influence, was more organizationally solid than the MVR of today, due to linkages to organized labor. AD's contingent of workers was formally incorporated into the party in the form of the Labor Bureau, and their union experience and identity enhanced the sense of discipline that was a party trademark. The collective character of AD's national leadership also contributed to the viability of its internal structure. In contrast, the MVR is in many ways a personalistic party centered on one individual. Unlike the case of AD, the MVR failed to provide leadership or direction to mass mobilizations that were inspired by Chávez or act in his name. This shortcoming was evident in oil worker demonstrations, squatter movements, and student protests, especially the takeover of the Central University of Venezuela in early 2001. In short, the obstacles to organizing the social class that represented Chávez's base of support were a major liability of the *chavista* movement. Such difficulties complicated the "original sin" of *chavismo,* which was that its emergence outside the military was divorced from civilian institutions (as discussed by Margarita López Maya in Chapter 4). This context explains the special challenges *chavismo* faced in building new institutions to replace the old ones it so thoroughly condemned.

Democratic Prospects

Chávez's record on democracy and the efforts to deepen it were far from uniform or consistent. Undoubtedly, his government scored pluses for some initiatives and minuses for others. In Chapter 8, Alvarez describes a government that deserves praise for tolerance of free speech but has arrested promising trends toward needed decentralization. Chávez's efforts to eradicate clientelism and corruption in the judicial system and to democratize the labor movement were commendable, but his means lent themselves to abuses by new actors. Critics of Chávez accused his government of compromising the integrity of the judiciary, but it is difficult to see how any government could have taken on corruption in the courts without inviting charges of interference. The opposition rightfully criticized the Chávez government for failing to formulate charges against corrupt officials, both those belonging to the MVR and those of former administrations.

The human rights record is equally complex. Human rights organizations continued to criticize the police and other security forces, sometimes harshly, but Chávez generally refrained from deploying security forces against the people. The president accepted demands to investigate human rights violations by the military during flood relief operations in December 1999 in the state of Vargas, even though this action precipitated the break from the government of three of his oldest and closest allies. In the aftermath of the April 2001 coup attempt, Chávez acknowledged that some of his supporters were responsible for some of the violence but denied having ordered the armed forces to fire on demonstrators. An independent commission was established to investigate deaths. Its findings were likely to greatly influence the democratic image of the president at home and abroad.

The institutional makeup of Venezuelan democracy also had advances and reverses during the first three years of the Chávez presidency. The Bolivarian constitution, inspired by an innovative, "protagonistic" conception of democracy, included three major offices (called the "Civic Power") charged with "preventing, investigating, and sanctioning activity that runs against public ethics and administrative morality." By "protagonistic democracy," Chávez and his followers had in mind a more participatory system that would allow citizens more initiative in formulating government policy and more constitutional mechanisms for checking the abuses of officeholders. The Bolivarian constitution contained many of the traditional checks and balances associated with liberal, Madisonian norms, but it put more responsibility for holding government accountable in the hands of the people through the Civic Power.

However, as Alvarez and García-Guadilla point out, many key appointments requiring consultation with civil society were made via political deals resembling the highly criticized mode of behavior prevalent during the Punto Fijo era. Although Chávez took office as a civilian through elections, he privileged the armed forces as an institution in many ways and incorporated domestic development projects into their mission. On the one hand, this helped place the armed forces visibly at the side of the people in a way consistent with certain historical myths (e.g., those surrounding the nineteenth-century caudillo Ezequiel Zamora). President Chávez also broke new ground by naming an influential civilian as defense minister. On the other hand, as Norden argues in Chapter 5, Chávez risked further politicizing internal military affairs and promotions, thus contributing to the militarization of politics and politicization of the military.

Democracy's Credibility:
Popular Expectations and Performance

Any evaluation of the impact of *chavismo* on democracy needs to go beyond discussion of the government's record on human rights and respect for democratic institutions. It is necessary to measure the gap between what Chávez and his movement offered the Venezuelan people and what he and his government delivered. The credibility of any democratic system hinges on the success of the nation's leaders in fulfilling electoral promises and avoiding accusations of demagoguery. This is particularly true with an elected leader who claims to be a revolutionary democrat and breaks with long-established political practices and institutions.

Economic performance and the long-term process of transformation also shape attitudes toward the political system. Conventional wisdom suggests a corollary as well: if the poor, the ones Chávez called *"el soberano,"* did not see substantial improvement in their lives, they might have been expected to turn on the president. As Márquez and Roberts argue, *chavistas* and Venezuelans in general blamed corruption for the economic crisis and expected things to improve once the former lieutenant colonel had driven the old political elite from power.

Prior to the decline in oil prices in the second half of 2001, there was evidence of a modest reversal in the deterioration of the economy and of social conditions. A survey in March 2001 showed that over 900,000 Venezuelans had escaped extreme poverty during the previous year, equivalent to a drop of 4 percentage points (*Venezuela al Día,* July 2001, www.venezuelaaldia.com). However, this improvement took place in the context of success in oil policy and higher prices. If Bernard Mommer's pessimistic view of the oil *apertura* is correct (see Chapter 7), Chávez faced an uncertain economic future, even with higher oil prices, because inherited contracts limit Venezuela's share of profits for years to come.

In highly polarized Venezuela, critics of Chávez had little interest in hearing good economic news. Were oil prices higher in 2001? Not because he helped revitalize the Organization of Petroleum-Exporting Countries (OPEC), but because the stars were properly aligned over the marketplace. Had inflation, after nearing triple digits toward the end of the Caldera era, not stabilized at about 10 percent? The reason lay not in fiscal discipline (government spending was actually below targets in 2000), but in the Central Bank's injection of dollar reserves from "windfall" oil rents into the economy to shore up the local currency. Had President Chávez not significantly reduced the international debt? Only by drawing down reserves and borrowing internally, said the opposition. Had not the country's credit rating improved? Were not bond ratings higher? Again, only because of oil prices and recourse to reserve accounts. Besides, critics argued, the bond ratings were not as high as they would have been with a "reliable" president. Did investment flows into Venezuela not increase in 2000? Yes, but not into employment-generating industries, and not enough to prevent capital flight.

We do not mean to suggest that there is a simple relationship between economic performance and political support. A factor difficult to measure is just how poor Venezuelans weighed economic hardship against a sense that Chávez's concerns about their well-being were genuine, not mere demagoguery. How the president was *perceived,* not just how the economy was lived, had a direct bearing on popular support, on his political future and the legitimacy of the new system he sought to install. Had the president's sincerity been successfully challenged because of his personal lifestyle or his failure to carry through on his social priorities, he would certainly have become widely viewed as a demagogue. Amazingly, despite polls showing rising disapproval of the president's performance, the poor rushed to the presidential palace to add their weight to international disapproval of the attempted coup in April 2002.

There were also more concrete reasons why the opposition did not succeed in breaking Chávez's special appeal to the popular sectors and convincing most of its members that Chávez really was a demagogue. The president kept his promise of a constituent assembly, offered significant new initiatives to fund grassroots enterprises, and continued to lambaste the neoliberal policies that speak to the needs of only the "included" minority. He avoided pandering to popular expectations of quick solutions to economic problems. His policies may have been implemented incompletely or flawed, but they reinforced in the popular mind that President Chávez represented a sharp break with a discredited past and privileged lower-class interests over those of the wealthy and the middle class. The key, says Alejandro Moreno, a Salesian priest and social psychologist who lived more than a decade in a Caracas barrio, is that the president addressed himself to "the people," not to elites. Moreno adds: "What is important is not what he speaks but what speaks inside him. In him speaks the convivial relations of popular Venezuela, of convivial man. . . . An elderly woman expressed it very well: 'for me, it's like my own son is president'" (1998: 5). These statements illustrate Chávez's remarkable abilities as a social communicator. Alberto Muller Rojas, a former general who served as chief of staff for the 1998 electoral race, says that the Chávez political persona is no public relations invention but was "self-constructed" without the aid of extensive polling, focus groups, or expensive foreign consultants that better-financed campaigns utilize (Producto Online, 1999).

As several of our contributors point out, Chávez mobilized subaltern sentiments deeply ingrained in Venezuelan national identity, especially when he appealed to powerful historical myths embodied in Simón Bolívar,

Simón Rodríguez, and Ezequiel Zamora. To counter the domination of mass media by the opposition, Chávez used his presidential authority to require radio and television networks to transmit his addresses and presentations, which often took on an extended conversational tone. Punctuated by friendly asides to studio workers, he discussed foreign affairs, tutored the masses in interpretations of Venezuelan history, told anecdotes about challenges faced by humble people, dispensed patronage to solve their problems, and responded, often in nationalist and populist terms, to his critics, referring to them as *"la oligarquía"* and *"los escuálidos."* Middle-class Venezuelans may have found the programs tedious, but they presented the country as once again shaping world events, not merely at their mercy. In both style and substance, Chávez conveyed to the economically excluded the notion that this president took *them* into his confidence.

Chávez's standing in public opinion polls was an important indicator as to whether the nonprivileged sectors, which represented a majority of the population, perceive Chávez's discourse as self-serving and devoid of substance. To the consternation of Chávez's detractors, predictions that his political appeal would disappear rapidly in the absence of rapid improvements in social conditions failed to prove correct in his first two years in office. Then the year 2001 witnessed a steady decline in Chávez's popularity, which to a certain extent may be considered normal for any president during a midterm period (Gil Yepes, 2001). This tendency, however, raised some important questions: Would Chávez indeed turn to more authoritarian or demagogic methods if his popularity continued to decline? Was there reason to think he could sustain enough support to carry him through eleven more years in office, as he projected? Did the polls adequately measure all relevant attitudes about his rule?

Finally, Chávez's credibility hinged on whether Venezuelans perceived that real changes had taken place and formed part of a new model with which they could identify. Just as the new strategy of import substitution and government interventionism shored up democratic credibility in the 1960s when democracy was under attack from the guerrilla left, the Chávez government faced a similar challenge to engender confidence in the future.

More specifically, democratic stability in the context of a radical discourse depended on the development of a new model along with new policies. For example, foreign policy and the government's positions toward OPEC represented two ruptures with the past. Oil prices responded positively to the government's turnabout on OPEC and production. In addition, Chávez employed bold rhetoric about a "multipolar" world, at the same time that he carefully avoided anti-U.S. language and made it clear that Venezuela welcomed foreign investments. In the area of economic policy, however, the changes and successful outcome were much more problematic, as Buxton shows in Chapter 6. Indeed, the government's adversaries on the left, and different currents within the labor movement, have character-ized the Chávez administration's economic policies as a continuation of the neoliberalism first implemented by Carlos Andrés Pérez in 1989.

Venezuela at the Crossroads: Modernization, Polarization, and the Future of Democracy

The debate over economic models and strategies of development (such as neoliberalism and state interventionism) places in evidence conflicting visions of modernization, national identity, and the role Venezuela should play within the hemisphere and global order. Discussion focuses largely on the terms in which the nation inserts itself in the global structure. Nevertheless, the controversy over "modernization" is not new in Venezuela, even though the word became a neoliberal catchword in the 1990s. Indeed, the issue predates "globalization" and for Venezuelans dates back to the outset of the modern period in 1936.

The model of political modernization bequeathed by the French Revolution and the Enlightenment suggests that Latin America will progress only after its traditional, personalist culture is replaced by a civic culture, one populated by rational, educated citizens capable of competing in both the economic and the political marketplace. Consistent with the concept of polyarchy as developed by Robert Dahl (1971), this notion of democracy envisions citizens articulating their interests through freely formed organizations in civic society. Acción Democrática was supposed to lead Venezuela through such a transformation. AD's founder, Rómulo Betancourt, believed that the overwhelming majority of Venezuelans would use the vehicle of universal suffrage to empower the state to confront "oil imperialism," capture a "just share" of profits generated by the nation's subsoil, and invest them in a project of social and economic modernization.

This modernizing project did transform Venezuela in many ways, but the democracy that fully emerged in the form of *puntofijismo* developed into a clientelistic system dependent on oil (as discussed by Daniel Hellinger in Chapter 2). The end result was captured in the well-worn phrase of Juan Carlos Rey (1989): a "populist system of reconciliation." This system never fully overcame extreme class inequality, and proved ill equipped to cope with neoliberalism and globalization. In short, the Punto Fijo system failed to complete the project of modernization that was closely associated with oil nationalism and pacted democracy.

Neoliberals departed from the vision of modernization and the strategy for achieving it put forward by Betancourt's generation, but they also repre-sented the antithesis of the ideals articulated by Chávez. Neoliberals and much of the middle class tended to believe that Chávez, not global economic injustices, was preventing them from securing a place in the new world order. The middle class, clinging to its precarious foothold in the "modern" world, regarded Chávez as anathema. They portrayed Venezuelan society as pathologically distorted—economically and psychologically—by the oil boom. This theme is common in academic discourse, as was espoused in Terry Karl's often-cited study of petro-states (1997). For neoliberals (though not for Karl), only tough medicine administered by the invisible hand of the world market can provide therapy. They characterized Chávez as an anachronism, a populist caudillo resisting the inexorable pull of the Washington consensus. If only Chávez had abandoned his myopic, outdated populism and embraced neoliberal modernization, the economy would have overcome dependence on oil and begun to incorporate Venezuela's masses into the middle class and into modern economy and society.

These arguments—and the barbarism-modernism dichotomy that lurks behind them—are misleading to the extent that they ignore the complexities of the current situation and portray actors along Manichaean lines. We have argued consistently in this book that the Chávez government, far from fitting into ready-made categories associated with Alberto Fujimori, Juan Domingo Perón, or Fidel Castro, is a rather unique and complex phenomenon. At the level of discourse and to a certain extent of action, Chávez defended democracy and capitalism, but at the same time intended to radically transform both of them. Chávez sought to achieve national insertion into the international economy under conditions completely defined by his government. His overriding goal of national sovereignty implied stiff terms imposed on foreign interests, but also interconnectedness, as shown by his determination to attract foreign capital and his support for regional integration. Chávez's opponents argued that his more exacting requirements on investments (as illustrated by new oil legislation), nationalistic rhetoric, and tampering with democratic institutions would scare off foreign capital and set the U.S. government against Venezuela. His supporters maintained that the nation should not spurn modernization, but added that when the specifics are formulated outside the country, the end product is continuing social polarization and dependence and is thus hardly worth the required sacrifices. In short, the feasibility of the *chavista* modernization strategy— vaguely articulated beyond oil policy and mixing participatory democracy with a strong role for the military—is debatable in a world in which global capital and the model of liberal democracy predominate. But this uncertainty and unpredictability is precisely what makes the Venezuelan process so intriguing and important to understand.

References

Agüero, Felipe (1995). "Debilitating Democracy: Political Elites and Military Rebels," pp. 136–162 in Louis Goodman, Johanna Mendelson Forman, Moisés Naím, Joseph S. Tulchin, and Gary Bland, eds., *Lessons of the Venezuelan Experience*. Baltimore: Johns Hopkins University Press.

Alexander, Robert Jackson (1982). *Rómulo Betancourt and the Transformation of Venezuela*. New Brunswick, NJ: Transaction Books.

———(1964). *The Venezuelan Democratic Revolution: A Profile of the Regime of Rómulo Betancourt*. New Brunswick, NJ: Rutgers University Press.

Alfredo Keller and Associates (2000). *Estudio cuantitativo de opinión pública en las diez principales ciudades de Venezuela*. Caracas: Alfredo Keller and Associates, April.

Alvarez, Angel E. (1996a). "La crisis de hegemonía de los partidos políticos venezolanos," pp. 131–154 in Angel E. Alvarez, ed., *El sistema político venezolano: Crisis y transformaciones*. Caracas: Universidad Central de Venezuela.

———ed. (1996b). *El sistema político venezolano: Crisis y transformaciones*. Caracas: Universidad Central de Venezuela.

Ameringer, Charles (1977). "The Foreign Policy of Venezuelan Democracy," pp. 335–358 in John D. Martz and David J. Myers, eds., *Venezuela: The Democratic Experience*. New York: Praeger.

Arriagada Herrera, Genaro (1986). "The Legal and Institutional Framework of the Armed Forces in Chile," pp. 117–143 in J. Samuel Valenzuela and Arturo Valenzuela, eds., *Military Rule in Chile*. Baltimore: Johns Hopkins University Press.

Arrioja, José Enrique (1998). *Clientes Negros: Petróleos de Venezuela bajo la generación Shell*. Caracas: Los Libros de El Nacional.

Arvelo Ramos, Alberto (1998). *El dilema del chavismo: Una incógnita en el poder*. Caracas: Catalá-Centauro.

Asamblea Nacional Constituyente, República de Venezuela (1999). *Gaceta Constituyente (Diario de Debates)*. No. 2 (May 8, 1999), Sesión Ordinaria, Caracas.

Ayala Corao, Carlos (1994). "La democracia venezolana frente a la participación política," pp. 79–110 in Ricardo Combellas, ed., *Venezuela: Crisis política y reforma constitucional*. Caracas: Universidad Central de Venezuela.

Baena, Cesar, Roberto Blanco, Pavel Gómez, and Hector Malavé (1998). "Todo lo que usted quería saber sobre: Datos básicos para un debate." *Debates IESA* 4, no. 1: 35–43.

Baloyra, Enrique A., and John D. Martz (1979). *Political Attitudes in Venezuela: Societal Cleavages and Political Opinion*. Austin: University of Texas Press.

Banko, Catalina (1996). *Las luchas federalistas en Venezuela*. Caracas: Monte Avila Editores.

Baptista, Asdrúbal (1997). *Bases cuantitativas de la economía venezolana, 1830–1995*. Caracas: Fundación Polar.

Baptista, Asdrúbal, and Bernard Mommer (1987). *El petróleo en el pensamiento económico venezolano: Un ensayo*. Caracas: Ediciones IESA.

Bartolini, Stefano, and Peter Mair (1990). *Identity, Competition, and Electoral Availability: The Stabilisation of European Electorates, 1885–1985*. Cambridge: Cambridge University Press.

BCV (Banco Central de Venezuela) (2001). "Informe de fin de año del Banco Central de Venezuela." www/bcv.org.ve (accessed January 22, 2001).

Bergquist, Charles (1986). *Labor in Latin America: Comparative Essays on Chile, Argentina, Venezuela, and Colombia*. Stanford: Stanford University Press.

Betancourt, Rómulo (1978). *Venezuela: Oil and Politics*. Boston: Houghton Mifflin.

Blanco, Carlos (1993). "Las transformaciones del estado venezolano," pp. 63–81 in Carlos Blanco, ed., *Venezuela, del siglo XX al siglo XXI: Un proyecto para construirla*. Caracas: Editorial Nueva Sociedad.

Blanco Muñoz, Agustín (interviewer) (1998). *Habla el comandante*. Caracas: Universidad Central de Venezuela.

Bolívar, Ligia, and Magaly Pérez Campos (1996). "El sistema de derechos humanos en la Constitución de 1961 y propuestas de reforma," pp. 33–129 in Angel E. Alvarez, ed., *El sistema político venezolano: Crisis y transformaciones*. Caracas: Universidad Central de Venezuela.

Boué, Juan Carlos (2002). *The Market for Heavy Sour Crude Oil in the U.S. Gulf Coast*. Oxford: Oxford Institute for Energy Studies.

———(1998). *The Political Control of State Oil Companies: A Case Study of the Vertical Integration Programme of Petróleos de Venezuela (1982–95)*. Oxford: Unpublished manuscript.

Bravo, Douglas, and Argelia Melet (1991). *La otra crisis, otra historia, otro camino*. Caracas: Original Editores.

Burgess, Katrina (1999). "Loyalty Dilemmas and Market Reform: Party-Union Alliances Under Stress in Mexico, Spain, and Venezuela." *World Politics* 52, no. 1 (October): 105–134.

Burggraaff, Winfield, and Richard L. Millett (1995). "More Than Failed Coups: The Crisis in Venezuelan Civil-Military Relations," pp. 54–78 in Louis Goodman, Johanna Mendelson Forman, Moisés Naím, Joseph S. Tulchin, and Gary Bland, eds., *Lessons of the Venezuelan Experience*. Baltimore: Johns Hopkins University Press.

Buxton, Julia (2001). *The Failure of Political Reform in Venezuela*. Aldershot, England: Ashgate.

Caballero, Manuel (2000). *La gestión de Chávez: 40 años de luces y sombras en la democracia venezolana*. Madrid: Catarata.

Calderón, Fernando (1986). *Los movimientos sociales ante la crisis*. Buenos Aires: Consejo Latinamericano de Ciencial Sociales.

Cámara de Diputados (1994). *Informe sobre pobreza y marginalidad*. Caracas: Cámara de Diputados.

Canache, Damarys (2002a). "From Bullets to Ballots: The Emergence of Popular

Support for Hugo Chávez." *Latin American Politics and Society* 44, no. 1 (spring): 69–90.

——(2002b). *Venezuela: Public Opinion and Protest in a Fragile Democracy.* Coral Gables, FL: North-South Center.

Canache, Damarys, and Michael Kulisheck, eds. (1998). *Reinventing Legitimacy: Democracy and Political Change in Venezuela.* Westport, CT: Greenwood Press.

CEPAL (Comisión Económica para América Latina y el Caribe) (2001). *Perspectivas de América Latina en el nuevo contexto internacional de 2001.* Santiago: CEPAL.

——(2000). *Anuario estadístico de América Latina y el Caribe.* Santiago: United Nations.

——(1999). *Estudio económico de América Latina y el Caribe, 1998–1999.* Santiago: CEPAL.

CESAP (Centro al Servicio de la Acción Popular) (1995). "Informe sobre el Seminario Reforma Constitucional o Asamblea Constituyente, supuestos y realidades." Mimeo. Caracas: CESAP, March 30–31.

——(1992a). "Editorial: La Asamblea Constituyente o como escuchar a la sociedad." Special edition of *Revista Juntos: Por la Constituyente* (Caracas), April.

——(1992b) "Encuentro por la Asamblea Constituyente." *Revista Juntos: Por la Constituyente* (Caracas) 3, no. 12 (July).

Chávez, Hugo (1993). *Mensaje bolivariano.* Yare: Ediciones MBR-200, no. 1 (February–May).

Collier, David, and Ruth Berins Collier (1991). *Shaping the Political Arena: Critical Junctures, the Labor Movement, and Regime Dynamics in Latin America.* Princeton: Princeton University Press.

Colomina, Marta (2001). "Las soberanas negritas de Acción Democrática." *El Universal* (Caracas), February 4, sec. 2, p. 8.

Combellas, Ricardo (1994). "La reforma constitucional en Venezuela: Retrospectiva de una experiencia frustrada," pp. 9–31 in Ricardo Combellas, ed., *Venezuela: Crisis política y reforma constitucional.* Caracas: Universidad Central de Venezuela.

Consultores 21 (2000). Survey cited in *Veneconomy.* Caracas: Consultores 21, September.

—— (1997). *Estudio de temas municipales.* Caracas: Consultores 21, February.

Coppedge, Michael (1994). *Strong Parties and Lame Ducks: Presidential Partyarchy and Factionalism in Venezuela.* Stanford: Stanford University Press.

——(1993). "Partidocracia y reforma en una perspectiva comparada," pp. 139–160 in Andrés Serbin, Andrés Stambouli, Jennifer McCoy, and William Smith, eds., *Venezuela: La democracia bajo presión.* Caracas: Instituto de Estudios Sociales y Políticos (INVESP), North-South Center (University of Miami), Editorial Nueva Sociedad.

COPRE (Comisión Presidencial para la Reforma del Estado, República de Venezuela) (1988). *La reforma del estado: Proyecto de reforma integral del estado.* Caracas: Editorial Arte.

Cornia, Giovanni Andrea (1998). *Liberalization, Globalization, and Income Distribution.* Working Paper no. 157. Helsinki, Finland: UNU/Wider, November.

Coronil, Fernando (1997). *The Magical State: Nature, Money, and Modernity in Venezuela.* Chicago: University of Chicago Press.

Corrales, Javier (2000). "Presidents, Ruling Parties, and Party Rules: A Theory on the Politics of Economic Reform in Latin America." *Comparative Politics* 32, no. 2 (January): 127–149.

Crisp, Brian F. (2000). *Democratic Institutional Design: The Powers and Incentives of Venezuelan Politicians and Interest Groups.* Stanford: Stanford University Press.

——(1998). "Development Strategy and Regime Type: Why Doesn't Democracy Matter?" *Studies in Comparative International Development* 33, no. 1 (spring): 8–41.

——(1997). "Presidential Behavior in a System with Strong Parties: Venezuela, 1958–1995," pp. 160–198 in Scott Mainwaring and Matthew Soberg Shugart, eds., *Presidentialism and Democracy in Latin America.* Cambridge: Cambridge University Press.

Crisp, Brian F., and Daniel H. Levine (1999). "Venezuela: Características, crisis y posible futuro del sistema democrático." *América Latina Hoy: Revista de Ciencias Sociales* no. 21 (April): 5–24.

——(1998). "Democratizing the Democracy? Crisis and Reform in Venezuela." *Journal of Interamerican Studies and World Affairs* 40, no. 2 (summer): 27–61.

Crisp, Brian F., Daniel H. Levine, and Juan Carlos Rey (1995). "The Legitimacy Problem," pp. 139–170 in Jennifer McCoy, Andrés Serbin, William C. Smith, and Andrés Stambouli, eds., *Venezuelan Democracy Under Stress.* New Brunswick, NY: Transaction Books.

Dahl, Robert (1971). *Polyarchy: Participation and Opposition.* New Haven: Yale University Press.

De la Cruz, Rafael, and Armando Barrios (1998). "Descentralización en perspectiva," pp. 225–254 in Rafael De la Cruz, ed., *Venezuela: Realidades y perspectivas un pacto para la descentralización.* Caracas: Ediciones IESA.

Diamond, Larry D., Jonathan Hartlyn, and Juan J. Linz (1999). "Introduction: Politics, Society, and Democracy in Latin America," pp. 1–70 in Larry Diamond, Jonathan Hartlyn, Juan J. Linz, and Seymour Martin Lipset, eds., *Democracy in Developing Countries: Latin America,* 2d ed. Boulder: Lynne Rienner.

Díaz, Rolando (2001). "Revolución sin sindicatos?" *Revista SIC* 65, no. 638 (September–October): 252–254.

Diccionario de historia de Venezuela (1997). 3 vols. Caracas: Fundación Polar.

Dix, Robert H. (1989). "Cleavage, Structures, and Party Systems in Latin America." *Comparative Politics* 22, no. 1 (October): 23–37.

Duverger, Maurice (1954). *Political Parties: Their Organization and Activity in the Modern State.* London: Methuen.

Economist Intelligence Unit Country Report: Venezuela (2000). 1st quarter. London: Economist Intelligence Unit.

Ellner, Steve (2001). "The Radical Potential of Chavismo in Venezuela: The First Year-and-a-Half in Power." *Latin American Perspectives* 28, no. 5 (September): 5–32.

——(2000). "Polarized Politics in Chávez's Venezuela." *NACLA: Report on the Americas* 33, no. 6 (May–June): 29–33.

——(1999a). "The Assault on Benefits in Venezuela." *NACLA: Report on the Americas* 32, no. 4 (January–February): 18–19.

——(1999b). "The Heyday of Radical Populism in Venezuela and Its Aftermath," pp. 117–137 in Michael Conniff, ed., *Populism in Latin America.* Tuscaloosa: University of Alabama Press.

———(1999c). "The Impact of Privatization on Labor in Venezuela: Radical Reorganization or Moderate Adjustment?" *Political Power and Social Theory* 13: 109–145.

———(1999d). "Obstacles to the Consolidation of the Venezuelan Neighbourhood Movement: National and Local Cleavages." *Journal of Latin American Studies* 31, no. 1 (February): 75–97.

———(1997). "Recent Venezuelan Political Studies: A Return to Third World Realities." *Latin American Research Review* 32, no. 2: 201–218.

———(1996a). "Democracia y tendencias internas en partidos políticos en Venezuela." *Nueva Sociedad* 145 (June): 42–54.

———(1996b). "Political Party Factionalism and Democracy in Venezuela." *Latin American Perspectives* 23, no. 3 (summer): 87–109.

——— (1995). *El sindicalismo en Venezuela en el contexto democrático (1958–1994)*. Caracas: Fondo Editorial Tropykos.

———(1993). *Organized Labor in Venezuela, 1958–1991: Behavior and Concerns in a Democratic Setting*. Wilmington, DE: Scholarly Resources.

———(1989). "Venezuela: No Exception." *NACLA: Report on the Americas* 23, no. 1 (May): 8–10.

"Encuesta realizada por *El Universal* a empresarios privados" (2001). www.el-universal.com (accessed March 5, 2002).

Enright, Michael J., Antonio Francés, and Edith S. Saavedra (1996). *Venezuela: The Challenge of Competitiveness*. New York: St. Martin's Press.

Espinasa, Ramón (1999). "El marco fiscal petrolero venezolano," *Revista del Banco Central de Venezuela*. Foros 3: 259–303.

Espinasa, Ramón, and Bernard Mommer (1992). "Venezuelan Oil Policy in the Long Run," pp. 103–126 in James P. Dorian and Fereidun Fesharaki, eds., *International Issues in Energy Policy, Development, and Economics*. Boulder: Westview Press.

Europa World Yearbook (2000). London: Europa.

Evans, Ronald (1998). *Desnutrición en Venezuela: Periodo 1990–1996*. Caracas: Instituto Nacional de Nutrición.

Evers, Tilman (1985). "Identity: The Hidden Side of New Social Movements in Latin America," pp. 43–71 in David Slater, ed., *New Social Movements and the State in Latin America*. Amsterdam: CEDLA.

Francés, Antonio (2001). "Venezuelan Private Enterprise in the 1990s." Unpublished manuscript.

Friedman, Elisabeth J. (2000). *Unfinished Transitions: Women and the Gendered Development of Democracy in Venezuela, 1936–1996*. University Park: Pennsylvania State University Press.

Fundación Pensamiento y Acción (1996). *Cultura democrática en Venezuela: Informe analítico de resultados*. Caracas.

Gabinete Social (2001). *Discusión de los anteproyectos de leyes de seguridad social: Informes y conclusiones*. Caracas: June.

García-Guadilla, María Pilar (2002). "El movimiento ambientalista y la constitucionalización de nuevas racionalidades: Dilemas y desafíos." *Revista Venezolana de Economía y Ciencias Sociales* 7, no. 1 (January–April): 113–132.

———(2001). "Nuevos actores, viejas prácticas: Clientelismo en la planificación urbana local." Manuscript, forthcoming in *Latin American Perspectives*, 2002.

———(2000a). "Actores, organizaciones y movimientos sociales en la Venezuela del 2000: Logros, problemas y desafíos." Seminario Internacional Venezuela:

Alcances, límites y desafíos del actual sistema político. Universidad de Salamanca, Spain, November.

——(2000b). "Efectos del modelo de gestión del Municipio Chacao sobre la eficiencia y la legitimidad política." *América Latina Hoy: Revista de Ciencias Sociales* no. 24 (April): 55–65.

——(1992). "The Venezuelan Ecology Movement: Symbolic Effectiveness, Social Practices, and Political Strategies," pp. 150–170 in Arturo Escobar and Sonia Alvarez, eds., *The Making of Social Movements in Latin America: Identity, Strategy, and Democracy*. Boulder: Westview Press.

—— ed. (1991). *Ambiente, estado y sociedad: Crisis y conflictos socioambientales en América Latina y Venezuela*. Caracas: Universidad Simón Bolívar–CENDES.

García-Guadilla, María Pilar, and Jutta Blauert (1992). "Environmental Social Movements in Latin America and Europe." *International Journal of Sociology and Social Policy* 12, special issue.

García-Guadilla, María Pilar, and Monica Hurtado (2000). "Participation and Constitution Making in Colombia and Venezuela: Enlarging the Scope of Democracy?" Paper presented at the Twenty-second International Congress of the Latin American Studies Association, Miami, FL, March 16–18.

García-Guadilla, María Pilar, and Ernesto Roa Carrero (1996). "Gobernabilidad, cambio político y sociedad civil: El proceso constituyente en Venezuela." *Revista Venezolana de Economía y Ciencias Sociales* 2, nos. 2–3 (May–August, September–December): 85–112.

—— (1995). *Interviews with the Civil Society Organizations*. Caracas: Unpublished manuscript.

García-Guadilla, María Pilar, and Nadeska Silva Querales (1999). "De los movimientos sociales a las redes organizacionales en Venezuela: Estrategia, valores e identidades." *Politeia* 23, no. 2: 7–27.

Garrido, Alberto (2001). *Mi amigo Chávez: Conversaciones con Norberto Ceresole*. Caracas: Ediciones del Autor.

——(1999). *Guerrilla y conspiración militar en Venezuela*. Caracas: Fondo Editorial Nacional.

GAU (Grupo de Investigación en Gestión Ambiental y Urbana) (2000). *Entrevistas: Organizaciones sociales y proceso constituyente, 2000*. Caracas: Cátedra de Participación Ciudadana de Estudios Generales y Postgrado en Ciencias Políticas: Curso de Nuevos Actores Sociopolíticos y Proceso Constituyente, Universidad Simón Bolívar.

Gil Yepes, José Antonio (2001). "Public Opinion, Political Socialization, and Regime Stabilization." Paper delivered at the Twenty-third International Congress of the Latin American Studies Association, Washington, DC, September.

Gómez Calcaño, Luis (1991). "Estado, ambiente y sociedad civil: Convergencias y divergencias," pp. 155–181 in María Pilar García-Guadilla, ed., *Ambiente, estado y sociedad: Crisis y conflictos socioambientales en América Latina y Venezuela*. Caracas: Universidad Simón Bolívar–CENDES.

——ed. (1987). *Crisis y movimientos sociales en Venezuela*. Caracas: Editorial Trópicos.

Gómez Calcaño, Luis, and Margarita López Maya (1990). *El tejido de Penélope: La reforma del estado en Venezuela (1984–1988)*. Caracas: CENDES-APUCV-IPP.

Gott, Richard (2000). *In the Shadow of the Liberator: Hugo Chávez and the Transformation of Venezuela*. London: Verso.

Gramsci, Antonio (1971). *Selections from the Prison Notebooks.* Edited and translated by Quintin Hoare and Geoffrey Nowell Smith. New York: International Publishers.

Guevara, Rafael M. (1983). *Petróleo y ruina: La verdad sobre el contrato firmado entre PDVSA y la Veba Oel A.G.* Caracas: Ediciones del Instante.

Habermas, Jungen (1981). "New Social Movements." *Telos* 49 (fall): 33–37.

Hagopian, Frances (1990). "'Democracy by Undemocratic Means'? Elites, Political Pacts, and Regime Transition in Brazil." *Comparative Political Studies* 23, no. 2 (July): 147–170.

Hartlyn, Jonathan (1998). "Political Continuities, Missed Opportunities, and Institutional Rigidities: Another Look at Democratic Transitions in Latin America," pp. 101–120 in Scott Mainwaring and Arturo Valenzuela, eds., *Politics, Society, and Democracy: Latin America.* Boulder: Westview Press.

Hellinger, Daniel C. (2000). "Nationalism, Oil Policy, and the Party System." Paper presented at the Twenty-second International Congress of the Latin American Studies Association, Miami, FL, March 16–18.

———(1996). "The *Causa R* and Venezuela's Nuevo Sindicalismo in Venezuela." *Latin American Perspectives* 23, no. 3 (summer): 110–131.

——— (1991). *Venezuela: Tarnished Democracy.* Boulder: Westview Press.

———(1984). "Populism and Nationalism in Venezuela: New Perspectives on Acción Democrática." *Latin American Perspectives* 11, no. 4 (fall): 33–59.

Hellinger, Daniel, and Dorothea Melcher (1998). "Venezuela: A Welfare State Out of Gas." Paper presented at the Twenty-first International Congress of the Latin American Studies Association, Chicago, September 24–26.

Herman, Donald L. (1988). "Democratic and Authoritarian Traditions," pp. 1–15 in Donald L. Herman, ed., *Democracy in Latin America: Colombia and Venezuela.* New York: Praeger.

Hillman, Richard S. (1994). *Democracy for the Privileged: Crisis and Transition in Venezuela.* Boulder: Lynne Rienner.

Huntington, Samuel P. (1968). *Political Order in Changing Societies.* New Haven: Yale University Press.

——— (1957). *The Soldier and the State.* Cambridge: Harvard University Press.

IESA (Institute for Higher Studies in Management) (2001). "Indicadores económicos y sociales." www.iesa.edu.ve/scripts/macroeconomia and www.iesa.edu.vc/macroeconomia.soc (accessed March 2002).

ILO (International Labour Organization) (1998). *Labour Overview: Latin America and the Caribbean.* Lima: ILO.

——— (1997). *World Labour Report 1997–98: Industrial Relations, Democracy, and Social Stability.* Geneva: ILO.

Inter-American Development Bank (1997). *Latin America After a Decade of Reforms.* Washington, DC: Inter-American Development Bank.

Jácome, Francine (2000). "Venezuela: Old Successes, New Constraints on Learning," pp. 99–129 in Jennifer L. McCoy, ed., *Political Learning and Redemocratization in Latin America.* Coral Gables, FL: North-South Center.

Karl, Terry Lynn (1997). *The Paradox of Plenty: Oil Booms and Petro-States.* Berkeley: University of California Press.

——— (1996). "Dilemmas of Democratization," pp. 21–47 in Roderic Ai Camp, ed., *Democracy in Latin America: Patterns and Cycles.* Wilmington, DE: Scholarly Resources.

—— (1995). "The Venezuelan Petro-State and the Crisis of 'Its' Democracy," pp. 33–58 in Jennifer McCoy, Andrés Serbin, William C. Smith, and Andrés Stambouli, eds., *Venezuelan Democracy Under Stress*. New Brunswick, NY: Transaction Books.

——(1987). "Petroleum and Political Pacts: The Transition to Democracy in Venezuela." *Latin American Research Review* 22, no. 1: 63–94.

Kelly, Janet (2000). "Thoughts on the Constitution: Realignment of Ideas About the Economy and Changes in the Political System in Venezuela." Paper presented at the 2000 meeting of the Latin American Studies Association, Miami, March 16–18, 2000.

Kissinger, Henry (2001). *Does America Need a Foreign Policy: Toward a Diplomacy for the Twenty-first Century*. New York: Simon and Schuster.

Kornblith, Miriam (1998). *Venezuela en los 90: La crisis de la democracia*. Caracas: Ediciones IESA.

——(1992). "Reforma constitucional, crisis política y estabilidad de la democracia en Venezuela." *Politeia* (Caracas) 15: 121–170.

Kornblith, Miriam, and Daniel H. Levine (1995). "Venezuela: The Life and Times of the Party System," pp. 37–71 in Scott Mainwaring and Timothy R. Scully, eds., *Building Democratic Institutions: Party Systems in Latin America*. Stanford: Stanford University Press.

Lander, Luis E. (2001). "Venezuela's Balancing Act: Big Oil, OPEC, and National Development." *NACLA: Report on the Americas* 34, no. 1 (January–February): 25–30.

Lerner, Elisa (1995). "Venezolanos de hoy en día: Del silencio posgomecista al Ruido Mayamero," pp. 2–18 in Moisés Naím and Ramón Piñango, eds., *El caso Venezuela: Una ilusión de armonía*. Caracas: Ediciones IESA.

Levine, Daniel H. (1995). Review of *Democracy for the Privileged* by Richard Hillman. *American Political Science Review* 89, no. 1 (March): 229–230.

——(1994). "Goodbye to Venezuelan Exceptionalism." *Journal of Interamerican Studies and World Affairs* 36, no. 4 (winter): 145–182.

——(1989). "Venezuela: The Nature, Sources, and Future Prospects of Democracy," pp. 247–289 in Larry Diamond, Juan J. Linz, and Seymour Martin Lipset, eds., *Democracy in Developing Countries: Latin America*. Boulder: Lynne Rienner.

——(1978). "Venezuela Since 1958: The Consolidation of Democratic Politics," pp. 89–109 in Juan J. Linz and Alfred Stepan, eds., *The Breakdown of Democratic Regimes: Latin America*. Baltimore: Johns Hopkins University Press.

——(1973). *Conflict and Political Change in Venezuela*. Princeton: Princeton University Press.

Levine, Daniel H., and Brian F. Crisp (1999). "Venezuela: The Character, Crisis, and Possible Future of Democracy." *World Affairs* 16, no. 3 (winter): 123–165.

López Maya, Margarita (2000). "The Venezuelan Caracazo of 1989: Popular Protest and Institutional Collapse." Paper presented in "Social Movements Conference: Are Social Movements Reviving?" International Sociological Conference no. 48, Manchester Metropolitan University, November 3–5.

——(1999). "La protesta popular venezolana entre 1989 y 1993 (en el umbral del neoliberalismo)," pp. 211–235 in Margarita López Maya, ed., *Lucha popular, democracia y neoliberalismo: Protestas populares en América Latina en los años de ajuste*. Caracas: Nueva Sociedad.

——(1997). "The Rise of Causa R in Venezuela," pp. 117–143 in Douglas A.

Chalmers, Carlos M. Vilas, Katherine Hite, Scott B. Martin, Kerianne Piester, and Monique Segarra, eds., *The New Politics of Inequality in Latin America: Rethinking Participation and Representation*. Oxford: Oxford University Press.

——— (1994). "Venezuela: El impacto de sus reformas políticas durante el lapso crítico de 1989–1993." *Cuadernos del Cendes* 26 (May–August): 40–54.

López Maya, Margarita, Luis Gómez Calcaño, and Thais Maingón (1989). *De Punto Fijo al Pacto Social Fondo*. Caracas: Editorial Acta Científica Venezolana.

López Maya, Margarita, and Luis E. Lander (2000a). "La lucha por la hegemonía en Venezuela: Violencia, protesta popular y el futuro de la democracia." Unpublished manuscript.

——— (2000b). "La popularidad de Chávez: ¿Base para un proyecto popular?" *Cuestiones Políticas* (Maracaibo, Venezuela) 24 (January–June): 11–36.

——— (2000c). "Refounding the Republic: The Political Project of Chavismo." *NACLA: Report on the Americas* 33, no. 6 (May–June): 22–28.

——— (1999). "Triunfos en tiempos de transición: Actores de vocación popular en las elecciones venezolanas de 1998." *Cuestiones Políticas* (Maracaibo, Venezuela) 22 (January–June): 107–132.

López Maya, Margarita, David Smilde, and Keta Stephany (2001). "Protesta y cultura en Venezuela: Los marcos de acción colectiva en 1999." Oxford: Unpublished manuscript.

Luttwack, Edward (1968). *Coup d'Etat: A Practical Handbook*. Cambridge: Harvard University Press.

Machín, Haidée (2001). *1er borrador de elementos para el anteproyecto de ley orgánica de participación ciudadana*. Caracas: Manuscrito del Equipo Comunitario Técnico de Apoyo para la Participación.

Mainwaring, Scott P. (1999). *Rethinking Party Systems in the Third Wave of Democratization: The Case of Brazil*. Stanford: Stanford University Press.

Mainwaring, Scott P., and Timothy R. Scully (1995). "Introduction: Party Systems in Latin America," pp. 1–34 in Scott Mainwaring and Timothy R. Scully, eds., *Building Democratic Institutions: Party Systems in Latin America*. Stanford: Stanford University Press.

Mainwaring, Scott P., and Jorge Viola (1984). "Los nuevos movimientos sociales, las culturas políticas y la democracia: Brasil y Argentina en la década de los ochenta." *Revista Mexicana de Sociología* 47, no. 101 (October–December): 35–84.

Márquez, Patricia (1999). *The Street Is My Home: Youth and Violence in Caracas*. Stanford: Stanford University Press.

Martz, John D. (1999–2000). "Political Parties and Candidate Selection in Venezuela and Colombia." *Political Science Quarterly* 114, no. 4 (winter): 639–659.

——— (1995). "Political Parties and the Democratic Crisis," pp. 31–53 in Louis Goodman, Johanna Mendelson Forman, Moisés Naím, Joseph S. Tulchin, and Gary Bland, eds., *Lessons of the Venezuelan Experience*. Baltimore: Johns Hopkins University Press.

——— (1966). *Acción Democrática: Evolution of a Modern Political Party in Venezuela*. Princeton: Princeton University Press.

MBR-200 (1996). "Agenda alternativa bolivariana (una propuesta patriótica para salir del laberinto)." Pamphlet. Caracas: MBR-200, July.

——— (1994a). "Asamblea Nacional Constituyente Bolivariana." N.p.

———(1994b). "Consejo popular constituyente 'Exposición de motivos.'" Unpublished manuscript. Caracas: MBR-200.

——— (1994c). "La esperanza en la calle." Pamphlet. Caracas: MBR-200.

———(1994d). "Poder constituyente (propuesta Táchira)." Barinas: MBR-200, June.

———(1994e). *Por Ahora ¡Y para siempre!* (Party periodical from the central region) no. 2, year 1.

McCoy, Jennifer L. (1999). "Chávez and the End of 'Partyarchy' in Venezuela." *Journal of Democracy* 10, no. 3 (July): 64–77.

———(1989). "Labor and the State in a Party Mediated Democracy." *Latin American Research Review* 24, no. 2: 35–67.

Medina, Medófilo (2001). "Chávez y la globalización." *Revista Venezolana de Economía y Ciencias Sociales* 7, no. 2 (May–August): 115–128.

Medina, Pablo (1999). *Rebeliones.* Caracas: Piedra, Papel o Tijera.

——— (1988). *Pablo Medina en entrevista.* Caracas: Ediciones del Agua Mansa.

Melcher, Dorothea (2000). "Seguridad social y derechos laborales en las reformas neoliberales en Venezuela," pp. 259–293 in Anita Kon, Catalina Banko, Dorothea Melcher, Maria Cristina Cacciamali, *Costos sociales de las reformas neoliberales en América Latina.* São Paolo: Pontifícia Universidade Católica de São Paulo.

Mendoza Potellá, Carlos (1995). *El poder petrolero y la economía venezolana.* Caracas: Universidad Central de Venezuela.

Merkel, Peter (1981). "Democratic Development, Breakdowns, and Fascism." *World Politics* 34, no. 1 (October): 114–135.

Mettenheim, Kurt von, and James Malloy, eds. (1998). *Deepening Democracy in Latin America.* Pittsburgh: University of Pittsburgh Press.

Ministerio de la Secretaria (1999). *Constitución de la República Bolivariana de Venezuela.*

Molina, José E., and Carmen Pérez B. (1999). "La democracia venezolana en una encrucijada: Las elecciones nacionales y regionales de 1998." *América Latina Hoy: Revista de Ciencias Sociales* no. 21 (April): 29–40.

Mommer, Bernard (2002a). *Global Oil and the Nation State.* Oxford: Oxford University Press.

———(2002b). "Venezuela: A New Legal and Institutional Framework in Oil." *Middle East Economic Survey* 45, no. 1 (January 7): D1–D3.

———(2001a). *Fiscal Regimes and Oil Revenues in the UK, Alaska, and Venezuela.* OIES Paper no. WPM 27. Oxford: Institute for Energy Studies, June.

———(2001b). "Grafting Liberal Governance on the Oil-exporting Countries: Will the Transplant Take Root?" Forty-second Annual Convention of the International Studies Association, Chicago. www.isanet.org/paperarchive.html (accessed August 24, 2002).

———(1999). *Oil Prices and Fiscal Regimes.* OIES Paper no. WPM 24. Oxford: Institute for Energy Studies.

———(1998). *The New Governance of Venezuelan Oil.* OIES Paper no. WPM 23. Oxford: Institute for Energy Studies.

———(1988). *La cuestión petrolera.* Caracas: Editorial Tropykos.

Moreno, Alejandro (1998). Editorial. *Heterotopia* 4, no. 10 (September–December): 5–16.

———(1997). "Desencuentro de mundos" *Heterotopia* 3, no. 6 (May–August): 11–38.

Moros Ghersi, C. A. (1986). "La problemática de la educación superior en Venezuela: Factores causales y soluciones," pp. 149–173 in C. A. Moros Ghersi, ed., *La crisis: Responsibilidades y salidas*. Caracas: Editorial Expediente, Cátedra Pío Tamayo, Universidad Central de Venezuela.

Moros Ghersi, C. A., ed. (1986). *La crisis: Responsibilidades y salidas*. Caracas: Editorial Expediente, Cátedra Pío Tamayo, Universidad Central de Venezuela.

Mulhern, Alan (2000). "The PYMI Experience in Venezuela." Paper presented at the Twenty-second International Congress of the Latin American Studies Association, Miami, FL, March 16–18.

Murillo, María Victoria (2001). *Labor Unions, Partisan Coalitions, and Market Reforms in Latin America*. Cambridge: Cambridge University Press.

—— (2000). "From Populism to Neoliberalism: Labor Unions and Market Reform in Latin America." *World Politics* 52, no. 2 (January): 135–174.

—— (1997). "From Populism to Neoliberalism: Labor Unions and Market-Oriented Reforms in Argentina, Mexico, and Venezuela." Ph.D. diss., Harvard University.

Myers, David J. (1998). "Venezuela's Political Party System: Defining Events, Reactions, and the Diluting of Structural Cleavages." *Party Politics* 4, no. 4 (October): 495–521.

—— (1996). "Venezuela: The Stressing of Distributive Justice," pp. 227–269 in Howard J. Wiard and Harvey F. Kline, eds., *Latin American Politics and Development*. Boulder: Westview Press.

Naím, Moisés (2001a). "High Anxiety in the Andes: The Real Story Behind Venezuela's Woes." *Journal of Democracy* 12, no. 2 (April): 17–31.

—— (2001b). "La Venezuela de Hugo Chávez." *Venezuela Analítica*. www. analitica.com (accessed July 9, 2001).

—— (1993). *Paper Tigers and Minotaurs: The Politics of Venezuela's Economic Reforms*. Washington, DC: Carnegie Endowment for International Peace.

Naím, Moisés, and Antonio Francés (1995). "The Venezuelan Private Sector: From Courting the State to Courting the Market," pp. 165–192 in Louis Goodman, Johanna Mendelson Forman, Moisés Naím, Joseph S. Tulchin, and Gary Bland, eds., *Lessons of the Venezuelan Experience*. Baltimore: Johns Hopkins University Press.

Naím, Moisés, and Ramón Piñango, eds. (1985). *El caso Venezuela: Una ilusión de armonía*. Caracas: Ediciones IESA.

Neuhouser, Kevin (1992). "Democratic Stability in Venezuela: Elite Consensus or Class Compromise?" *American Sociological Review* 57, no. 1 (February): 117–135.

Njaim, Humberto, Ricardo Combellas, and Angel E. Alvarez (1998). *Opinión pública y democracia en Venezuela*. Caracas: Universidad Central de Venezuela.

Norden, Deborah (1998). "Democracy and Military Control in Venezuela: From Subordination to Insurrection." *Latin American Research Review* 33, no. 2: 143–165.

—— (1996). "The Rise of the Lieutenant Colonels: Rebellion in Argentina and Venezuela." *Latin American Perspectives* 23, no. 1 (summer 1996): 74–86.

Nordlinger, Eric (1977). *Soldiers in Politics: Military Coups and Governments*. Englewood Cliffs, NJ: Prentice-Hall.

O'Donnell, Guillermo (1997). *Contrapuntos: Ensayos escogidos sobre autoritarismo y democratización*. Buenos Aires: Paidós.

—— (1994). "Delegative Democracy." *Journal of Democracy* 5, no. 1 (January): 55–69.

————(1993). *Modernization and Bureaucratic Authoritarianism: Studies in South American Politics.* Berkeley: University of California Press.

Ojeda, William (2001). *La "V" por dentro: Caras nuevas, vicios viejos.* Caracas: Solar Ediciones.

Organización Panamericana de la Salud (1998). *Análisis sectorial de agua potable y saneamiento Venezuela.* Caracas: Organización Panamericana de la Salud.

Ovalles, Omar (1987). "Movimientos de cuadro de vida en la Venezuela actual," pp. 83–106 in Luis Gómez Calcaño, ed., *Crisis y movimientos sociales en Venezuela.* Caracas: Editorial Trópicos.

"Pacto de Punto Fijo" (1989). *Documentos que hicieron historia: Vida Republicana de Venezuela (1810–1989).* Vol. 2. Caracas: Ediciones Presidencia de la República.

Parker, Dick (2001). "Populismo radical y potencial revolucionario." *Revista Venezolana de Economía y Ciencias Sociales* 7, no. 1 (January–April): 13–44.

Peeler, John A. (1992). "Elite Settlements and Democratic Consolidation: Colombia, Costa Rica, and Venezuela," pp. 81–112 in John Higley and Richard Gunther, eds., *Elites and Democratic Consolidation in Latin America and Southern Europe.* Cambridge: Cambridge University Press.

Penfold-Beccera, Michael (2001). "El colapso del sistema de partidos en Venezuela: Explicación de una muerte anunciada," pp. 36–52 in José Vicente Carrasquero, Thais Maingón, and Friedrich Welsch, eds., *Venezuela en transición: Elecciones y democracia, 1998–2000.* Caracas: CDB Publicaciones.

Pérez Perdomo, Rogelio (1995). "Corruption and Political Crisis," pp. 311–333 in Louis Goodman, Johanna Mendelson Forman, Moisés Naím, Joseph S. Tulchin, and Gary Bland, eds., *Lessons of the Venezuelan Experience.* Baltimore: Johns Hopkins University Press.

Pérez Perdomo, Rogelio, and Ruth Capriles (1991). *Corrupción y control: Una perspectiva comparada.* Caracas: Ediciones IESA.

Producto Online (1999). "Boina imagen." www.producto.com.ve/184 (accessed December 10, 2001).

Provea (Programa Venezolano de Educación Acción en Derechos Humanos) (2000). *Situación de los derechos humanos en Venezuela: Informe annual.* Vol. 12. http://derechos.org.ve/situa/anual (accessed February 22, 2001).

Provea (1992a). "Editorial: ¿Quién le teme a la voluntad popular?" *Referencias* (Caracas) 4, no. 46 (August).

Provea (1992b). "Reforma y referendum: PROVEA se suma al NO." *Referencias* (Caracas) 4, no. 46 (August).

Pulido de Briceño, Mercedes (1999). *Balance social 1999: Del simplismo ramplón a la complejidad del bienestar.* www.gumilla.org.ve/sic/sic2000/sic621/sic621.pulido.htm (accessed March 2001).

Queremos Elegir (1994). "Comunicación enviada al Presidente del Congreso Nacional, Eduardo Gómez Tamayo." Caracas: Queremos Elegir, June 3.

Rangel, José Vicente (2001). Interview on *Globovisión.* June 12.

Ray, Talton F. (1969). *The Politics of the Barrios of Venezuela.* Berkeley: University of California Press.

República de Venezuela (1995). *Venezuela ante la cumbre mundial sobre desarrollo social.* Caracas.

Rey, Juan Carlos (1993). "La crisis de legitimidad en Venezuela en el enjuiciamiento y remoción de Carlos Andrés Pérez de la Presidencia de la República." *Boletín Electoral Latinamericano* 9 (January–June): 67–112.

————— (1989). *El futuro de la democracia.* Caracas: Serie Estudios Colección Idea.

——— (1972). "El sistema de partidos venezolanos." *Politeia* 1: 175–135.

Riutort, Matías (2001). "El costo de erradicar la pobreza," pp. 15–26 in *Pobreza: Un mal posible de superar: Resumenes de los documentos del proyecto pobreza,* vol. 1. Caracas: Universidad Católica Andrés Bello.

——— (1999). *El costo de erradicar la pobreza.* Proyecto Pobreza at http://omega.manapro.com/pobreza/index1.htm (last accessed March 2001).

Roberts, Kenneth M. (2002). "Social Inequalities Without Class Cleavages in Latin America's Neoliberal Era." *Studies in Comparative International Development* 36, no. 4 (winter): 3–33.

———(2001). "La descomposición del sistema político venezolano visto desde un análisis comparativo." *Revista Venezolana de Economía y Ciencias Sociales* 7, no. 2 (May–August): 183–200.

———(1995). "Neoliberalism and the Transformation of Populism in Latin America: The Peruvian Case." *World Politics* 48, no. 1 (October): 82–116.

Robinson, William I. (1996). *Promoting Polyarchy: Globalization, U.S. Intervention, and Hegemony.* Cambridge: Cambridge University Press.

Romero, Anibal (2000). "De las FAN a la FA: Los militares y la 'Revolución' Chavista." *Venezuela Analítica.* www.analitica.com (accessed June 14, 2000).

——— (1997). "Rearranging the Deck Chairs on the Titanic: The Agony of Democracy in Venezuela." *Latin American Research Review* 32, no. 1: 7–36.

———(1994). *Decadencia y crisis de la democracia.* Caracas: Panapo.

———(1986). *La miseria del populismo: Mitos y realidades de la democracia en Venezuela.* Caracas: Centauro.

Salamanca, Luis (1999). "Protestas venezolanas en el segundo gobierno de Rafael Caldera: 1994–1997," pp. 339–364 in Margarita López Maya, ed., *Lucha popular, democracia y neoliberalismo: Protestas populares en América Latina en los años de ajuste.* Caracas: Editorial Nueva Sociedad.

———(1995). "La incorporación de la Confederación de Trabajadores de Venezuela al sistema político venezolano: 1958–1980." *Revista de la Facultad de Ciencias Jurídicas y Políticas* 95: 189–399.

Santana, Elías (1986). *El poder de los vecinos.* Caracas: Ediciones Ecotopia.

Santana, Elías, and Luis Perroni (1991). "La visión ambiental desde el movimiento vecinal," pp. 293–317 in María Pilar García-Guadilla, ed., *Ambiente, estado y sociedad: Crisis y conflictos socioambientales en América Latina y Venezuela.* Caracas: Universidad Simón Bolívar–CENDES.

Santodomingo, Roger (2000). *La conspiración 98: Un pacto para llevar a Hugo Chávez al poder.* Caracas: Alfadil Ediciones.

Sartori, Giovanni (1997). *¿Qué es la democracia?* México: Editorial Patria, S.A.

———(1976). *Party and Party Systems: A Framework for Analysis.* New York: Cambridge University Press.

Scott, Alan (1990). *Ideology and the New Social Movements in Latin America.* London: Unwin Hyman.

Silva, Nadeska (1999). "Democracia, descentralización y concepciones de ciudadanía en Venezuela." Master's thesis, Universidad Simón Bolívar, Caracas.

Sinergia (2001). *Propuesta de proyecto de ley elaborada desde UPALE.* Caracas: Sinergia.

———(1999). *Primera, segunda y tercera mesa nacional sociedad civil: Presentación de propuestas para la Asamblea Constituyente.* Vols. 1–3. Caracas: Sinergia, August and September.

Slater, David (1985). *New Social Movements and the State in Latin America.* Amsterdam: CEDLA.

Smith Perera, Roberto (1995). ¿*Venezuela: Visión o caos?* Caracas: Planeta.

Sosa Abascal, Arturo (1989). "¿Qué fue lo que pasó?" *Revista SIC* 52, no. 520 (May): 101–117.

Sosa Abascal, Arturo, and Eloi Lengrand (1981). *Del garibaldismo estudiantil a la izquierda criolla: Los orígenes del proyecto de A.D. (1928–1935).* Caracas: Ediciones Centauro.

Sosa Pietri, Andrés (1998). "Venezuela, el 'Tercermundismo' y la OPEP." *Venezuela Analítica.* www.analitica.com (accessed March 2002).

Stambouli, Andrés (1980). *Crisis política: Venezuela 1945–1958.* Caracas: Editorial Ateneo de Caracas.

Sunkel, Osvaldo (1994). "La crisis social de América Latina: Una perspectiva neoestructuralista," pp. 128–181 in Eduardo S. Bustelo, Felix Bombarolo, and Horacio E. Caride, eds., *Pobreza y modelos de desarrollo en América Latina.* Buenos Aires: Programa de Fortalecimiento Institucional y Capacitación de Organizaciones no Gubernamentales.

Target Global Research (1998). *Estudio de opinión pública a nivel nacional.* Ciudad de Valencia, Venezuela: Target Global Research, October.

Torre, Carlos de la (2000). *Populist Seduction in Latin America: The Ecuadorian Experience.* Athens: Ohio University Center for International Studies.

Touraine, Alan (1987). *Actores sociales y sistemas políticos en América Latina.* Santiago: PREALC/OIT.

Trinkunas, Harold Antanas (1998). "Crafting Civilian Control of the Armed Forces: Poltical Conflict, Institutional Design, and Military Subordination in Emerging Democracies." Ph.D. diss., Stanford University.

Uribe, Gabriela, and Edgardo Lander (1991). "Acción social, efectividad simbólica y nuevos ámbitos de lo político en Venezuela," pp. 69–104 in María Pilar García-Guadilla, ed., *Ambiente, estado y sociedad: Crisis y conflictos socioambientales en América Latina y Venezuela.* Caracas: Universidad Simón Bolívar–CENDES.

Urquijo, José I. (2000). *El movimiento obrero de Venezuela.* Caracas: Organización Internacional del Trabajo.

Véliz, Claudio (1980). *The Centralist Tradition of Latin America.* Princeton: Princeton University Press.

"Venezuela's Chávez Won't Tone Down Campaign for New Constitution" (1999). www.cnn.com (accessed December 2, 2000).

Vilas, Carlos (2001). "La sociología latinoamericana y el 'caso' Chávez: Entre la sorpresa y el déjà vu." *Revista Venezolana de Economía y Ciencias Sociales* 7, no. 2 (May–August): 129–145.

Villasmil, Marcos (2000). "Un nuevo partido D.C. para Venezuela?" *Nueva Política* (Caracas) nos. 71–72: 177–190.

Werz, Nikolaus (2001). "Chávez en la prensa europea y estadosunidense." *Revista Venezolana de Economía y Ciencias Sociales* 7, no. 2 (May–August): 147–155.

Weyland, Kurt (1996). "Neoliberalism and Neopopulism in Latin America: Unexpected Affinities." *Studies in Comparative International Development* 31, no. 3 (fall): 3–31.

Wiarda, J. Howard, and Harvey F. Kline (1996). "Conclusion: Latin America and Its Alternative Futures," pp. 531–538 in J. Howard Wiarda and Harvey F. Kline, eds., *Latin American Politics and Development,* 4th ed. Boulder: Westview Press.

World Bank (1994). *World Development Report.* New York: Oxford University Press.

Zago, Angela (1992). *La rebelión de los ángeles.* Caracas: Fuente Editores.
Zapata, Roberto G. (1996). *Valores del venezolano.* Caracas: Ediciones Conciencia 21.

Periodicals

El Nacional (Caracas daily)
El Universal (Caracas daily)
La Jornada (Mexico City daily)
Latin American Weekly Report
New York Times
Proceso (Mexico City daily)
Revista SIC (Caracas monthly)
Tal Cual (Caracas daily)
Veneconomy (Caracas monthly)
Venezuela al Día (Miami, www.venezuelaaldia.com)
Venezuela Analítica (www.analitica.com)
Washington Post

The Contributors

Angel E. Alvarez is a professor in the Faculty of Juridical and Social Sciences at the Universidad Central de Venezuela. Among his many books are *Estrategias de propaganda electoral en las campañas de 1958, 1963 y 1968; Los dineros de la política;* and (coauthor) *La institución presidencial.* He has also published many articles on Venezuelan electoral processes and is a frequent columnist in Venezuelan newspapers.

Julia Buxton is lecturer in politics at Kingston University, UK. She is author of *The Failure of Political Reform in Venezuela* and coeditor (with Nicole Phillips) of *Developments in Latin American Political Economy.* She has published several articles on democratization in Venezuela.

Steve Ellner is author of *Venezuela's Movimiento al Socialismo: From Guerrilla Defeat to Electoral Politics; Organized Labor in Venezuela, 1958–1991: Behavior and Concerns in a Democratic Setting;* and (coeditor) of *The Latin American Left: From the Fall of Allende to Perestroika.* He has taught economic history at the Universidad de Oriente in Venezuela since 1977.

María Pilar García-Guadilla is a Venezuelan sociologist, environmentalist, and urban planner. She is a professor at the Universidad Simón Bolívar in Caracas, Venezuela, and holds a Ph.D. from the University of Chicago. She has written extensively on social movements in Latin America and is editor of *Retos para la democracia y el desarrollo: Movimientos ambientalistas en America Latina y Europa.*

Daniel Hellinger is author of *Venezuela: Tarnished Democracy* and was the coordinating editor for *Post-Bonanza Venezuela,* an edition of *Latin American Perspectives.* He is the author of many scholarly articles on

Venezuela and is the past president of the Venezuela Studies Section of the Latin American Studies Association. He is professor of political science at Webster University in St. Louis, Missouri.

John V. Lombardi is chancellor and professor of history at the University of Massachusetts, Amherst. He served as dean of international programs and dean of arts and sciences at Indiana University, Provost, at the Johns Hopkins University, and as president of the University of Florida. He is a specialist in Latin America with a special interest in Venezuelan history, especially of the nineteenth century, and is the author of many books and articles.

Margarita López Maya holds a doctorate in social sciences from the Universidad Central de Venezuela (UCV), where she is presently full professor. She is editor of the journal *Revista Venezolana de Economía y Ciencias Sociales,* published by the UCV's School of Social Science. Her publications include (editor), *Protesta popular en América Latina en los años de ajuste;* "Alcaldías de izquierda en Venezuela: Gestiones locales de la Causa Radical (1989 y 1996)," in Beatriz Stolowicz (editor), *Gobiernos de izquierda en América Latina;* and several articles in *NACLA: Report on the Americas.*

Patricia Márquez holds a Ph.D. in sociocultural anthropology from the University of California at Berkeley and is associate professor in organizational behavior at the Institute for Higher Studies in Management (IESA) in Caracas. Her publications include *The Street Is My Home: Youth and Violence in Caracas.* She is coauthor of *Heratenea: El nuevo género de la gerencia.*

Bernard Mommer is a Venezuelan mathematician with a doctoral degree in social science from the University of Tübingen, Germany. After teaching at several Venezuelan universities for many years, he was appointed senior adviser for strategic planning and coordination for Petróleos de Venezuela in 1991. Since 1995 he has held a senior research fellowship at the Oxford Institute for Energy Studies, and is currently an adviser to the Venezuelan minister of energy and mines, and to the secretary-general of OPEC. His publications include *Die Ölfrage, The New Governance of Venezuelan Oil, Global Oil and the Nation State.*

Deborah L. Norden received her Ph.D. in political science from the University of California at Berkeley in 1992 and is currently assistant professor of political science at Whittier College. She has published widely on civil-military relations, democratization, and political parties in Latin

America. Her publications include *Military Rebellion in Argentina*, and articles in *Comparative Politics, Latin American Research Review, Journal of Inter-American Studies and World Affairs, Armed Forces and Society, Party Politics*, and elsewhere. She is currently completing a book on U.S.-Argentine relations with Roberto Russell.

Kenneth Roberts is associate professor of political science at the University of New Mexico. He is the author of *Deepening Democracy? The Modern Left and Social Movements in Chile and Peru*. His research on party systems and populism in Latin America has been published in the *American Political Science Review, World Politics, Comparative Politics, Comparative Political Studies*, the *Latin American Research Review*, and other journals and edited volumes.

Index

About the Book

The radical alteration of the political landscape in Venezuela following the electoral triumph of the controversial Hugo Chávez calls for a fresh look at the country's institutions and policies. In response, and challenging much of the scholarly literature on Venezuelan democracy, this book offers a revisionist view of Venezuela's recent political history and a fresh appraisal of the Chávez administration.

Steve Ellner is professor of economic history at the Universidad de Oriente in Venezuela, where he has taught since 1977. His many publications include *The Latin American Left: From the Fall of Allende to Perestroika* (coedited) and *Venezuela's Movimiento al Socialismo: From Guerrilla Defeat to Electoral Politics.* **Daniel Hellinger** is professor of political science at Webster University. He is author of *Venezuela: Tarnished Democracy* and coordinating editor of *Post-Bonanza Venezuela,* a special issue of *Latin American Perspectives.*